HOW NOT TO WRITE
THE HISTORY OF
URDU LITERATURE

And Other Essays on Urdu and Islam

Ralph Russell

OXFORD
UNIVERSITY PRESS

OXFORD
UNIVERSITY PRESS

YMCA Library Building, Jai Singh Road, New Delhi 110 001

Oxford University Press is a department of the University of Oxford.
It furthers the University's objective of excellence in research, scholarship,
and education by publishing worldwide in

Oxford   New York
Athens   Auckland   Bangkok   Bogota   Buenos Aires   Calcutta
Cape Town   Chennai   Dar es Salaam   Delhi   Florence   Hong Kong   Istanbul
Karachi   Kuala Lumpur   Madrid   Melbourne   Mexico City   Mumbai
Nairobi   Paris   Sao Paolo   Singapore   Taipei   Tokyo   Toronto   Warsaw

with associated companies in

Berlin   Ibadan

ISBN   0 19 564749 1

Typeset by Eleven Arts, Keshav Puram, Delhi 110 035
Printed in India at Pauls Press, New Delhi 110 020
and published by Manzar Khan, Oxford University Press
YMCA Library Building, Jai Singh Road, New Delhi 110 001

PREFACE

This book, like its predecessor, *The Pursuit of Urdu Literature* (1993), is essentially a collection of articles published in quite a wide range of periodicals and books over the last thirty years or so. But there are some which had never been published, and those that have, have been read through again and amended where necessary. However, there was very little that needed changing.

The arrangement of the materials is as follows: Marion Molteno's article surveys much of my work on Urdu and thus provides a setting for the rest of the book. Part Two, in effect, sets out the main aspects of my approach to Urdu and its literature and to the people and organizations which have been concerned with promoting it. And Part Three, will, I hope, make clear the spirit in which I have myself approached my life's work. From the days of my first encounter with Urdu in 1942 it has been my constant desire to communicate as fully as possible with the people whose language and literature it is. I do not believe there is any other satisfactory basis for fruitful study, and those pieces in this Part which give some picture of my interaction with the people who speak and write Urdu are intended to provide the background to the more formal articles.

Some of the material in this volume was written without any thought of publication, and some without any thought that publication might one day require me to give detailed references for passages, written either by others or by myself, which I quoted. At the publisher's request I have wherever possible found and supplied these references, but I have not been able to do so in every case, and must apologize for such gaps as remain.

RALPH RUSSELL

CONTENTS

PART ONE

⚜ 1 ⚜

RALPH RUSSELL
Teacher, Scholar, Lover of Urdu
Marion Molteno

Thomas More [to an ambitious young man]: 'Be a teacher! You'd be a fine
teacher. Perhaps, a great one.'
[Ambitious young man]: 'And if I was, who would know it?'
Thomas More: 'You, your pupils, your friends, God. Not a bad public that.'
From A Man for All Seasons *by Robert Bolt*

INTRODUCTION

Ralph Russell's work for Urdu began over forty years ago, and
still continues. For more than thirty years he taught at the
School of Oriental and African Studies (SOAS) at the
University of London, and has published extensively, earning a
reputation as one of the foremost western scholars of Urdu literature.
He is best known for works undertaken with Khurshidul Islam on
the poets Mir and Ghālib.

But his influence has been felt far beyond the world of scholarship.
An inspiring teacher, he has received from generations of students a
disciple-like devotion. Among Urdu speakers he holds a special place
of affection and admiration as one of the few English speakers who
has taken the trouble to learn to speak their language with complete
facility. He has continually looked beyond the world of university

* Originally published in *The Annual of Urdu Studies* 6 (1987):11–29.

studies: his writings and translations have made Urdu literature accessible to a readership with no knowledge of the language; he has pioneered the teaching of Urdu to teachers, social workers and others who work with Urdu-speaking communities in Britain; and in recent years has devoted a major part of his time to pressing for Urdu to be adequately taught in schools.

His unique contribution to Urdu has come about because he combines great scholarship with unusual qualities and a clear sense of commitment to certain ideals. I hope that others will assess his work from a more strictly scholarly point of view; in this article I want to look at it in the wider context of the man himself, and the convictions which have inspired him to work as he has done. I will follow the method he and Khurshidul Islam used in their *Ghalib: Life and Letters* and 'wherever possible . . . let the story emerge from his own words'.[1]

Fortunately it is possible to do this, because of what one of his colleagues described as his 'autobiographical approach' to the study of language and literature. When asked to comment on the work of a twentieth-century poet or short story writer, he begins, 'I first met Faiz/Krishan Chandar/Manto in 1949 . . .', and proceeds to tell us about this meeting, and his first response to the writer's work. The approach has much to recommend it: by speaking so directly about his own experience he has helped many others over the initial barriers to understanding. There is the added advantage that, scattered through the voluminous output of articles, duplicated notes and prefaces to books, we have a unique record of his own reflections about his life work for Urdu.

'THE LANGUAGE OF THE RULER AND THE RULED'

Ralph Russell's contact with Urdu speakers began when he was conscripted during the Second World War, and sent to serve on attachment to the Indian Army.

I learnt Urdu during the war years because I wanted to communicate, in the fullest possible sense of the word, with those who could not communicate through any other medium. I took it as axiomatic that they, like every other language community in the world, would have things to teach me. They did. That they and their literature have taught me more than I could have ever expected has been a bonus on top of that. I want to help others, at *every* level, to have access to what Urdu speaking people can give them, and a means of communicating what they in turn can give to Urdu speaking people.[2]

This desire, maintained consistently over forty years, has informed all his work for Urdu. The driving force came from his political values. As a student his energies were taken up with work for the communist movement. He had always enjoyed literature, and had studied both Latin and Greek with enjoyment, but had no academic ambition. The idea of becoming an Urdu scholar would never have occurred if his political sympathies had not first been engaged. Even before arriving in India he was convinced of the justice of the Indian struggle for independence, and everything he saw of the behaviour of the British in India reinforced this. The dismissive attitude of his fellow army officers towards the people and culture around them made him very angry. Though they were all expected to learn some Urdu, few took this seriously. The only available course books reflected

a world in which every Britisher was in some sense a representative of the ruling power, whose needs could be met by textbooks which, as a student once complained, 'all seemed to be written in the imperative' . . .[3]

Years later in Lahore, when asked to assess the contribution British scholars had made to the study of Urdu, he said:

When the relationship between two peoples is not that of independence and equality, but of ruler and ruled, sympathetic interest in the culture of the subject people never flourishes in the ruling nation; and the fact that this *was* the relationship between your people and mine has meant that the British contribution to Urdu studies has been relatively limited . . . How many hundreds of thousands of British people must have lived and worked in the subcontinent during the nearly two centuries of British rule? And of all those hundreds and thousands what proportion ever achieved any really deep sympathy with—let alone any substantial knowledge of—the culture of the peoples over whom they ruled?[4]

He was one of the few who did. For three years he spoke Urdu daily, becoming completely fluent at an everyday level, and using the language as a means of coming closer to the people he was working with. It was only after he had returned to Britain at the end of the war that the idea of academic study arose. He heard of a studentship to do a degree in Urdu at SOAS, with the possibility of a lecturership thereafter. He applied, for it seemed to offer a way of keeping in touch with the people and politics of the subcontinent. As his study progressed, he began to envisage more clearly how his work as a teacher of Urdu could help towards changing the attitudes among his fellow British he had so fiercely rejected. He would do away with the language of command and complaint, and prepare new materials for 'the kind of people . . . who want to communicate with Urdu speakers on terms of mutual respect'.[5]

Before starting to teach he insisted on a year's study leave in India, so that he could learn from Urdu speakers. Though the request surprised the SOAS establishment, it was granted. The year 1949–50 was spent at Aligarh, and was immensely formative—perhaps chiefly in introducing him to Khurshidul Islam, who became his life-long friend and collaborator. As, with Khurshidul Islam's help, his understanding of Urdu literature deepened, so did his desire to make it accessible to other English speakers. This is reflected in a talk he gave in Delhi, in Urdu, shortly before his return, in the course of which he said:

there is much in Urdu literature which English speaking readers could immediately appreciate if they could read it in English translation. I hope in the future when I have acquired sufficient competence . . . that I, with other English speakers who will learn Urdu from me, will be able to undertake the work of producing good, readable translations. Meanwhile I can at least help and encourage English students so that they can begin reading Urdu literature—in Urdu.[6]

This talk, entitled *'Urdu kā Mustaqbil'* [The Future of Urdu], was published in the Delhi paper *Nai Raushni*. It foreshadows quite strikingly certain qualities which have characterized Ralph's work ever since. Most prominent is a type of confidence which comes from having committed yourself to work you think important. He did not hesitate to take on controversy, attacking scholars who used unnecessarily high-flown Urdu and so removed the language of literature from that of ordinary people. Nor did he appear to think it incongruous that as a young Englishman, with no experience of teaching or writing about Urdu, he should address Urdu scholars about the future of their language. When he talked of the contribution he personally hoped to make to that future, he did so without any trace of self-importance; he simply regarded it as his responsibility to analyse the situation in which he found himself, and drew conclusions as to where he should put his efforts.

'LITERATURE FOR ORDINARY MEN AND WOMEN'

In 1951 Ralph began teaching at SOAS. Almost immediately afterwards, the lecturer responsible for Urdu studies died, and Ralph took his place. He remained for the next eighteen years SOAS's only full-time permanent lecturer in Urdu. Working alongside him was a succession of 'overseas lecturers' on short-term contracts: Hamid Hasan Bilgrami, Khurshidul Islam, Aziz Ahmad, Ebadat Brelvi, and Khalid Hasan Qadiri. Most of their students were undergraduates, doing a BA in Urdu (in most cases starting with no knowledge of the language) or taking Urdu as a subsidiary subject towards another degree.

As he started teaching, Ralph was convinced that the key to the study of both language and literature was to take as broad a view as possible. In notes prepared for students he wrote:

as you yourself will soon come to feel, you cannot study Urdu satisfactorily without acquiring more knowledge about the people who speak it—of their history, culture, and social life, and of the countries where they live.[7]

If for the moment his students were not able to have the person-to-person contact with speakers of the language which he thought so essential, their interest would have to be stimulated by other means:

The best way of doing this is to make available in English translations those Urdu literary works which are most likely to arouse such interest.[8]

It was several years before he got round to doing anything concrete to achieve this. In describing his first years at SOAS he afterwards wrote:

I think my concept of my job during this period was too limited. I met all teaching requirements adequately, and left it at that, neither reading widely nor doing anything much towards producing articles let alone books for publication.[9]

The person who jolted him out of this state was Khurshidul Islam, whom he had met on study leave in Aligarh:

it is to him above all others that I owe most of such understanding of the ghazal as I possess, and 1950 marks the beginning of what I trust will be a life-long collaboration.[10]

It did indeed remain that. From 1953 to 1956 Khurshidul Islam joined him at SOAS as an overseas lecturer, and on each of Ralph's subsequent study leaves he based himself at Aligarh so that they could spend as much time as possible working together. Their friendship was founded on two shared passions, which have continued to fuel the life-long working partnership. The first is a love of literature:

Our tastes and interests and judgements, and the range of our reading in literature in general are so similar that a more ideal collaboration could hardly be imagined.[11]

They shared, also, a conviction that to offer Urdu literature to English readers in a form in which they could adequately appreciate it would be an immensely worthwhile task, with implications far beyond the field of literature itself. They both believed that the barriers to appreciation were political as much as linguistic. English speaking readers were unconscious heirs to the attitudes of the Raj, summarized so forcefully by Macaulay in his Minute on Indian Education in 1835: 'A single shelf of a good European library . . . [is] worth the whole native literature of India and Arabia.' Over a hundred years later those literatures were still almost unknown to an ordinary educated reader in Britian. Khurshid and Ralph were convinced that this situation could be changed:

The Bible, the Arabian Nights, and the Rubaiyat of Omar Khayyam are all works of Oriental literature, and successive generations of English speaking readers have been moved, inspired, and entertained by them. It is worth stressing that *the chief reason for this has been that they have approached these works with respect,* knowing of the power they have exercised over millions of readers before them and expecting to experience something of this power themselves. There are things in them which they do not understand or appreciate, but they generally assume (and for the most part correctly) that this is because of an insufficient knowledge of their background, and they do not allow these things to stand in the way of their enjoyment. (Emphasis added.)[12]

Already while on study leave in India, Ralph had been on the lookout for works which would make a direct appeal to western readers, something closer in both form and content to what they were used to. He had met many of the leading writers connected with the Progressive Movement, and felt that the best of their short stories would be ideal for this purpose—reflecting the social concerns of the day and giving a vivid picture of daily life. By 1958 he had translated stories by Ismat Chughtai, Krishan Chander, and Rajinder Singh Bedi; and soon after, Aziz Ahmad's novel *Aisī Bulandī, Aisi Pastī*.

Now he and Khurshidul Islam planned to tackle the much more complex task of presenting Urdu poetry to an English readership. Together they conceived of a series of books which would introduce to English readers a selection of the work of Urdu's greatest writers; they would not assume

in the readers any previous knowledge of the subject . . . [but only] a readiness to make that minimum mental effort which is required of any man who wants to understand and appreciate the literature of a people and an age which are not his own.[13]

While aware of the difficulties, they were confident of what they could achieve together:

In translating, where every nuance of every word and phrase, in both the language of the original and that of the translation, can be important, we can do together what neither of us could do alone, for both of us know both languages well, and each of us has one of them as his mother tongue; and we can therefore hope to understand fully what the Urdu intends and to convey that intention as fully as English allows.[14]

They knew it would not be sufficient to provide translations; they would also need to help their readers surmount obstacles of form and poetic convention by setting the poetry against the background of the society and age that had produced it:

Our own experience of teaching Urdu literature to English and European students show that once the historical setting has been explained, the main obstacles to an appreciation of the literature are overcome.[15]

They began work first on three of the leading eighteenth-century poets—Mir Hasan, Sauda, and Mir Taqi Mir. Through selections from these three poets they would introduce the reader also to three major genres of Urdu poetry—*maṣnavī* (the narrative verse), *hajv* (the satire), and, above all, the ghazal. It was many years before they had completed the book to their satisfaction, and still more years before it was finally published, as *Three Mughal Poets.*

Three Mughal Poets is a unique book. There exists in English no better introduction to Urdu poetry, yet it has nothing of the superficiality often associated with introductory books; its scholarly nature is unquestionable. The greatest achievement is the section on Mir, which occupies half the book. Extracts from Mir's poetry are woven into an extended essay on the attitudes and way of life of the poet-lover who is the central figure in much of Urdu poetry. The text linking the quotations is so deeply informed by the values which underlie the poetry that readers are scarcely aware of a voice other than the poet's. The translations have an unobtrusive dignity; while never sacrificing naturalness in the English, they remain exceptionally faithful to the original.

It is scarcely surprising that the book received recognition from Urdu scholars; but that was not what mattered most to the authors. Ralph wrote:

I am happy to say that it won the admiration and praise of men and women who before they read it did not even know what Urdu was—including an economist, a mathematician, a school-teacher and housewife and mother of a young family—and no scholar's praise could bring us such satisfaction as their praise does.[16]

Once work on Mir had been completed, they turned to the great nineteenth-century poet Ghālib:

We have for many years believed that if once the barrier of language could be satisfactorily surmounted and Ghālib's prose and verse made available to a world audience, his work would win him a place in world literature which historical circumstance has hitherto denied him; and it is this belief which has inspired us to undertake the present work.[17]

They planned two volumes: the first would include a selection from Ghālib's prose; the second would introduce the reader to both his

Urdu and Persian poetry, starting with his ghazals. Volume I—*Ghālib: Life and Letters*—published in 1969, is a work of great craftsmanship. It serves three distinct purposes at once. Firstly, it introduces the reader to the wealth of Ghālib's prose writing through extremely fine translations. Secondly, the extracts are arranged so that, together with the interlinking text, they tell the story of Ghālib's life. The transitions between Ghālib's own writing and the authors' text are so smoothly achieved that there is no sense of interruption—one has the sense of meeting Ghālib himself throughout. Finally, we gain an understanding of the age in which Ghālib lived. His writings offer plenty of raw material for this, but the skill of the author lies in providing sufficient background explanation of the social milieu to enable readers to understand why Ghālib thought and felt as he did.

With volume I complete, they began reading, selecting, and translating Ghālib's poetry for volume II. This work has continued, off and on, for twenty years. They have had to contend with the difficulties of communicating across continents, and repeated delays from pressure of more immediate tasks. But they have not been prepared to compromise with their painstaking attention to detail in order to produce the book more quickly. Pending publication of the full work, Ralph has published articles on their work on Ghālib, and edited a volume entitled *Ghalib: The Poet and His Age*.[18] But he has never considered undertaking the work of interpretation on his own:

In the ghazal, more perhaps than in any other field, we in the West need to realize that, without guidance from those who are steeped in its tradition, we understand, at a generous estimate, about as much as an intelligent fourteen-year old understands of Donne.[19]

He has been sharply critical of western scholars who 'failed to draw adequately upon expert help from Urdu speakers which would very willingly have been given'[20] and quotes a story from Sa'di's *Gulistān:*

. . . the great Muslim scholar al-Ghazali was asked, 'How did you attain to so high a degree of learning?' He replied, 'Anything I did not know. I felt no shame in asking.'[21]

He is an equally severe critic of those Urdu speakers who in attempting to popularize Urdu literature sacrifice faithfulness to the original.

Their desire that someone should 'do full justice' to Ghālib has prevented them from losing heart about a project that has taken so much longer than they had anticipated.

Neither Ralph nor Khurshidul Islam regard their collaborative work as anything like complete. They feel confident that the method they have developed—both of working together, and of the style of presentation—can be successfully applied to other poets. In 1972, they took time off work on Ghālib to produce a major article on the satirical verse of Akbar (1846–1921),[22] which shares many of their characteristics: a blend of translations from Akbar's poetry with a perceptive view of the society against which his satire was directed. In 1974 Ralph wrote:

A good many other things have long awaited attention . . . The most substantial, and most difficult, has been the second volume of our work on Ghālib . . . This is the only major, comprehensive study in depth of any Urdu writer I can reasonably hope to make before I die—though you never know your luck.[23]

In 'On Translating Ghālib' Ralph provides a thought-provoking analysis of the variety of ways in which translators approach their complex task:

A translator tries to get as close as he can to an unrealizable ideal, and to produce in English what Ghālib would have written himself had English, and not Urdu, been his mother tongue.[24]

On the strength of his work on Mir and Ghālib, Ralph has been described as 'the leading western scholar of Urdu literature'.[25] He says his initial reaction to this tribute was one of surprise—followed by pleasure at the recognition that it was true. Perhaps the surprise is accounted for by the fact that he does not think of himself as operating alone. In 1984, in a speech paying tribute to Khurshidul Islam's work he said that people who knew *him* rather than Khurshid assumed that it was he who had done the major share of their work, while those who had more contact with Khurshid assumed that the credit went largely to *him*. Ralph has always insisted that their work and thought have been so intertwined as to be inseparable:

We . . . [have always] worked in the closest collaboration, selecting, reading, and discussing together every line of the poetry we were attempting to present, and modifying the final text until we were both completely satisfied with it.[26]

Their combined reputation has for years rested largely on two books: quantity of output clearly has little to do with it. What gives their work its unusual quality is the values that have inspired it. In terms of ghazal imagery they see themselves as the *'āshiq*—the true lover who serves his love with wholehearted, unswerving dedication: but it is also the people for whom they interpret it—the many thousands of English speakers, unknown to them individually yet powerfully imagined, who through their work will come to know and respect the literature to which Urdu speakers feel a passionate attachment. Their scholarship serves this deep commitment; and therein lies its significance.

'WHAT ARE PROBLEMS TO US ARE NOT PROBLEMS TO THEM'

When in 1950 Ralph had considered what he could contribute to the future of Urdu, he had identified two roles: the first was to produce translations; the second, to '. . . help and encourage English students so that they can begin reading Urdu literature—in Urdu'.[27]

He did not underestimate the difficulty of the second task. Years later he commented: 'when I came into the field of Urdu studies almost everything for the English speaking student of the post-independence era still remained to be done . . .'[28]

One of the first things to be done was to remove the straight-jacket of a badly designed syllabus. His predecessor, A.H. Harley, had taught only that literature which he in turn had learnt many years before in Delhi from a man he referred to namelessly, as 'my old Munshi'. The result was some astonishing omissions: no mention of Iqbal; none of the many excellent stories by Premchand, or by the Progressives. In other words, the syllabus omitted precisely the type of literature which Ralph felt sure would make the most direct appeal and be easiest for learners to read.

Within a few years he had broadened the syllabus to include not only these works but also some of the earlier classics such as *Zahr-e 'Ishq* and *Umrāō Jān Adā*, which Harley's 'old Munshi' and indeed Harley himself had perhaps considered unsuitable fare for a young student, being on themes of illicit love and the life of a courtesan. But in addition to extending the syllabus, Ralph also increased students' range of choice within it:

You are welcome to read and discuss my own proposals . . . and equally welcome to put forward proposals of your own . . . If any of you want to pursue an interest in the field of Urdu which the syllabus does not adequately cater for, I am quite prepared to help you do this, and am at the same time more than willing to press for modification in the syllabus to allow scope for such interests.[29]

Above all he hoped to free them from the tyranny of an examination-oriented approach, so that they could respond more naturally to what they read:

I know that if you read literature at a university you are bound to give due weight to the consideration that you have to pass examinations in it, and to recognize that this obliges you to study aspects that do not particularly interest you. But even so, you still have quite a lot of time to do what *does* interest you, and to experience the enjoyment that comes from reading the great works which add something to your whole being, enlarging both your capacity to enjoy life and your ability to understand more fully yourself, and other men and women, and the world around you.[30]

Ralph communicates this approach by example. He teaches students to read as if they are encountering the author, one human being meeting another on equal terms:

It is important that you learn what a great poem or play or novel meant to the man who wrote it and to the people and the age he wrote it for; but in a sense, it is even more important to think what it means to YOU—you, who belong to a different age and a different people, and who even as an individual are in some measure different from any other individual regardless of the age and the people to which you belong—and who despite all these things find that the greatest works of literature can speak directly to you. In the last resort, both the pleasure and the profit of reading derive from the sense of what the things you read mean to you personally.[31]

Many teachers pay lip service to this idea; Ralph takes it literally.

Nevertheless he is keenly aware that students with a western background have many obstacles to overcome before they can be expected to respond positively to Urdu literature. As a teacher, he wanted to ensure that his students did not give up in the face of such difficulties. Eventually this would require the removal of all possible obstacles in the student's way. These obstacles may be briefly summed up in the statement that most of the facilities which exist for the student of, say, French, do not exist for the student of Urdu. Dictionaries and grammars are out of date: only a very few clearly printed and annotated texts, prepared specifically for the English student, are in existence . . . On a whole range of topics with which the student needs to be familiar if he is to understand Urdu literature, no satisfactory treatment in English exists. The Urdu script is a formidable difficulty to the new student.[32]

The first step was to learn to read fluently—for which students needed a plentiful supply of simple reading material, *not* chosen primarily for literary merit. He had been on the lookout for such materials from his first study leave in India in 1949. He felt that his students needed 'the Urdu of the normal, humdrum situations of contemporary life'. He was excited to discover in Khwaja Hasan Nizami's prolific writings short pieces aimed at people with no literary education, and wrote to him in 1985:

You may perhaps not have realized that, in just the same way that your books are useful to the general public, so they have a special importance for any foreign student . . . Not only is their language that of idiomatic Delhi speech; it is in addition extremely pure and simple. So it seems to me that for English students such as myself there could not be better reading material.

To his students he said:

Many Urdu speakers will smile at the choice of such books, but for your purposes they are excellent. You are not primarily concerned with the personalities and viewpoints of the authors.[33]

What mattered was learning to read independently.

He eventually published a partial collection of such material as *Readings in Everyday Urdu*.[34] But this is one of the many tasks for Urdu that he regards as unfinished.

There were other technical hurdles which he tried to help learners overcome:

A good many western students of Urdu, having completed a course in the elements of the language, want as soon as possible to make the acquaintance of its poetry. They soon find themselves confronted with many difficulties, and one of the most frustrating is the discovery that they cannot generally appreciate its rhythms.[35]

He knew that he was in a better position to help than someone who had grown up with Urdu poetry:

[The student] is not likely to find that his Urdu speaking friends can help him much . . . The great majority, not only of those who appreciate Urdu poetry, but also of those who write it, could not name any of the metres they use, nor tell you how they are scanned. But then they do not really need to know these things, because they appreciate the rhythms very well—so well, in fact, that if you misquote a line of verse—even if it is a line they have never heard—they will often tell you at once that you are misquoting, 'because it doesn't scan': after which they will suggest what the correct version probably is, and recite a line, which, to your English ear, is indistinguishable in its rhythm from the one you had recited.[36]

To answer these questions he produced *A Primer of Urdu Verse Metre*. The book is far less known than it deserves to be, largely because it was published by the author and, therefore, not widely distributed. It presents Urdu's complex metrical system in simple terms: 'at a stage when all the Urdu [a student] is assumed to have is what he has acquired in an elementary language course'.[37] But in Ralph's work simplicity is never achieved at the cost of oversimplification. *A Primer of Urdu Verse Metre* does not avoid troublesome details: it explains them. Instead of merely presenting an academic description of Urdu metre in general terms, the *Primer* gives a practical training in how to work out the metre of any ghazal students might encounter. And throughout, technical considerations are made to serve the more fundamental aim:

I have in every case chosen poems and verses which I hope you will enjoy, and not verses which merely illustrate the points I am making about the metre.[38]

He was, however, under no illusion that once his students had the technical tools they required, they would necessarily like what they read. In the most sustained and significant of his 'autobiographical' pieces, 'The Pursuit of the Urdu Ghazal', he described his own first reactions:

It is now more than twenty years ago that I was first introduced to the Urdu ghazal—the classical Urdu lyric—and found with something like dismay that there was almost nothing about it which I understood and liked (p. 107).

It was clear to him that if his Urdu-speaking friends loved the ghazal there must be something in it to love:

It was possible that they were all wrong, but much more likely that the fault lay in me, in my continuing inability to understand exactly what the ghazal was all about . . . I never ceased to think that I could one day hope to appreciate the ghazal as my Urdu speaking friends did (p. 110).

But few of them were able to help him, because:

What are problems to us are not problems to them, and no one can solve a problem when he cannot see that it is there (p. 124).

One of Ralph's major contributions to the study of Urdu literature has been that he pinpointed exactly which factors were responsible for his own lack of appreciation—and by extension were likely to hinder others. As he writes in the same essay:

I am convinced that to understand and appreciate the ghazal is the most difficult task that confronts the modern western student of Urdu literature, and as my own understanding increased, I have become equally convinced that this is a task which once accomplished brings the greatest reward (p. 107).

His determination to share this reward with others has inspired not only his face-to-face teaching, but also a prolific output of articles: on the ghazal, on the society that produced it,[39] and spreading out from that, on all the issues in Urdu literature that he has pondered over. He has written on the development of the Urdu novel from roots quite unlike that of the novel in the West,[40] on Iqbal's often contradictory political message[41], on Faiz's poetry which both reflects present-day political concerns and yet is rooted in the classical ghazal tradition.[42] (Many of these articles, slightly modified, are now chapters in *The Pursuit of Urdu Literature*.) His particular strength lies in perceptive analysis of the social and political ideas of a particular age, and how they gave rise to certain trends in literature. Articles such as 'Strands of Muslim Identity in South Asia'[43] or 'Leadership in the All India Progressive Writers' Movement'[44] cannot easily be classified; they are not conventional essays in literary criticism, but they provide far more useful insights. One of their chief characteristics is fearlessness. In one of his more controversial articles, 'Aziz Ahmad, South Asia, Islam and Urdu', he criticized those scholars—both western and South Asian—who are

> too timid in stating truths, and sometimes very important truths, that their knowledge of Urdu has taught them. I sometimes have the impression that in the field of Islamic studies more than most, scholars feel a need to be 'diplomatic' (which, let us face it, is only a polite way of saying 'less than completely honest') so that influential people will not be offended. Well, no sensible person would advocate giving offense unnecessarily or stating honest conclusions in deliberately offensive language, but neither should one forget what Hardy, quoting St Jerome, stressed in his Explanatory Note to *Tess*— that 'if an offense comes out of the truth, better is it that the offense come than that the truth be concealed'.[45]

The 'truths' he feels a particular interest in discovering and sharing are ways of thinking which commonly exhibit themselves in Urdu literature, and which western readers therefore need to understand. Some of these are the kind of things that many people recognize to be the case, but few would put in print. Ralph, however, feels differently:

> I am not a professional historian, merely one who as a teacher and student of Urdu literature has an interest in all aspects of the history and the social and cultural life of the people who produced and still produce it.[46]

His reputation for being an inspired teacher and interpreter of Urdu literature stems from two closely related features. First, his strong desire that learners should make their own direct personal response to literature, regardless of their inexperience; and secondly, his recognition of the handicaps which this inexperience imposes. By analysing the obstacles so perceptively he equips learners to respond more fully. What were problems for him cease to be problems for those who follow after him.

'COMMUNICATING ON TERMS OF MUTUAL RESPECT'

Language learning at SOAS was traditionally seen as no more than a tool for the study of literature. Language ability as such was tested only in written translation. Ralph was in total disagreement with this approach. He had never lost sight of his original motivation for taking up work in Urdu—to enable people 'to communicate with Urdu speakers on terms of mutual respect'. 'My primary aim,' he insisted, 'is to teach people to speak Urdu.'[47]

On first taking up his post he had pressed for changes in the syllabus which would have given much greater emphasis to language teaching—specifically spoken language. But it was not until the early 1960s that he and other teachers who shared these views succeeded in getting the degree period lengthened from three years to four, with the first year being set aside entirely for language teaching. This opened up new possibilities, and Ralph was quick to make use of them, convinced that even in a totally English-speaking environment he could find ways to help his students learn to speak fluently:

There are few people who, in a relaxed atmosphere, cannot be given the necessary self-confidence to take the plunge and start speaking . . . It is possible, if students are prepared to make the effort, to get them speaking fluently right from the start, and I think that this is the most important thing a teacher has to do.[48]

There were several aspects to 'getting them speaking'. One basic assumption was that people will speak more readily—in any language—if there is something they want to say:

They want as soon as possible to be able to say correctly . . . *meaningful* statements, of however elementary a kind; and I see no reason to frustrate this desire.[49]

In the initial stages his lessons were designed to give carefully graded spoken practice. He was both patient in helping students overcome their hesitation about speaking, and forceful in refusing to let them take refuge in a book-learning approach. He insisted that grammatical accuracy, far from hindering fluency, actually increased confidence in using the language. But all such grammatical teaching should arise in natural contexts:

. . . in general I have avoided teaching great slabs of formal grammar, just as I avoided teaching the sound system and the script en bloc. Instead I have explained in relation to each fresh set of Urdu sentences the new grammatical points that arise, and have left systematic statement to follow some time later . . . In short, I have aimed at giving students, as far as possible what they want and need, and refraining from giving them what they do not want and do not need.[50]

He developed a style of teaching which made the most of the fact that the teaching groups were small. He would bombard students with personal questions—about themselves, their studies, their daily activities—questions to which they were bound to have ready answers. He became very skilled at keeping this within the range of what he knew a particular group of students had learnt to say in Urdu, so they got the maximum amount of practice with the minimum frustration.

The teaching of reading and writing was similarly linked as closely as possible to what students might need to say. Ralph's teaching materials include no artificial dialogues to illustrate grammatical points, but students' own conversations with him, written down and used as reading passages. He enlisted the help of his colleague, Khalid Hasan Qadiri,[51] to ensure that the Urdu in the passages was natural and idiomatic, and could be used by other students as models for saying similar things about themselves.

In the early stages, the emphasis in teaching materials was overwhelmingly on what students themselves might want to say. As their competence increased, Ralph began to use reading materials also to foster the broad view which he thought so essential to any language learner:

I have tried as far as possible to select themes which teach you something relevant and useful . . . For example, a passage may illustrate some facet of Pakistani and Indian Muslim ways of life which the average British student doesn't know about or hasn't thought about, or may point contrasts between the social conventions of English speaking peoples and those of Muslims.[52]

These were not passages written by outside observers: the material he collected was almost all

the work of native speakers of the language, and a good proportion of it . . . (was) uttered without any thought of its suitability or otherwise for teaching purposes: or from books and papers written for the general Urdu-reading public.[53]

Perhaps the most remarkable of his range of materials was a collection of taped interviews, built up over the years in an attempt to provide students with more opportunity to hear Urdu spoken. The recordings are of conversations between himself and Urdu speakers talking about their lives, their work, their experiences—from dramatic political events such as the traumas of the Partition, to simple descriptions of everyday routines. These interviews were woven into his language teaching, with written exercises based on them.

Through all these varied language teaching materials runs the unstated but very clear theme of 'communicating on terms of mutual respect'. This was not simply a matter of learning to make the appropriate polite noises. No doubt 'respect' for others implies being prepared to take their views seriously; but there is no 'communication' unless you also think as seriously about your own values and are prepared to share them with others. Ralph's students quickly realize that he is not simply a teacher of a language in the limited sense, but someone who is interested in *them*. His quite unusual personal directness creates an atmosphere in which there are no taboo subjects, and no pressure on students to come to certain conclusions; and this is the most positive atmosphere in which to explore cultural values different from one's own.

In 1974 he published *Essential Urdu*, putting together all the introductory materials, dialogues, reading passages and taped interviews that he had been using—and testing—for five years. It is a coursebook that defies categorization. I know of no language teaching book as personal—and yet as unpretentious. Ralph describes his technique very simply by saying that he was determined to 'write as one normal adult speaking to others'.[54] It retains something of the impact a teacher can usually have only through personal contact.

Essential Urdu achieves this effect because real people fill the book; his students are there in the transcripts of actual conversations—on things they really wanted to talk about, in an atmosphere which was free and informal. Just as important, Ralph himself is present throughout—not as 'the author', but as a human being. He includes short extracts about his own life and daily routine, and personal notes written to him by Urdu speaking friends. He chats to the learner in print as he might do in person, and the exercises are interspersed with conversational advice on how to tackle each stage of language learning— the vigour with which he expresses himself face-to-face spilling over into the text in underlinings. The advice is detailed and practical, but never dull, for it expresses so clearly his conviction that to learn a language well, and be able to use it to get to know other people better, is a deeply satisfying and worthwhile task.

Essential Urdu was published and distributed by the author; as a result, like *A Primer of Urdu Verse Metre*, it is not as widely known as it deserves to be. If it were to be republished now, would it be out-of-date? How relevant can a book published in 1974—and originally conceived in the immediately post-1947 period—be to learners today?

Firstly, the methods on which it is based will not date. It follows no fashion of language teaching methodology, but simply provides a common-sense response to the needs of learners in Britain, taking full account of the limits of what is possible. In terms of content, the book reflects a style of teaching which kept growing in response to changing conditions; materials first prepared for full-time Urdu students were adapted to include the interests of the growing number of students with personal rather than academic reasons for learning, or those who planned to live or work for a while in the subcontinent. The collection of extracts and recorded interviews, too, grew and changed; some are old, some are very recent—and many are timeless. An interview about Hindu-Muslim riots at the time of Independence was relevant to students in the early 1950s because these happenings were so recent: for learners in the 1980s an interview like this is oral history, thirty years old—but still highly relevant if they are to understand the feelings of any Urdu speaker who was alive at that time, or indeed of the children of those who lived through that period.

Fundamentally, less has changed than people like to think. The Raj has been gone for many years, and there are now few Urdu coursebooks left which teach only the language of command and complaint. But Britain now has a sizeable community of Urdu speakers, permanently resident—and many members of the 'host' British community display towards Indians and Pakistanis the same assumption of superiority, the same disregard for what another culture might have to offer. At the time *Essential Urdu* was published Ralph had not yet begun to have contact on any significant scale with the new immigrant communities. But in his Preface he looked forward to his book being used by a new category of students 'consisting of people who want to achieve a better relationship with Urdu speaking immigrants in Britain'.

The values that underlie *Essential Urdu* are entirely relevant in the present era.

'A NEW, MAJOR AND UNEXPECTED DEVELOPMENT'

For anyone studying or teaching a South Asian language in Britain, the early 1970s marked a major turning point. As increasing numbers of South Asians settled in Britain, university students for the first time had the prospect of using the languages they were studying in a British context. More fundamentally, English people who had previously had no contact with speakers of other languages were now— as teachers, social workers, health workers, etc.—working closely with speakers of Asian languages.

Ralph was one of the few academics who saw the importance of these far-reaching changes, and adapted his work priorities accordingly. Within a few years he had pioneered short intensive courses in spoken Urdu for people whose work brought them into contact with Urdu speakers. At the same time he established contact with local Urdu speaking communities, and took a lead in pressing for their children's educational needs to be more adequately met—and particularly for Urdu to be taught in the schools.

Though Ralph's new community-linked work has taken a major part of his time and energy for the past fifteen years, inevitably slowing down his academic writing, he has welcomed the opportunities it has brought, describing it as

a new, major and unexpected development in my life . . . that I can increasingly [share my knowledge] not at an elite or specialized level, but at a level which enables e.g. English speaking school teachers to communicate with people of Pakistani and Indian peasant stock, makes me very happy.[55]

Characteristically, he does not see the practical and academic aspects of his work as competing areas in any fundamental sense. They are simply different aspects of the same commitment. He is not at all bothered that most of his teaching in recent years—both for English speaking adults and for children from Urdu speaking backgrounds— has necessarily been confined to the beginner level: this is no less important to him than the study of Mir and Ghālib:

Some readers may wonder that I, who for thirty-two years taught Urdu at the university level, should attach so much importance to the kind of developments I have described. I do so because I am convinced that sooner or later from *all* categories I have mentioned, will come men and women who will develop a real love of the language and will find ways of going forward to the stage where they can read, appreciate and enjoy its great literature and interpret it to ever wider audiences. In other words, if we work as we should, we shall be creating a great reservoir from which Urdu scholars and Urdu writers of the future will be drawn.[56]

NOTES AND REFERENCES

1. Ralph Russell and Khurshidul Islam, *Ghalib: Life and Letters* (Cambridge: Harvard University Press and London: Allen and Unwin, 1969), p. 9.
2. 'The British Contribution to Urdu Studies', *Oriental College Magazine* (Lahore), Centenary Number (1974), p. 3.
3. *Essential Urdu: A Course for Learners in Britain* (published by the author, 1974), p. i.
4. 'The British Contribution to Urdu Studies', p. 179.
5. *Essential Urdu*, p. ii.
6. 'Urdu kā Mustaqbil', *Nai Raushni*, 4(1):2.
7. 'Notes for Undergraduates Beginning the Study of Urdu' (unpublished, 1974).
8. 'Urdu Studies in England' (unpublished, 1951).
9. 'The Pattern of My Life and Work' (published by the author, 1974), p. 8.
10. 'The Pursuit of the Urdu Ghazal', *Journal of Asian Studies* 29(1): 111.
11. 'On Translating Ghalib', *Mahfil* 5(4): 74.
12. Ralph Russell and Khurshidul Islam, *Three Mughal Poets* (Cambridge: Harvard University Press and London: Allen and Unwin, 1968), p. xviii.
13. Ibid., p. xv.
14. 'On Translating Ghalib', *Mahfil* 5(4): 74.
15. *Three Mughal Poets*, p. xix.
16. 'The British Contribution to Urdu Studies', p. 186.
17. *Ghalib: Life and Letters*, p. 9.
18. London: Allen and Unwin, 1972.
19. Review of *An Anthology of Classical Urdu Love Lyrics* by D. Matthews and C. Shackle, *South Asian Review* 6 (1): 78.
20. 'The British Contribution to Urdu Studies', p. 188.
21. Review of *An Anthology of Classical Urdu Love Lyrics* by D. Matthews and C. Shackle, *Journal of the Royal Asiatic Society* 1.
22. 'The Satirical Verse of Akbar Ilahabadi', *Modern Asian Studies* 8 (1): 1–58.

23. 'The Pattern of My Life and Work', p. 10. The materials that were to have comprised *Ghalib, Volume II* are now being published in a number of separate volumes. *Selections from the Persian Ghazals of Ghalib* containing English translations by Russell and Urdu translations by Iftikhar Ahmad Adani was published in 1997 by the Pakistan Writers' Co-operative Society in collaboration with Anjuman Taraqqi-e-Urdu.

24. 'On Translating Ghālib', *Mahfil* (East Lansing), 5(4) (Ghālib issue): 74

25. D. Matthews and C. Shackle, *An Anthology of Classical Urdu Love Lyrics* (London: Oxford University Press, 1972), p. 1.

26. *Three Mughal Poets*, p. xxii.

27. *'Urdu kā Mustaqbil'*, p. 2.

28. 'The British Contribution to Urdu Studies', p. 185.

29. 'Notes on Urdu for B.A. Students Entering the Second Year' (unpublished, 1970).

30. 'The Pursuit of the Urdu Ghazal', p. 111.

31. Ibid.

32. 'Urdu Studies in England', pp. 3–4.

33. *Essential Urdu*, p. 153.

34. Published by the author, 1979.

35. *A Primer of Urdu Verse Metre* (published by the author, 1974), p. 1.

36. Ibid.

37. Ibid.

38. Ibid., p. 23.

39. 'The Urdu Ghazal in Muslim Society', *South Asian Review* 3(2): 141–9.

40. 'The Rise of the Modern Novel in Urdu', *New Orient* (Prague), 7: 33–9; republished as 'The Development of the Modern Novel in Urdu', in T.W. Clark, ed. *The Novel in India* (London: Allen and Unwin), pp. 102–41.

41. 'Reflections on Khizr-i-Rah', Iqbal Centenary Celebrations, Lahore (unpublished).

42. Review of *Poems by Faiz* translated by Victor G. Kiernan, *Modern Asian Studies* 6(3): 353–78.

43. *South Asian Review* 6(1): 21–32; republished in this volume (chapter 13).

44. In B.N. Pandey, ed. *Leadership in South Asia* (Delhi: Vikas, 1977), pp. 104–27; republished in this volume (chapter 5).

45. 'Aziz Ahmad, South Asia, Islam and Urdu', in M. Israel and N. Wagle, eds, *Islamic Society and Culture* (New Delhi: Manohar, 1983; republished in this volume—chapter 7), p. 67.

46. Ibid., p. 63.
47. *Essential Urdu*, pp. ii–iii.
48. Ibid., p. iii.
49. Ibid.
50. Ibid., pp. iv–v.
51. Ralph considered himself very fortunate to have the assistance of Dr Qadiri, who had joined the staff at SOAS in 1965 just when the preparation of language teaching materials became a major priority. Their working relationship, based on complete mutual respect, has been close and continuous ever since.
52. 'Notes on Urdu for B.A. Students Entering the Second Year', p. 4.
53. *Essential Urdu*, pp. vi–vii.
54. Ibid., p. ii.
55. 'The Pattern of My Life and Work', p. 3.
56. 'Urdu in Britain: A Note', *Pakistan Studies* 1(2): 63.

❧ PART TWO ☙

⚜2⚜

HOW NOT TO WRITE THE HISTORY
OF URDU LITERATURE

When I was in Pakistan in 1965 I was told of the publication of a new, full-scale history of Urdu literature, written in English by Muhammad Sadiq and published by Oxford University Press.[1] I looked forward with some excitement to reading it. As a student in 1946–49, I had encountered Ram Babu Saksena's *A History of Urdu Literature*,[2] and T. Grahame Bailey's *A History of Urdu Literature*[3] at that time the only histories available in English. I read both with mounting amazement and indignation—amazement because it passed my understanding how people who had such a poor opinion of Urdu literature could want to write a history of it, and indignation because a student who as yet could not read Urdu with facility would obviously turn to these books in the first instance and find, as I did, that anything more likely to *discourage* the study of Urdu literature would be difficult to imagine. I hoped, therefore, that this new book would be very different.

When I saw the book and read it my hopes turned to disappointment and anger. I began to ask myself, more strenuously than before: Why do these people write like this? Why can't they see all the things that are so glaringly wrong with what they write? And I promised myself that I would one day write an article on how not to write the history of Urdu literature, or at any rate how not to write it for English-speaking readers.

* Originally published in *The Annual of Urdu Studies* 6 (1987): 1–9.

Let us first see how Saksena sets the tone to which I take so strong an exception. He introduces his reader to Urdu poetry in a chapter (chapter 3) entitled 'General Characteristics of Urdu Poetry'. In its nine pages we are told that 'old Urdu poetry [was] an imitation of Persian poetry' and that

its range is very limited for it sank into the ruts of old battered Persian themes and adorned itself with the rags of the cast off imagery of Persian poetry having absolutely no relation to India, the country of its birth . . .

This greedy absorption and servile imitation invests Urdu poetry with a sense of unreality and often is the cause of its debasement' (p. 23).

This last sentence is the first in a paragraph headed 'The defects of such an imitation', and three pages (23–5) are then devoted to a listing and elaboration of these defects. The paragraph headings read:

1. It made Urdu poetry seem unnatural.
2. It made Urdu poetry rhetorical.
3. It made Urdu poetry conventional.
4. It made Urdu poetry mechanical, artificial and sensual.
5. It made Urdu poetry unnatural. [Yes, once again—RR].

This last paragraph is worth quoting almost in full:

Not only did imitation make poetry conventional, rhetorical, artificial and sensual but it made it what is worse, unnatural . . . the vitiated and perverse poetry of the Persian celebrating the love of a man for a boy of tender years was copied without excuse or justification. The boy is regarded as a mistress and his [beauty is] . . . celebrated with gusto in a sensual manner revolting to the mind (p. 25).

He goes on to review the main forms of poetry, mostly in the same derogatory way, and then in a final half-page, to the reader's astonishment, informs him that

Urdu poetry, however, with all its limitations and at its best is sublimely emotional and makes a powerful appeal to sentiment. It is very sweet and subtle and is pre-eminent in its special sphere (p. 31).

Grahame Bailey's overall tone is much the same. He tells us : the range of Urdu poetry is still very circumscribed (p. 101). And he complains that the ghazal, which most lovers of Urdu literature, including me, regard as perhaps its greatest achievement 'is characterized by . . . monotonous sameness of subject, the theme of love . . .' (p. 41). (True, he makes this comment on the ghazal of 'The Age of Hatim'. But he tells us of Hatim's successors, Mir and his contemporaries, that they 'had nothing new to say' (p. 42), and that in the period of Mushafi and Insha (who came after Mir) 'there was no real advance' (p. 42). And of course, this 'monotonous theme' characterizes the ghazal to this day.)

Sadiq, too, follows in the same tradition. He tells us that the ghazal 'stands very low in the hierarchy of literary forms' (p. 20). (He doesn't tell us what this hierarchy is, or what other forms stand where in it, but at any rate the 'very low' is clear enough.)

A common feature of all three books is the constant pointing of contrasts between Urdu literature and English—always to the detriment of Urdu. These contrasts are both general and particular. Thus Saksena writes:

The range of Urdu poetry is limited. Nature so fruitful a theme for poets of West had not much inspiration for Urdu bards. There are no Briants [Who's he? I've never heard of him—RR], no Whittiers, no Thompsons in Urdu. There is no rapturous adoration of nature like Wordsworth (p. 29).

Or

The Masnavis . . . are said [By whom?—RR] to supply the place of epic and drama but fall very short of the requirements of those two great forms of literature . . . a mere knowledge of the essentials of drama would disclose that *Masnavi* do not even mean [*sic*] an approach to it (p. 30).

Similarly, Grahame Bailey tells us:

Epics can hardly be said to exist . . . There is no dramatic poetry . . . If the Urdu writers of today would make a study of Shakespeare, Milton, Tennyson and Browning, they might create a whole new world for their readers (pp. 101–2).

In Sadiq this contrast is repeated ad nauseum. Practically every writer is compared and contrasted with European writers. I quoted a typical example in a review I wrote of the second (1984) edition of his book.[4] He writes:

Akbar has not the geniality of Dickens or Fielding. He stands between the two extremes—not an Aristophanes, or a Cervantes, or a Rabelais, much less a Dickens or a Meredith, but a cross between Thackeray and Swift (pp. 403–4).

I commented:

The words tell us nothing relevant except that Akbar is lacking in geniality for Dr Sadiq does not tell us what his 'two extremes' are, or what qualities are in his view exemplified by the authors in his impressive list, or what he thinks 'a cross' between the last two produces. This constant parading of Western parallels and (more often) contrasts (invariably to the detriment of Urdu) is not merely annoying; it suggests at every step the relevance of comparisons which are in fact not relevant at all. It is rather as though one were to write a history of the nineteenth-century English novel proclaiming on every page that Dickens cannot compare with Tolstoy or Gaskell with Dostoevsky. Of course they cannot; but what rational critic *does* compare them? (Orwell has aptly remarked that to ask if you prefer Dickens to Tolstoy is like asking whether you prefer a sausage to a rose—'their purposes barely intersect'.)

In this article it will be relevant to look at the passage more closely and see exactly what Sadiq is telling us.

First, he is telling us that he has read all these authors, or at any rate sufficient of their works to form a judgement of their characteristic features. I don't doubt that he has, though the reader only has his word for it. But what has this to do with Akbar Ilahabadi?

Secondly, he is telling us, in effect, that we too, like him and all other truly educated people, have read these works, know the major qualities of all these writers, and so, of course, don't need to have them spelt out. Well, perhaps we do, or perhaps we don't. My own case is that I have read (in Greek, fifty years ago, at school) one play of Aristophanes (*The Frogs*), Cervantes' *Don Quixote* (but not his other works), Rabelais' *Gargantua and Pantagruel*, nine of Dickens's fifteen novels, nothing at all of Meredith, one novel of Thackeray (*Vanity Fair*), and Swift's *Gulliver's Travels*, *A Modest Proposal* and a few shorter pieces of his verse and prose. I belong to Sadiq's generation, and grew up aspiring to read those works of literature which our generation was taught to value most. Even so, as you see, I don't score anything like full marks on Sadiq's list. It seems probable that younger readers, whose reading has been different from ours (and not necessarily worse than ours) would probably score even poorer marks. And the chances are that we are expected to feel ashamed of our deficiencies or at any rate awestruck by Sadiq's immense range. Well, we may be or we may not be. Personally, I'm not. Nobody has read everything he'd like to have read, because everyone has a lot to do in life besides reading books, and there just isn't time to do all you'd like to do, let alone read all you'd like to read. So *everyone* has gaps in his reading, and while that may be a cause of mild regret it is certainly no cause for shame. And anyway the judgements that Sadiq, or I, or anyone else may have made of these writers may be interesting, but again, what have they to do with Akbar Ilahabadi? I am reasonably competent to make judgements about, say, two-thirds of the works that Sadiq lists for comparison, and I can't see much point in comparing any of them with any of the others, let alone with Akbar. There is, as far as I can see, no name in the list except Swift to whom reference is in any way relevant. And that reference too is totally unnecessary. What needed to be said about Akbar could perfectly well have been said (and would far better have been said) without reference to any other author whatsoever. And this is not all. I noted in a review of the first edition:

Within two pages (308–10) we are told of Akbar that he is 'like the Tractarians in England', that 'What S.A. Brooke says of Matthew Arnold is true of Akbar also', that 'his strictures . . . remind one of Carlyle' and that 'This reminds me of what Trollope writes of Thackeray'. [5]

All these comparisons are present in the second edition too (pp. 396–7). Readers may be impressed, but they are more likely to feel disappointed, and even irritated, and to wish that they could have an account of Akbar by someone whose heart was not in so many other places at the same time.

If you're going to write about Akbar, study *Akbar*, and tell people what they want to know about him, assuming in them only an intelligent, sensitive interest in literature and a desire to know about a worthwhile writer that they don't yet know about. In all probability you won't need to refer to any other writer at all. If you do, let it be a writer whose works you can reasonably expect your reader to have read, and let your reference be one which is both intelligible in itself and really helpful to the understanding of Akbar.

I have quoted at length from Sadiq because he is the star performer in this childish game of showing off. Grahame Bailey is, as we have seen, just as prone as the other two to make comparisons with English, but he is not guilty of the constant parading of knowledge in which Sadiq indulges, probably because as a man whose mother tongue is English, born and bred in Britain, he doesn't feel the same compulsion to display his knowledge of English literature (or, more precisely, of books *about* English literature, because it is these that Sadiq constantly quotes). But Saksena, albeit in a more limited way than Sadiq, suffers from the same childish desire to show off. Thus he writes of Farhad that 'he dug through a second Athos' (pp. 23–4). All that it was relevant to say was that he dug through a mountain. Why 'a second Athos'? The only reason can be that he wanted to show that he knew something about ancient Greece. But what student of Urdu literature needs to know that? It is ironical that one who considers it a grave defect in Urdu that all its literary references are to Persian legend, and that this makes it un-Indian (as if one were to condemn *Paradise Lost* as un-English because all of its references are to Hebrew, Greek and Roman legend), thinks it quite alright to use metaphors which assume a knowledge of Greek and Latin references—to talk about 'Athos' when all he needed to say was 'a mountain' and talk of 'Venus and Bacchus' (p. 28) when what he means is simply 'love and wine'.

What Grahame Bailey does share with the other two is the assumption, which they seem to think a self-evident fact, that the only literature which really deserves the name of literature is that which educated English readers of their and my generation have traditionally prized—that is English literature, plus those classics of ancient Greece and Rome and of the European middle ages and renaissance long available to English readers in English translation. Well, everyone is entitled to his own point of view, but this particular point of view is one that disqualifies you from writing a worthwhile history of Urdu literature. People want to know what Urdu literature has to offer them, not to be told three times on every page what it *doesn't* offer them. How it compares or doesn't compare with English (or any other) literature is totally irrelevant.

Totally irrelevant—but since writers on Urdu literature regularly make the comparison let me digress to say a few words about it. The literature which Saksena, Sadiq and Co value so highly is, they tell us, far richer both in quantity and in quality than Urdu literature is. Yes, on the whole *of course* it is. And the reasons are obvious. English in approximately its present form, has been the language of major works of poetry and prose literature since the sixteenth century; Urdu, in approximately its present form, has been the language of such literature in poetry since the early eighteenth century and in prose for little more than a hundred years. People who have English as their mother tongue and speak roughly the same language as that of English literature number hundreds of millions; people who have Urdu as their mother tongue are nowhere near as numerous. Speakers of English are mostly literate. Speakers of Urdu are mostly not. Speakers of English can, for the most part, afford to buy books, at any rate occasionally. Speakers of Urdu mostly can't—not even books on cheap paper, badly calligraphed and badly bound. In the English-speaking world popular fiction writers can make a comfortable living by writing. Their Urdu counterparts will commonly be published in editions of at the most 1500 copies, and making a living by writing and thus being able to devote their whole time to it, is out of the question. So of course English literature is richer and more abundant. And what relevance does this have for the would-be historian of Urdu literature? None at all. Absolutely none. His job is to tell us what Urdu literature has contributed, and still contributes, to the world's stock of worthwhile writing.

And now let us return to how *not* to do it. One could illustrate how not to do it from the treatment accorded by these three historians to every single genre; but it is their treatment of the *marsiya*—the long poem on one or other episode in the tragedy of Karbala—that illustrates most clearly what is wrong. Let us first see what they say about it.

Saksena here gives us a pleasant surprise: in his 'General Characteristics' chapter he abandons (only for five lines, it is true) his prevailing tone of censure or damning with faint praise and tells us that the Urdu *marsiyas* are 'excellent' (p. 30).

Not so Grahame Bailey, however. He writes:

They are essentially religious . . . under Anis and Dabir the marsiya became practically a form of epic having however this limitation that it must always revolve round the death of Hasan, Husain and the members of their family.

Subject to this limitation, which is a very serious one, marsiyas take in Urdu the place that epic poetry occupies in western lands . . . They suffer of course from their narrowness; every character is either friend or enemy, altogether good or entirely evil, and the only emotions are those which would be brought out by such a tragedy as that of Karbala (p. 61).

He graciously concludes: 'Yet with all that, there is nothing so admirable in Urdu poetry as the marsiya.'
And now Sadiq:

The *marsiyas* are not organic wholes. They are like strings of beads, the poet exhausting all his strength on a single episode at a time without treating the subject as a whole. They suffer, besides, from a conscious tendency to overdo the pathetic. Most of them are marred by cheap sentimental effects and seldom, if ever, rise to the austere heights of tragic sentiments (p. 40).

His fuller treatment (chapter X) runs to twenty-five pages, in which praise is mixed with blame. But he too echoes all of Grahame Bailey's criticisms and adds some of his own. Thus he considers 'excessive tearfulness' to be inconsistent with 'manliness fortitude and endurance' (p. 212). He says he has 'a long list of grievances against Anis, both in regard to his style and sentiment' (p. 213). This list includes 'the use of colloquialisms, cheap endearments and sob-stuff' (p. 213) and of 'debased erotic imagery' (p. 216).

Let us take these adverse criticisms one by one.

The *marsiya* isn't really an epic. Quite true. But who says that it ought to have been? Urdu has no epic like those of Homer and Virgil and Milton. So what? So nothing. Classical Greek and Latin and English have no *marsiya*. So what? So nothing. Grahame Bailey and Co would think you mad if you criticized the epic for not being a *marsiya* and they would be right. What they don't realize is that it is no less mad to criticize the *marsiya* for not being an epic. An epic is an epic and a *marsiya* is a *marsiya* and no literature is under any obligation to have every genre that every other literature has.

The *marsiyas* don't tell a connected, coherent story. Quite true. But who says they should? And how come that people who find this 'limitation' . . . 'a very serious one' appear to find exactly the same feature in the European epic quite unexceptionable? Neither the *Iliad* nor the *Odyssey* nor the *Aeneid* nor *Paradise Lost* tell a connected, coherent story of the kind that Grahame Bailey seems to think the *marsiya* should tell. They tell parts of a story. They don't need to tell it in full because their audience knows the full story already. And so does the audience of the *marsiya*.

The *marsiyas* 'suffer . . . from their narrowness; every character is either . . . altogether good or entirely evil.' So? Isn't the same feature evident in the greater part of *Paradise Lost*?

As for the 'tearfulness' versus 'manliness' theme. Sadiq is treating modern Western convention as a universal, eternal one. Dorothy Sayers made an apt response to this kind of narrow attitude, when she wrote, in the introduction to her translation of *The Song of Roland*:

I think we must not reckon it weakness in him [Charlemagne] that he is overcome by grief for Roland's death, that he faints upon the body and has to be raised by the barons and supported by them while he utters his lament. There are fashions in sensibility as in everything else. The idea that a strong man should react to great personal and national calamities by a slight compression of the lips and by silently throwing his cigarette into the fireplace is of very recent origin. By the standards of feudal epic, Charlemagne's behaviour is perfectly correct. Fainting, weeping and lamenting is what the situation calls for.[6]

With regard to Sadiq's other 'grievances' all that can be said is that he is entitled to his own taste and his own opinion, but that neither I nor most of those who value Urdu literature would agree with him. Anis's use of colloquialisms is in no way inappropriate; his endearments are *not* 'cheap'; and his use of erotic imagery is not 'debased'. (One suspects that to Saksena, Grahame Bailey and Sadiq sentiment which is 'erotic' is by definition also 'debased'—just as homosexual love, rightly accepted as legitimate in, for example, both ancient Greece and Shakespeare's sonnets is, to Saksena, 'revolting to the mind'.)

The English reader doesn't want, and doesn't need, to be told all this stuff. He needs to know what the *marsiya* is, who were the poets who wrote it, what impelled them to write, who they wrote for, how it was conveyed to its audience, and in what context and on what occasion. But this information is either missing from Sadiq and Co or where it is supplied, is supplied with vague and/or disparaging remarks.

Grahame Bailey tells us that it is 'a religious poem'. Sadiq, rightly and properly, gives us an outline of the story of the Karbala tragedy. He further tells us that the reason why the *marsiya* is in the form it is 'is not clear' (p. 209) and that 'Probably' this 'was dictated by the requirements of the mourning assemblies' (p. 209). On the contrary, it is entirely clear, and there is no 'probably' about it. What he suggests is not 'probably' but quite certainly (and, one might add, obviously) the case.

The *marsiya* can be read, or listened to, at any time, but it is intended above all to be recited in that month of the year when Husain's martyrdom took place and to give expression to the grief and the sense of tragedy which all Muslims, and especially Shia Muslims, feel when that anniversary comes round. This emotional atmosphere is all-pervading. The audience knows every detail of the Karbala story and can respond at once to every detail of every episode which the poem presents. Not only the intense emotional tone of the poem, but its very form is determined by this situation. Look at any of Anis's *marsiyas* and you can almost *see* it being recited. It is composed in six-line stanzas, and the rhyme scheme is AAAABB CCCCDD and so on throughout the poem. The first four lines, often in the gorgeous language which people all over the world think appropriate to such solemn occasions, build up to a climax, like great clouds massing in the sky, and the last two, often in simple language which makes an immediate, forceful impact, are like the torrential rain which falls as the clouds burst. There is naturally a pause before the next stanza is presented, which gives time for the tears and cries of grief of the audience to subside.

Disparaging critics often belittle the *marsiya* as a poem composed 'merely' to make you weep. Why on earth should that be considered a defeat? Isn't the tragedy of Karbala one to which any sensitive person would react in this way? I am not a Shia, not a Muslim, and not even a believer in any religion. I became an atheist at the age of fifteen and have continued one over all the years I have lived since then. But I am moved by the spectacle of *any* people, of any religion or none who will endure suffering and death before they will betray the principles by which they live. So the *marsiya* moves me too, and will move any person of strong feeling and firm conviction who is open to receive what it has to give him and doesn't let irrelevant display of his profound understanding of English literature get in the way. (I may remark in passing that the 'erotic' sentiment to which Sadiq objects is entirely relevant to the *marsiya* theme. The hero of the ghazal too is the man who will suffer and die before he will forsake the woman, or the God, or the ideals he loves.) And once again, those who object to the extravagant grief of the *marsiya* reciter and his hearers might care to be reminded that the characters, reciters, and listeners of Homer (who belongs to the European tradition and so is, quite rightly, admired by Sadiq and Co) also display this extravagant grief. Read in the Book XVIII of the *Iliad* how Achilles responds to the news of the death of Patroclus, and read in Plato's *Ion* the account of the extravagant emotions with which the rhapsodes (professional reciters) recited Homer's poems to an equally emotional audience.

One could continue on these themes much longer. But it is time to conclude with some remarks of how to write in English a history of Urdu literature. First I would have all would-be historians who belong to the Urdu-speaking community consider carefully whether they have the necessary qualifications for writing such a history. I would say to them: If you don't think much of Urdu literature, please don't go to the trouble of writing a history of it. You are under no obligation to do so, and it would be much better for all concerned if you spared yourself the labour and your readers disappointment; because a man who is interested enough in Urdu literature to open a book on the subject does so hoping to find an answer to the question, 'What has Urdu contributed to the world's literature?' If your answer to this question is, in effect, 'Precious little; certainly not nearly as much as its admirers think, and in any case very much less than English has contributed'—then I respectfully suggest that you are not the person to write its history in English. If, holding this opinion, you still feel moved to write about Urdu literature, surely you should follow the example of your soul-mate Kalimuddin Ahmad and write *in Urdu,* for those who can read Urdu literature. In this way you may perhaps persuade them to revise their (in your view) false estimate of it and either abandon the study of a literature which has so little to commend it and cultivate a taste for English literature instead, or else at least to learn from the study of English (as Grahame Bailey suggests) the kind of writing with which they may attempt to enrich their own language. These things are primarily matters of concern to people who already know Urdu literature, and not to your English readers.

In short, don't embark upon a history of Urdu literature in English unless you genuinely feel that Urdu literature has something substantial to give the world and you want to help people understand what that something is.

If you do feel that, and are confident that you can write a good history, there are still things that you need to think about. First, 'literature' covers a vast range of writing. Don't try to cover it all. Give major coverage to major writers, writers who produce that kind of literature which makes a writer really great, the kind of literature that has the power to *change* you, enlarging both your capacity to enjoy life and your ability to understand more fully yourself, and other men and women, and the world around you. By all means include lesser writers too, but let the space you give a writer always be proportionate to his greatness.

Secondly, since you are writing in English, make the most of your medium: realize how many millions of people in how many different countries you can reach and, as far as you can, write for them all, bearing in mind that it will be through your book that most of them will be making the acquaintance of Urdu literature for the first time, and assuming only that they *want* to know—not that they already do know—something of the subject. If you are an academic you may have fallen prey to the absurd, but, alas, very widespread idea that you need to display to a (you hope) admiring audience how extremely learned and original you are. Actually you don't need to and shouldn't want to do that even in writing for an academic audience. And you must certainly not do it in a work of this kind. Tell your readers what they need and want to know—and only that.

Thirdly, realize that Urdu literature is the product of a kind of society and of a history of which most of your readers will know very little. So set the literature in its social and historical perspective. Tell them what they need to know of these things if they are to understand and appreciate it—and, for example, don't be coy about love. Your readers need to know that the love which Urdu poetry celebrates is, in the eyes of the society in which it was written, illicit love. Otherwise, they'll think Urdu love poetry very odd stuff—which, of course, it isn't. (In my own case, it was more than three years after I first made the acquaintance of the ghazal before I encountered in Khurshidul Islam someone who was prepared to tell me plainly what it is all about.)

Well, that covers all that it seems appropriate to say in an article of this length. I must, however, just add a tailpiece to say that the publication in 1985 of *Urdu Literature,* by D. J. Matthews, C. Shackle and Shahrukh Husain,[7] marked the appearance at long last of a short account of Urdu literature written, by and large, as it should be written. Its one major defect, in my view, is that it does not perform adequately the task that my immediately preceding paragraph ['Thirdly, ...] explains and, for example, continues the tradition of coyness on the subject of love. For all that, it is a vast improvement on its predecessors, and a forerunner, I hope, of still better followers to come.

NOTES AND REFERENCES

1. Muhammad Sadiq, *A History of Urdu Literature* (Delhi: Oxford University Press, 1964; 2nd edition, 1984).
2. Allahabad: Ram Narain Lal, 1927.
3. Calcutta: YMCA Press, 1932.
4. Published in *Bulletin of the School of Oriental and African Studies,* 51(1) (1988).
5. *Asia Major,* XII/New Series (1966), p. 135.
6. Dorothy Sayers, tr. *The Song of Roland* (London: Penguin, 1957), p. 15.
7. London: Urdu Markaz.

❦3❧

AIJAZ AHMAD AND GHĀLIB

Aijaz Ahmad's *Ghazals of Ghalib: Versions from the Urdu*[1] is one of the modest crop produced by the celebrations of the centenary of Ghālib's death in 1969, and it is one of the most interesting. Someone conceived the idea that the way to present Ghālib's Urdu verse (the volume does not include any of his Persian) to the modern American public was to provide to a number of American poets, none of whom, I think, has any knowledge of Urdu, as much information as could be provided about Ghālib's originals, and ask them, where they felt inspired to do so, to re-create them in modern American verse. Personally, I am not sure that this is *the* way to do it, but it is certainly a legitimate and potentially valuable way, and an experiment which was well worth trying.

Accordingly it was decided to select someone competent to interpret Ghālib—that is, to convey to the chosen poets the sounds, the rhythms, the literal meanings, the necessary explanations, and the historical, social, cultural and literary background of Ghālib's verse. *Ghazals of Ghalib* is the result. After an Introduction we have thirty-seven ghazals (more accurately, extracts from ghazals) presented. In each case the Urdu text is followed by a literal translation, and usually by a note on 'Form' (which I shall discuss below), after which, couplet by couplet, we are given 'Essential vocabulary' and 'General explanation' wherever Mr Ahmad feels this to be necessary. Then follow the American poets' finished versions. Unlike Victor Kiernan's *Poems by*

* Originally published in the *Journal of the Royal Asiatic Society*, 1974, Part 1.

Faiz,[2] this book does not present the Urdu texts in Roman transliteration as well as in the Urdu script.

In a project of this kind the role of what one may call the interpreter of the original is clearly a key one, and his burden of responsibility clearly a very heavy one; and that being so, the interpreter needed to be selected with the greatest care to ensure as far as humanly possible that the person chosen should be one equipped with all the necessary knowledge and prepared to spare no effort to do full justice to the great poet in whose service he was to be enlisted. Had this been done, the method would have left little to be desired.

Unfortunately there is sufficient evidence to warrant the conclusion that Mr Ahmad was not, shall we say, an ideal choice. One's doubts are aroused on the very first page of the Editor's Note (p. v) by such vague and pretentious statements as 'It is impossible, and even pointless, to mention all the dictionaries one reads in the course of one's love affair with a language . . .', '. . . no Urdu dictionary compiled during the last fifty years is of any real value . . .', and 'I have, of course, read the usual scholarly commentaries . . .'; or, on p. xxvii, where he remarks of the researches of 'some Western orientalists' (unspecified) that 'what is common knowledge in Persia [*sic*] seems to be presented now as news'; or, on p. 75, where within a few lines we have references to 'the harder core of Islamic thought' (whatever that means) and to the 'totalization of knowledge' (whatever that means) in the 'Islamic, or Marxist-Sartrean' or 'very Hegelian' sense. We are thus presumably intended to receive the impression that here is a man who has ('of course') read practically everything, although for one of his attainments this was hardly necessary. Not surprisingly one finds as one reads on, ample reason to doubt whether this impression is correct, and to wonder whether rather sweeping generalizations are not often a cover for ignorance. One of the most striking grounds for this feeling is provided by Mr Ahmad's statement about the 'form' of his selected ghazals. Thirty of the thirty-seven bear a note headed 'Form'. (What this means we shall see in a moment.) Why seven lack any such note is not clear; all seven exemplify forms which are exemplified, and described, elsewhere in the selection too, but there is not so much as a 'Same as Ghazal . . .' to indicate this. Under the heading 'Form' in the great majority of cases appear the words 'Approximately . . . syllables' or words to the same effect. The word 'approximately' or 'about' occurs in every case. This in itself is noteworthy. As Mr Ahmad himself remarks (p. xvi), 'All the lines in a ghazal have to be of equal metrical length' and he (surely?) knows that only in a very few metres is the poet permitted such variations as the alternation of two short syllables for one long. Hence, read in terms of strict scansion, every line has, with rare exceptions, not an approximate, but an exact number of syllables. True, it is not recited in a way which stresses the scansion pattern unduly; *kaunse* will be *read* as *kaunse* and not as the *kaun(a)se* which it becomes for purposes of scansion. But if you are going to give a brief indication of the form of the line surely a statement of the basic metrical pattern is to be preferred to an 'approximate' syllable-count. It is no more difficult to say 'Metre: $-\cup- - |\cup-\cup-|--$' than it is to say 'Form: Approximately ten syllables to the line'. This is not all. Mr Ahmad seems to have used the word 'approximately' as an excuse for not bothering to count at all. Thus Ghazal XXXII (p. 144) which is in the metre just quoted, is said to have 'Approximately seven syllables to the line'. In fact it has ten to the line; eight of the ten lines quoted cannot in any conceivable way be read as lines of less than ten syllables, and the two that can, score respectively nine syllables (first line) and eight syllables (third line). I chose this ghazal at random, but further examination shows that such extraordinary mistakes are by no means rare. Thus almost exactly the same position emerges in relation to Ghazal XIII which is in the same metre as Ghazal XXXII, and is again said to have 'approximately seven syllables to the line'. As before, ten lines are quoted. As before, eight of them are of ten syllables. The remaining two are of nine syllables each. Examples of this kind of thing could be multiplied. Thus the note on the form of Ghazal VI reads, 'Each line of approximately fourteen syllables'. In fact the metre is of sixteen syllables; of the ten lines seven score that number as they would be recited, and the remaining three score fifteen each. Ghazal VII ('Each line of approximately fourteen short syllables') has a line of sixteen syllables, of which eight are short and eight long. Not only does Mr Ahmad not bother to count, he seems quite unaware of the recurrence of the same metre in numbers of ghazals. Thus Ghazals IV, X, XX, XXII, XXVI, XXVII, XXVIII, XXIX and XXXIII are all in the same metre (of fourteen syllables to the line), but Mr Ahmad's notes on their form are as follows: on IV and X there is no note at all; XX, XXII, XXVII, XXIX and XXXIII are said to have 'approximately twelve syllables to the line', XXVIII has 'approximately thirteen' and most surprising of all, XXVI bears the note 'Strongly stressed line [*sic*] of approximately seven syllables each'. The idea of seven as an approximation to fourteen is intriguing.

When we come to consider the selection Mr Ahmad has made we enter on difficult ground for two men of good taste may legitimately differ from each other, and no two men's selections are likely to coincide. In his Introduction (pp. xxvi–xxvii) he explains, for the most part very sensibly, the principles which governed his selection, but he goes on to say that 'in practically all cases' he has 'selected five or six couplets from within a ghazal'. He does not explain why he has thought this sort of uniformity desirable. And in fact the degree of uniformity has been understated. In all cases except one he chose precisely five couplets. The one exception is XXVIII which, though Mr Ahmad does not trouble to tell us so, is in fact a *qaṭa'*—a number of lines on a single theme—in contrast with the separate, independent couplets of the typical ghazal. There is one other apparent exception in XXXVII, which has only four couplets of text; but this is because Mr Ahmad discovered, after selecting his usual five, that the fifth couplet he had chosen was not by Ghālib at all, and so dropped it. Mr Ahmad's own words (on p. xxvii, in the same paragraph as that in which he explains his selection of five verses per ghazal) should have shown him that there is no rational justification for this 'five of each' principle, and the result reinforces this point, for it has not infrequently led to the inclusion of some rather light-weight verses to make up the quota. And there are some inexcusable pieces of carelessness. For instance, in XXXVII, where Mr Ahmad's belated discovery caused him to drop the fifth couplet he had originally selected, he has *not* dropped the 'General explanation' which accompanied it. And in XXV, the fifth couplet of text does not correspond to the 'Fifth couplet' explained and translated. (That in the text is the eighth in the full text of the ghazal in question, while that translated and explained—and, incidentally, incorrectly translated and explained—is the sixth.)

But let us grant Mr Ahmad the right to his own selection—and he uses a forceful argument when he points out that the existing *Dīvān* is itself a selection from which 'Ghālib had eliminated most of what [in his view—RR] lacked excellence' (p. xxvii)—and proceed to see how he has presented his results to his American collaborators.

Here too his work leaves a good deal to be desired. His reading of dictionaries seemingly too numerous to count and 'of course . . . the usual scholarly commentaries' seems to have left him on occasion singularly impervious to what they told him. A few examples: *khud-been* (in the very first couplet of Mr Ahmad's selection) does not mean 'one who seeks awareness of Self', but 'one who exults in her own beauty'. The one dictionary which Mr Ahmad praises, that of Platts (not 'Platt' as Mr Ahmad styles him on p. v) makes this clear, and indeed the word is so common an attribute of the beloved in the ghazal that his mistranslation is surprising. (In the third couplet of the same poem Mr Ahmad translates the word for 'known' as 'unknown'.) The suffix *sanj* (p. 81) does not mean 'doing' or 'having' but 'weighing, measuring'. *Subuk-sar* (on the same p. 81) does not mean 'humble', but 'lacking in dignity, cheap, contemptible', *nay o nosh* (p. 129) does not mean eating and drinking but 'music and drinking, music and wine', a pairing which is directly taken up and repeated in the couplet immediately following. Ghālib himself explained the meaning of the verse which Mr Ahmad gives on p. 97 (the second of XXI): since Mr Ahmad's own translation and general explanation make very little sense, it is not surprising that they bear no relation to Ghālib's own explanation. We must presume that Mr Ahmad was not aware that Ghālib *had* explained the verse. And yet this explanation is quoted at length on pp. 122–3 of the same Lucknow, 1932 edition of Ḥālī's *Yādgār-i-Ghālib* which Mr Ahmad recommends to his own 'interested reader' (p. v)—somewhat fatuously, since the whole purpose of his work is to introduce Ghālib to an audience that knows no Urdu, and *Yādgār-i-Ghālib* is in Urdu.[3]

There are other translations and explanations which, though they contain no actual misstatements, are quite inadequate. In Ghazal XV the imagery ('Picasso-like', thinks Mr Ahmad) of 'Daughters of the Bier' is quite inadequately explained: the translation does not even indicate that they are stars, and the 'General explanation' merely says that 'the three stars that go before the Bier are called "Banat". What 'the Bier' is, is not explained. (The reference is in fact to the Plough (or Great Bear) or the Little Bear. The three stars of the 'handle' are the 'Daughters' and the remaining four are 'the Bier'.) In XXXII the explanation of the verse about Khiẓar and Alexander completely misses the point, which is that Khiẓar is humanity's guide *par excellence*, and yet his guidance proved useless to Alexander. (The story of the water of immortality needed to be told here, but is not.)

Mr Ahmad's reading of other books which he has consulted seems to have been as careless as his reading of dictionaries and commentaries. For example he writes (on p. xiv) of 'the recent researches of Dr Ashraf, in India, which *prove*[4] that *at least* 27,000 persons were *hanged* during the summer of that one year in Delhi'. In fact, Dr Ashraf's only reference to this figure states simply: '*It is generally estimated* that 27,000 persons were *hanged or shot* in the city of Delhi alone.' This fondness of Mr Ahmad for the sweeping, extravagant, and would-be impressive statement is often in evidence, and leads him to write things that simply do not bear examination. Thus he tells us that Delhi in Ghālib's lifetime was 'a major focal point for countless traumatic crises' and that he was 'surrounded by constant carnage' (both statements on p. vii), and that in his time peasants revolted often enough for Ghālib to use peasant revolt as a metaphor in poetry (p. 30). None of these statements has more than a grain of truth in it, and the last is both untrue and ridiculous. (The verse in relation to which it is made has nothing to do with peasant revolt.) Similarly with Ghālib's more personal history: Mr Ahmad tells us that Ghālib's relations with his wife were 'at best, tentative, obscure, and indifferent' (p. xi), that 'the house in which he lived . . . was filled with nothing but rats and borrowed books' (p. 69), and that he consumed alcohol 'in vast quantities' (p. 35). Again, none of these statements contains more than a grain of truth, and the first is wholly incorrect.

A more fastidious reviewer, or a more pedantic scholar, could find many more grounds on which to impugn Mr Ahmad's competence. For instance, he would treat with derision pp. xxix–xxx where Mr Ahmad speaks of his 'literal translations' (thinking perhaps of transliterations and meaning, it seems, transcriptions, since this alone makes full sense in the context). But while his explanations of the pronunciation of Urdu consonants range from the almost useless to the positively misleading, I would not, bearing in mind that his book is for the lay reader and not for the scholar, have criticized his choice of, for example, 'ee' and 'oo' instead of the scholar's 'ī' and 'ū', had it not been for the fact that there seems to be no reason to quote Urdu words in any transcription at all; for the text is not transcribed, and is thus presumably intended for those who already know the Urdu script.

But Mr Ahmad has a pretty cordial dislike of scholars, fairly plainly hinted at in the present book and more frankly avowed elsewhere.[5] One knows what he means, and to a great extent I sympathize. (No one who has read and responded to W. B. Yeats's poem on Catullus and his editors—'Old, learned, respectable bald heads' who 'Edit and annotate the lines/That young men, tossing on their beds/Rhymed out in love's despair'—could do other than sympathize.) But there are scholars and scholars, and, *pace* Mr Ahmad, they include some who love and appreciate poetry. Even so, I would agree with Mr Ahmad that there was no need to choose an established scholar even of this kind for the work which was entrusted to him. What *is* necessary for such a project as this is to choose a man who is prepared to undertake the labour which is often involved in discovering what it was that Ghālib wanted to say and why he said it in the way he did. Only in this way can a man equip himself to understand, and to convey to others, *Ghālib's poem*, and not the poem which Ghālib's words, not infrequently misunderstood, convey to a reader who has not so equipped himself. Unfortunately, Mr Ahmad does not measure up to this requirement. Two illustrations will suffice. In his translation and explanation of the third couplet of Ghazal VI (p. 30—the statement to which reference was made above) it is Mr Ahmad's sympathy for peasant revolts (one, again, which I share, but which it is in the highest degree unlikely that Ghālib shared) that makes him read into the verse a meaning which is simply not there. A literal translation of the second line of the couplet would be: 'The hot blood of the peasant is the substance of the lightning of [i.e. the lighting that destroys] his crop'—not, as Mr Ahmad thinks, 'the potential electricity hidden in unthreshed corn'. The metaphor illustrates the concept, already stated in the first line, and perfectly intelligible with or without a background of peasant revolts, that within a man's own make-up are the qualities which will one day bring him to ruin. Similarly, in the second example: it is Mr Ahmad's modern imagination that reads into the fifth couplet of Ghazal VIII a reference to the censoring of mail (p. 39). In the convention of Ghālib's day the arrival of a letter unsealed meant that it brought the news of someone's death; the line does not mean that the letter had been opened by, or left open for the convenience of the censor. In both cases the commentaries which Mr Ahmad says that he has ('of course') read, make all this perfectly clear.

In short, one's early misgivings about Mr Ahmad are confirmed as one reads on. Pretension does indeed conceal incompetence. Gross carelessness, inaccuracy, mistranslation of words and lines, and incorrect and inadequate explanations all seriously impair the value of the materials on which the American poets had to rely. I have stressed these inadequacies both because this seems to me to be the aspect of the book to which, in a review for a learned journal, the main attention needs to be paid, and because it is necessary to drive home the point that in a project of this kind the selection of the interpreter of the original is of absolutely crucial importance. Let us hope that in any future project—the book is stated on the flap to be one of a series—we shall find that a great deal more awareness of this fact has been shown.

Where Mr Ahmad has shown so inadequate a sense of his responsibility it is a pleasure to be able to record that the harm done is much less than might have been feared. A great many of the verses Mr Ahmad has chosen are such as were within both his comprehension and his ability to explain reasonably adequately. And the fact that Ghālib was a poet and that Mr Ahmad's American collaborators are also poets (some, inevitably, better than others) guarantees that enough of the original poetry gets across in a sufficiently effective form to vindicate the project and to justify the labour, care, and money that have gone into it. The project was indeed a worthwhile one, and I share the deep satisfaction that Mr Ahmad feels at the American poets' response to Ghālib, for this testifies to the fact that Ghālib can speak to the modern English-speaking world in a way that evokes a deep response.

It was a good idea to include several translations of each piece in several styles, for tastes vary, and by presenting several re-creations of Ghālib's originals the editor has no doubt helped a wider circle of readers to appreciate them than would have been the case had he presented only one. The versions which make the strongest appeal to me are those of Adrienne Rich and W. S. Merwin. Others will doubtless have other preferences. Yet others may not respond very warmly to this kind of verse at all. One hopes that, for them, others will translate in other styles. And one hopes also that no one will condemn either these versions or others in other styles simply because they are not to his own particular taste. Ghālib has different audiences, even within the English-speaking world, and each of them perhaps needs, and should not be denied, its own style of translation.

NOTES AND REFERENCES

1. New York, London: Columbia University Press, 1971.
2. London: Allen and Unwin, 1971.
3. A similar piece of fatuity occurs on p. 68, where in a characteristically pretentious note a discussion of ambiguity reminds Mr Ahmad of 'Mr Empson' who we are told, 'should read these verses of Ghālib'—adding in the next breath that they need to be 'read in the original'. I may perhaps be permitted to remark at this point on Mr Ahmad's ignorance of, or ignoring of, a book which his interested reader *could* consult, *Ghālib: Life and Letters*, translated and edited by myself and Khurshidul Islam. He recommends three things to his readers (all of them in Urdu)—*Yādgār-i-Ghālib*, Ghālib's own letters, and the work of S.M. Ikram. These same three things form the main basis of our book. (For our grateful, and duly acknowledged, use of Ikram see p. 11 of our Introduction.) The book was published simultaneously by Allen and Unwin in Britain and Harvard University Press in the USA in October 1969. Mr Ahmad's Introduction is dated 15 April 1970, and his book was published in 1971.
4. Emphasis in this and the following quotation is mine.
5. See his article in *Mahfil*, v (4): 59–70.

THE URDU GHAZAL
A Rejoinder to Frances W. Pritchett
and William L. Hanaway

I have just read William L..Hanaway's review of my *The Pursuit of Urdu Literature*[1] in *The Annual of Urdu Studies* (*AUS*) 9 (1994), and was gratified by his generally favourable opinion of it. But his strong disagreement with my assessment of the ghazal together with a recent reading of Frances Pritchett's *Nets of Awareness*,[2] revived in me a long dormant feeling that I should respond to the criticism which she made a good many years ago, and in which he now joins her. (I first encountered it in her article 'Convention in the Classical Urdu Ghazal: The Case of Mir'.[3] I don't know whether she would still stand by every word of that, but she refers the reader of *Nets of Awareness* to it and clearly still holds the main line of her argument to be valid.) Then during the summer and autumn of 1994 I had an exchange of letters with Frances Pritchett in which further discussion of some of these issues figured and others were also raised. In her letter of 3 August 1994 she suggested that we might ask 'for space in the *AUS* for a kind of debate on the subject'. I am very glad to accept her suggestion.

Briefly, the difference between us is this: I with Khurshidul Islam, see the ghazal as essentially the love poetry of a society in which passionate, romantic love is necessarily illicit and is persecuted by the

* Originally published in *The Annual of Urdu Studies* 10 (1995): 93–109.

pillars of society; and in it the theme of love between two human beings is paralleled by the experiences of mystic love for God, the Divine Beloved (or, in secular terms, for a high ideal in life) similarly persecuted by the pillars of society. Frances Pritchett and William L. Hanaway on the other hand argue that 'this characterization is all wrong' (Hanaway), that it is 'impossible to consider the ghazal a social document' (Hanaway again) and that 'any attempt to move from poetic imagery to social reality . . . is destined to break down' (Pritchett). (Actually, to say that they argue this is to pay them a compliment they do not deserve. They don't argue; they just assert.)

But before I come to this major difference between us I think I should first clear the ground by taking up other points from Frances Pritchett's 1979 article and her recent book *Nets of Awareness* (a book of which, incidentally, despite reservations, I have a high opinion). In both she writes as though the views expressed in *Three Mughal Poets*[4] and 'The Pursuit of the Urdu Ghazal'[5] are mine. Of course they *are* mine, but—and this is an important point to which I shall return below—they are the views of not just Ralph Russell, but of Ralph Russell and Khurshidul Islam. In her 1979 article she makes the valid point that the 'I' of Mir's poetry is not necessarily the same as the actual Mir. Islam and I have accepted this, but, to quote *The Pursuit of Urdu Literature*, while this is true it is 'not very significant, because Mir was clearly prepared to have his readers think that it was himself he *was* writing of and so to identify himself with 'I' of the poems' (p. 54).

She goes on to say that in *Three Mughal Poets* 'Russell [i.e. Russell and Islam] makes [make] no further attempt to examine the facts of Mir's life' (p. 61). Indeed we don't, since that was not our aim. Our aim was to illustrate from the verse of Mir the typical course of love, regardless of whether the lover in these verses was always Mir, or the beloved was always Mir's beloved. She says, 'Russell's [i.e. Russell and Islam's] interpretative goals . . . require him [them] to claim a high degree of sociological accuracy for his [their] model' (p. 62). Yes, for reasons which I shall elaborate later, we do claim this; and I might add at this point that in my view the ghazal poets themselves support us. Because as I have had occasion to observe elsewhere (for example, in *Three Mughal Poets*, pp. 106–7) some of the great poets who wrote ghazals also wrote *maṣnavīs*, in which the course of love is portrayed essentially as *Three Mughal Poets* describes it. There is no reason to think that Mir's *maṣnavīs* are not, and every reason to think that Mōmin's are, essentially realistic stories, as is the story of Shauq's *Zahr-e 'Ishq*. (I used to have my Urdu students read *Zahr-e 'Ishq* before we came to the ghazals because that poem to a large extent spells out the situations of love of which the ghazal assumes previous knowledge.)

She goes on to contrast my (our) portrayal of Mir (although in *Three Mughal Poets* it is not claimed that Mir's verses always portray Mir) both with 'Andalīb Shādānī's and with Annemarie Schimmel's. I venture to say that, outside the USA, no one ever took Shādānī's 'sensational' article seriously, and his select verses no more prove Mir to have been essentially a pederast—a lover of boys—than other selections which could equally well have been made would prove him to have been essentially heterosexual. Not that Mir, or Urdu ghazal poets in general, would have disapproved of love of boys. And I am not, as Pritchett alleges, in the least 'uncomfortable' with the idea that Mir may have loved boys, handsome men, and courtesans as well as purdah-observing women. To him, and to ghazal poets in general, love is love—and as Ḥasrat Mōhānī put it,

> *muḥabbat khair-e muṭlaq hai baharḥāl*
> All love is unconditionally good . . .

Of course, this sentiment was not, and is not, shared by conventional society, and it is, unfortunately, those who uphold the values of conventional society who have predominated in the ranks of Urdu literary critics for the last hundred years and more. (I once remarked to 'Ibādat Barēlavī that the *ghazal* has fared badly at the hands of Urdu literary critics because the ghazal poet is an *'āshiq*—a lover—and his two main adversaries are the *shaikh* and the *dunyādār;* and the values of the literary critics have been either those of the *shaikh*—in modern terms, the fundamentalists—or those of the *dunyādār*—the worldly wise.) The conventional have always been uncomfortable with the ghazal, and traditionally the best that the poets could do when cornered by them was to defend themselves by alleging that, for example, detailed descriptions of sexual intercourse were *really* simply an allegory for divine love—as though this altered the fact that even if they were, they were *also* detailed descriptions of sexual intercourse. The approach of Ḥālī, Shiblī, and others to men's love for boys is motivated by the same desire to make respectable what *cannot be* made respectable. Pederasty in Urdu poetry, they allege, is a (now purely conventional) feature of Urdu poetry carried over from Persian in imitation of Persian convention. They knew perfectly well what everyone else knew (and knows)—that homosexual love, including pederasty, is one inevitable product of societies (like their own) in which there is strict segregation of the sexes, be it ancient Athens, South Asian Muslim society, the old British navy ('rum, buggery and the lash'), British public schools or (if contemporary American detective novelists are to be believed) prisons in the USA. And that is why Urdu poetry reflects it.[6]

Of Annemarie Schimmel, Pritchett writes, 'Schimmel's emphasis on the theme of 'the suffering lover' suggests an approach to classical ghazal poetry—including Mir's—very different from the one used by Russell and Islam' (p. 65). Oh? How does she make that out? Russell and Islam, it seems to me, emphasize the suffering lover just as much as Schimmel does. Where does Pritchett get the opposite impression from?

There are other points in Pritchett's article which need to be taken up. For instance, she expresses some surprise that 'Russell even feels able to identify in the character of Fancy Day [of Thomas Hardy's *Under the Greenwood Tree*] a girl who resembles in many ways the heroine of the Urdu ghazal' (p. 61). There is nothing surprising in that; in many ways she *does* resemble the heroine of the Urdu ghazal. And Pritchett is surely aware that I never suggested that there are not other ways in which she does not. She also writes that 'the question "Who is the beloved?" is a thoroughly unhelpful and misleading one if the answer expected' is anything like 'Russell's attempted reply—a girl like Fancy Day' (p. 72). Her very next sentences make it clear that this is a far from adequate description of 'Russell's attempted reply.' And ten years before she wrote these words I had made clear in 'The Pursuit of the Urdu Ghazal'—an article which presumably she had studied, since she refers to it in a footnote—what my view was. I quote the relevant extract here:

We can now put in comprehensive form the question, 'Who, or whàt is the beloved of the Urdu ghazal?' and can answer, 'Any person, or any ideal to

whom or to which the poet, whether in real life or in fantasy, is prepared to
dedicate himself, sacrificing himself for its (her, his) sake and willingly
accepting the hostility of his fellow men as an inevitable consequence of his
love' (pp. 119–20).

And now let me come to the central issue—that of conventions
and what they do or do not show. Pritchett, in her 1979 article, went
so far as to assert, 'It is precisely this conventionality of theme and
content that Russell [and Islam] is [are] unwilling to recognize in
Mir's ghazals' (p. 70). Oh? Where is her evidence for this? We are not
in the least unwilling to recognize the conventions of the ghazal. Where
is there anything in what we have written to suggest that we are?
Every student of the ghazal knows that ghazal poets write within strict
conventions, and that it is important to discuss their significance. So
I have no substantial quarrel with Hanaway when he writes in his
review that classical 'Persian [and Urdu] lyric poetry screens the direct
expression of emotions through a dense filter of conventions' (p. 256),
though I think that 'dense' is too strong a word.[7] What I do quarrel
with is his astonishing assertion in his very next sentence (echoing, as
we have seen, Pritchett's view). He writes, 'It is this process of
abstraction that makes it impossible to consider the ghazal a social
document . . . and to give the lover and beloved of the poetry direct
analogues in real life.' Oh? *How* does this 'abstraction' make this
'impossible'? This is something which needs to be argued, nor simply
asserted. (And I wonder what on earth it is that drives him and Pritchett
to assert this so emphatically.) It is as though one were to say,
'Shakespeare makes his characters speak in blank verse; this proves
that it is impossible to give them analogues in real life.' Of course it
doesn't prove anything of the sort. Neither Hanaway's assertion nor
the hypothetical assertion about Shakespeare either proves or disproves
either what Hanaway asserts or what Islam and I assert. It simply has
no relevance to either assertion. The use of conventions is the use of
conventions; it implies nothing about either the relevance or irrelevance
of the social context in which the poets write. The relevant question
to ask is: What are the emotions that the poets express through these
conventions? But before coming to that, let us see what these
conventions are and consider where they come from. In her *Nets of
Awareness* Pritchett tells us that 'people of the old culture felt able to

invoke attraction to beautiful boys . . . illicit heterosexual love, intoxication, apostasy, and other images of forbidden behaviour . . . as powerful, multivalent poetic images' (p. 175). Why *these* images? Why are beautiful boys, etc., etc., the images that the 'people of the old culture' invoked? And where do these images come from? Islam and I answer that where the Urdu ghazal is concerned, they come from the social reality that the poets experienced, from the experience, in fact or in fantasy, of love that was necessarily illicit love. The best that Pritchett and Hanaway can do is to tell us that they come from the conventions of Persian, Turkish and Arabic. Okay, they come from Persian, Turkish, Arabic. But where did the Persians, Turks and Arabs get them from? What real experiences did they represent? Islam and I didn't need to talk about Persian, Turkish and Arabic, but we would maintain that they were the product of a Persian, etc., 'social reality' similar to the 'social reality' which produced them in the Urdu ghazal. Pritchett and Hanaway should not content themselves with asserting (*not* arguing) that Islam and I are wrong; they should tell us where *they* think these things ultimately come from.

Pritchett says that these 'images of forbidden behaviour' are invoked as 'powerful, multivalent poetic images'. Images *of what?* What is it that the poets express through these conventions? Neither Pritchett nor Hanaway has anything much to tell us about this. Pritchett says in her 1979 article that the vision of Mir which emerges is not that which Russell and Islam portray 'but rather of Mir the consummate poet, who uses the traditional themes and conventions of the ghazal with brilliance, individuality, and intense emotional power' (p. 71). (Why 'but rather'? There is no contradiction between the two 'visions' she speaks of. Mir is both what we say he is *and* a 'consummate poet', etc.) She quotes with approval Muhammad Sadiq's judgment of Mir's verse as 'moving and powerful', verse which 'at its best comes from the heart and goes to the heart', but she is pretty vague about what she thinks this 'intense emotional power' is used to express. He expresses 'with simple dignity', she says, 'moods of melancholy, futility, pain and despair' (pp. 71–2). Yes, and much, much more besides, as *Three Mughal Poets* amply showed.

Pritchett and Hanaway tell us what they think ghazal poetry is *not* about, but have very little to say on what it *is* about. (A few days ago I was reading Lytton Strachey's essay on Johnson's *Lives of the Poets*, and felt I might equally say of Pritchett and Hanaway what he says of Johnson: 'Johnson never inquired what poets were trying to do; he merely aimed at discovering whether what they had done complied with the canons of poetry.'[8]

So much for Pritchett and Hanaway's published writings. In her as yet unpublished letter to me—the one in which she suggested an exchange of views in the *AUS*—Frances Pritchett presented her argument in more detail, and it is only fair to her that I should quote the relevant paragraphs at length. So here they are, followed by my rejoinder to them.[9]

To me the ghazal's reliance on its wonderful network of images and conventions makes it very clear that for most purposes, it is not derived from anything like the *actual* 'social conditions' of their personal and collective lives. After all, if the ghazal poet writes as a passionate lover (of people of both sexes and widely varying social conditions), he also depicts himself as a drunkard, a madman, an apostate from Islam, a caged bird, a hunted animal, and even a voice from beyond the grave. If we do not imagine him to be these latter things in reality, why do we imagine that he must be a passionate lover in reality? If any of these reflect actuality, it's surely at one remove, through conventions adopted and understood by all practitioners and enjoyers of the genre. Your attempt in *Three Mughal Poets* to construct an ideal-type love affair—the glimpse on the balcony, the secret messages, etc.—has sometimes reminded me of Freud's archetypal band of brothers who kill their father and thus give rise to the Oedipus complex. Can this primal event at all be located in history? Did it occur once and definitely (like the Fall), or repeatedly for everybody, or only conceptually? After all, we know that many Urdu poets began composing well before they reached puberty, and we know they were trained by technical methods that emphasized a mastery of the tradition rather than personal experience, and we know that their mushairah [*mushā'ira*] performances were deliberately made competitive and formally restricted, in a way that cut personal experiential input to a minimum. I believe I argue from a wealth of evidence that the classical ghazal is indeed a 'game of words'.

But of course I would never agree that it is *only* words. To me the central thrust of the ghazal is the exploration of states of passionate desire—and the experience of the radical, irrevocable unfulfillment of desire. The beloved's one chief role is to be absent. I know many ghazal-lovers whose lives have had almost nothing in common with the social conditions of medieval North India, who still find rich emotional and intellectual experience in the ghazal. I am certainly one of them!

To me it is like country-and-western music: the hero in a song always has to be a cowboy or a long-distance truck-driver, or something very similar, but nobody thinks that the song-writer, the singer, or the audience has to be. The delights of genres like this do not lie in their realistic depiction of particular social conditions but in their expression of shared human emotional experiences in literarily heightened ways. Maybe the inventors of the genre were cowboys, but their actual experience (to whatever extent it was reflected in the songs) is now entirely conventionalized for modern enjoyers of the genre.

The strong form of your argument I think is open to many objections. In a weaker form, however, I would argue that it becomes irrefutable but also undecidable. Even if people don't actually live the lives they depict in their poetry, maybe the original impulse for setting up those generic conventions was an actual set of social conditions? Maybe so and maybe not, but how to prove or disprove it? What would count as evidence, and would we have to start with the early Arabic ghazal? Persian ghazal? We are back looking for Freud's primal band of parricidal brothers. And what of the poet as apostate from Islam, as embracing Hinduism in fact—would some poet or group of poets ever have actually done this? And if not, how to explain such conventions?

Here, Frances Pritchett, is my response to what you write:

First, let me again ask *how* 'the ghazal's reliance on its . . . images and conventions makes it very clear that . . . it is not derived from anything like the *actual* 'social conditions' of their lives'? You must *argue* this, nor just state it.

Secondly, since I have never studied Freud (a statement which is neither a boast nor an apology) I cannot respond to this part of your argument.

Thirdly, I think that much of the rest of what you say supports my interpretation rather than yours. I shall return to this point later.

I hope you won't take it amiss if I say that I think the answers to most of your questions were given long before you asked them—in *Three Mughal Poets* (1968), 'The Pursuit of the Urdu Ghazal' (1969), and an article (which, however, you may not have seen) called 'The Urdu Ghazal in Muslim Society' (1970).[10] However, its essential points are again made in chapter 2 of my *The Pursuit of Urdu Literature* which you had read and reviewed (in gratifyingly favourable terms!) before you wrote the letter to which I am responding.

First let me take the case of the man who was/is in real life the illicit lover of another human being. You will surely not deny that there have been, and are, such people, even if we grant (as I do) that they constitute(d) a very small minority of their community. (Heloise and Abelard existed, though the vast majority of their contemporaries did not love and act as they did.) Surely you will also not deny that many of them will have been ghazal poets. *Their* ghazals will, within the ghazal conventions, have been the direct, literal expression of what they were actually feeling. Some of these poets will also have subscribed to the common mystic view that earthly love teaches divine love, [11] to the humanist, anti-fundamentalist concept of Islam, to the view that one may be a true lover of God even if one calls Him by some other name, and that *all* human beings should be united by love for one another. All these things are, I am convinced, literally true of Mīr, and if it is true that neither I nor anyone else can conclusively prove this, it is, so to speak, even more true that you can't produce the slightest evidence for your assumption that he was *not* the man his poetry describes himself as being.

In what terms does he so describe himself? Often with an exaggeration which is surely a feature of all language. When someone says, 'He's crazy about her', no one takes 'crazy' literally. When you say of someone who holds tenaciously to an outrageous opinion, 'He's completely mad', you don't mean that he's *literally* mad. Urdu is a language which, in my experience, is given to forthright, unqualified statement. (No Urdu speaker ever says, or even thinks, in such terms as 'The bulk of the evidence would perhaps tend to suggest . . .') And exaggeration, often of a more extreme kind than people bred in the English tradition can easily stomach, is a regular feature of Urdu, and more particularly of Urdu poetry, and is, so to speak, an extension of this forthright, unqualified style of expression. That being so, I'm surprised that you think it necessary to ask such questions as '. . . what of the poet as apostate from Islam, as embracing Hinduism in fact—would some poet or group of poets ever have actually done this? And if not, how to explain such conventions?' These things are from the very start entirely intelligible, exaggerated statements of a genuinely held belief. Take the verse quoted by Rusvā in *Umrā'ō Jān Adā* (where he, wrongly, it seems, attributes it to Ḥāfiẓ):

mai khur-o mushaf bisūz-o-ātish andar ka'ba zan
sākin-e butkhāna bāsh-o-mardum āzārī makun
Drink wine, burn the Qur'ān, set fire to the Ka'ba,
live in the idol-temple, and don't injure your fellow-men.

Every reader with a taste for poetry knows at once that the poet doesn't
mean his words to be taken literally. What he is saying is: 'Don't you
realize that if you injure your fellow-men you are committing an even
greater sin than you would be if you burnt the Qur'ān, etc.?'
     When Mir writes,

mīr kē dīn-o-mazhab kō ab pūchtē kyā hō? un-nē tō
qashqa khaincā dair mēṅ baiṭhā kab kā tark islām kiyā
Why do you ask now about Mir's religion? He has drawn the caste mark on
his forehead, settled in the temple, and long ago abandoned Islam.

he means by 'Islam'—and again everyone with a taste for poetry knows
this—the version of Islam upheld by what are nowadays called the
fundamentalists. The Hindu imagery is equally simple. The poet's
beloved, whether human or divine, is his idol, whom he worships. If
human, his/her beauty is one of the manifestations of God, and the
worship of beauty is the worship of God.[12] In a Hindu environment
what is more natural than that he should use a literal description of
Hindu practice as a metaphorical description of his own?
     The symbolism of the other things you instance is equally clear
and simple—and all of them are, if I may say so, quite adequately
explained in my writings from 1968 onwards. For madness see *Three
Mughal Poets,* pp. 154 and 193. For wine and intoxication see p. 195
of the same. The metaphors of the caged bird and of speaking from
the grave are too obvious to need explaining.
     So, my first point is that the ghazal can perfectly well be the poetry
of men who really were illicit lovers and men who really held some of
the main beliefs, derived from the doctrines of the Sufis, that the
ghazal expresses—anti-fundamentalist, valuing *all* human love, and
stressing humanism as an essential feature of true Islam. That these
beliefs were expressed in the symbols and metaphors we have been
discussing in no way changes the fact that these *were* their real, genuine
beliefs. There is no reason to doubt the essential truth of what Mir
says of himself in his *masnavīs* and in *Żikr-e-Mir,* and, through the

conventions of the form, in his ghazals. To ignore the fact—yes, *fact!*—
that many of the great ghazal poets had the experience, and held the
views which I have described, is to do them a grave injustice. We
know that Mōmin was the illicit lover of purdah women, as was Hasrat
Mōhānī. We know that Ghālib may have been so, and certainly was
the illicit lover of at least one singing-and-dancing girl. We know that
Ghālib's attitude toward Islam was, in real life, that of the ghazal poets,
and that he was a drinker of real, as well as metaphorical wine, and
that he wrote to Tufta, on 23 December 1859, 'I hold all mankind to
be my kin, and look upon all men—Muslim, Hindu, Christian—as
my brothers.'[13] So why the emphatic assertions of the ghazal's
remoteness from real life? For the greatest ghazal poets it is not in the
least remote from their real lives. What *makes* the great poets great is
that they mean what they say, and that somehow this comes across.
They are not simply manipulating conventional symbols. (The ones
that *aren't* great *are* doing that, and no more than that. But I shall
come to them later.) One of the reasons why it comes across to *me*,
and why I *know* that the great poets could really believe what their
ghazals said they believed is that *I* believe it. *I* believe that 'all love is
unconditionally good'—both heterosexual and homosexual; *I* believe
that humanism—not in my case religiously based—is the one unfailing
guide to moral conduct in all departments of life; *I* hate
fundamentalism; and *I* believe that one must be true to the people
and the ideals one loves, no matter what price one may have to pay.
No one can produce any convincing evidence that the great ghazal
poets did not also believe these things.

The ghazal has another very important relevance to social realities.
Part of its enormous appeal lies in the fact that it enables real lovers
(still to be found in appreciable numbers in South Asian Muslim
society and still in most cases—necessarily so in that society—illicit
ones) to express their feelings without being penalized for doing so.
The heroine of *Umrā'ō Jān Adā* rightly stressed the importance of this
where love for human beings is concerned.[14] In *The Pursuit of Urdu
Literature* I have shown how the ghazal is a 'licensed, institutionalized
form of passionate protest against the world in which poets and their
audiences were alike confined' (p. 46)—a sort of safety valve for them.
No one could prove that in real life their attitudes were those which

they expressed in their ghazals—which by no means proves that this was never the case. The position of the poet who really was an illicit lover was not unlike that of Pasternak under the Stalin regime when he gave public recitations of his translations of Shakespeare's sonnets. His audience would often call for the one which, in the original, begins, 'Tired of all this . . .' and includes such lines as, 'And art made tongue-tied by authority.' He, his audience, and 'authority' knew very well that he was speaking of Soviet society, but no one could prove it, and 'authority' knew very well that he could say that he was simply reciting a poem by one whom he, his audience, and 'authority' alike recognized as a great poet. Similarly the lover's audience might strongly suspect (and in some cases know) that he is speaking of his own experiences, safeguarded by a convention which made it impossible for anyone to prove this.

However, if one looks at the whole range of the members of South Asian Muslim society, the great majority were not and are not illicit lovers. And similarly, if one takes the whole range of ghazal poets— good, bad, and indifferent—the great majority are not and never have been true lovers of the kind the ghazal exalts. This too my writings have made perfectly clear. I hope I may be permitted a lengthy quotation from them. Thus on p. 117 of my article 'The Pursuit of the Urdu Ghazal' I wrote: ' . . . the deterrents against love which purdah society had [and has] at its disposal were generally quite effective to make most of its members hold back from so dangerous a course.' And on p. 118:

. . . qualities . . . which he hoped to find in a mistress—or would have hoped to find if he had dared to have one.

These last words foreshadow a fourth possibility. If the poet is writing of actual experience of love for a real person, the real person is either another man's wife or betrothed, or a boy, or a courtesan. But in many cases the 'beloved' must have had no existence at all except in the poet's fantasy. In this case, the question of real-life experience and real-life models simply does not arise; all is the product of the poet's imagination, and in his 'beloved' he paints the portrait of someone who in his real-life experience never existed and probably never will exist . . .

Finally, just to complete the picture, let it be said that there have no doubt always been ghazal poets who never had a fantasy beloved. For a tolerable performance at ghazal composition was regarded by many as a necessary part of the social equipment of a gentleman, in much the same way as a tolerable ability to play bridge is so regarded in some circles in the modern West. At this level, the ghazal is nothing more than evidence that its author has successfully acquired certain techniques.

It is not necessary to trace at any length the parallels in the mystic or quasi-mystic aspect of the ghazal. At the two extremes stand first, those poets who really were mystics—Mīr Dard is the example that comes most readily to mind—and, at the other end those who have no more loved their God than they have ever loved a woman, but who can handle the techniques with sufficient expertise to show that they are cultured gentlemen. In between, the possible diversity of range is great.

But there is more to be said about fantasy than I said there. Fantasy plays an important role in everyone's life, and the contrast between 'real experience' and 'fantasy experience' should not be overstressed. The exercise of fantasy is as much a part of everyone's real experience as the daily round of 'real' activities are. And here I come to your paragraph about country-and-western music and to my point that some of your points support my interpretation of the ghazal rather than yours. This one certainly does. In the first place, for lovers of country-and-western and lovers of the ghazal alike, it is the essential content of what is said or sung that is of primary importance, not the conventions with which that content is expressed. Then you say that the hero of country-and-western 'always has to be a cowboy or a long-distance truck-driver, or something very similar', and 'nobody thinks that the song-writer, the singer, or the audience has to be'. I entirely agree. Real truck-drivers did and do exist, and so did real cowboys (do they still?); but all the enthusiasts for country-and-western are concerned with is their image of an imaginary hero who has the qualities they vaguely assume his real-life prototype has, or once had, qualities which in fantasy they would like to feel that they too have, even if in real life they neither have them, nor, quite often, even *want* to have them. They want, in fantasy, and in some cases in real life, to experience (again in your words) 'shared human emotional experiences in literarily heightened ways'. Well, in all that substitute 'ghazal' for 'country-and-western' and 'lover' for 'cowboy or long-distance truck-driver' and it applies word for word. In your letter you are a bit more specific than you have been in your published writings about what 'shared human emotional experiences' form the subject of the ghazal, but let me say again that both you and Hanaway give short measure when it comes to telling us what the ghazal tells its readers; and no satisfactory account of the ghazal can be written unless the writer tells us what he or she thinks this is. Which brings me to a final point. I've got nothing against country-and-western songs, but I think that what they tell their audience and what that audience values, is less valuable than what the ghazal tells *its* audience and *its* audience values. And I don't agree with you that 'the central thrust of the ghazal is the exploration of states of passionate desire—and the experience of the radical, irrevocable unfulfillment of desire'. Of course, it *does* explore that, but the central thrust is the celebration of the heroism of the lover, who remains unshakeably true to his love, come what may.

So much for a direct reply to my critics. But I feel I cannot conclude without saying something about the general context in which this discussion must be set. This may be a delicate matter, but I think we need to consider who it is that says what, and what are their qualifications for saying it. So first, I need to revert to the point that what Pritchett and Hanaway regularly speak of as my assessment of the ghazal is not Ralph Russell's assessment but Ralph Russell and Khurshidul Islam's assessment. Frances Pritchett in her 1979 article explicitly assumed (perhaps understandably but nevertheless unjustifiably) that the relevant chapter in our *Three Mughal Poets* was 'chiefly Russell's work' (p. 60) and said that accordingly she identified it as such. I had occasion to write to her correcting this false impression and reaffirming that the views expressed were the joint views of both of us. Whether Hanaway was as aware (or as fully aware) of this as Pritchett was, I don't know. But she is still writing as though Khurshidul Islam's views aren't of any great relevance—whereas in fact they are of absolutely cardinal relevance. Because he knows and understands the Urdu ghazal and the poetry of all its major exponents better than Pritchett, Hanaway and I will ever know and understand it if all of us live to be a hundred, and there can be no justification for, so to speak, brushing him aside in this way. (Which of course is not to say that one is not entitled to disagree with him—provided that one can explain why.)

Secondly, something about myself. I was amused to read Pritchett's remark in her 1979 article, speaking of the picture of love which *Three Mughal Poets* presents: 'Its source is unclear, but it seems to be an abstraction made by Russell himself from a combination of Mu'amlat-e'Ishq and his own historical and sociological knowledge about the period' (p. 61). It evidently didn't occur to her that the source of my (and, let me repeat, Khurshidul Islam's) picture could be what in fact is was—his life experience and life-long study, and my own (much shorter and more limited but nonetheless relevant) experience and years of study. I am well aware that what I am about to say may be misunderstood as boasting, but I must take that risk all the same, because it is closely relevant to my argument. I know South Asian Muslim family and social life quite intimately—'from the inside', as they say. My close friendship with Khurshidul Islam began in 1949 and continued unbroken until 1986. During those thirty-seven years there was nothing—repeat *nothing*—about which we could not speak openly and honestly to each other, and no question, however intimate, which we could not ask each other in the complete certainty that we would receive a frank and honest answer. I have lived for two whole separate years, as a member of a South Asian Muslim family in which the wife was not highly educated, and came from a traditional background, and for shorter periods in similar families. I have numerous other close Indian and Pakistani friends, both in South Asia and in Britain. I have lived in South Asian villages as well as towns. And all of this experience is relevant to my (and Islam's) understanding of the ghazal, for, as Pritchett surely knows, the social conditions which Islam and I show as the soil from which the ghazal sprang are in all essentials the social conditions in which millions upon millions of South Asian Muslims still live, and there are quite a number of them known to me personally who have experienced all or most of the situations of love which *Three Mughal Poets* describes. I am reminded of the words of, I think, Mark Rutherford (a little-known nineteenth-century author who is a great favourite of mine) to the effect that to be a competent critic of literature, what you need even more than a knowledge of literature is a knowledge of life; and in this area I feel that I have this knowledge. Which is why, to quote Pritchett's words again, we 'claim a high degree of sociological accuracy' for our model.

Thirdly, we need to find out, and having found out, pay careful attention to, the assessment of South Asian Urdu scholars, beginning with those who have long been established in the universities of the USA. I know that at least one of them, C.M. Naim, at whose feet Pritchett once sat as a student, is evidently not of her opinion. In a letter which he wrote on 1 August 1989 (ten years after the publication of Pritchett's article) to a friend of mine, and which I have his permission to quote, he said, 'Russell's brilliant article ['The Pursuit of the Urdu Ghazal'] was like a godsend for me. It laid out the issue in detail, then offered useful analogs and suggestions, doing it all in the most lucid and cogent fashion. It had many new things even for an insider. Since then that article has headed the list of required readings for my students.' (I know of course that this doesn't necessarily imply that he agreed with it *in toto*.) What do the others think? I am struck by the fact that, so far as I know, none of them has published anything in support of the view which Pritchett and Hanaway so emphatically put forward. They are all of them people who, so to speak, grew up with the ghazal and their views would be of special interest. (I would especially like to know what Pritchett's close collaborator Shamsur Rahman Faruqi, for whose formidable range of learning I have a great respect, may have to say on the question.) If any of them like to regard this as something in the nature of a challenge, so be it. I know very well that there was a time when it would not have been profitable to invite Urdu speakers to discuss relaxedly the interpretations which I (and Khurshidul Islam) put forward. In the 1969 article to which Naim refers I wrote of my experiences in the University of Delhi in 1958, when in the course of a lecture on the ghazal I made a statement (which in my then innocence I thought unremarkable) that it was the poetry of illicit love. This was greeted with marked disapproval, conveyed to me (in suitably delicate terms) by the chairman, who (though I did not name him in my article) was none other than the illustrious K.G. Sayyidain. I wrote of this in my 1969 article: '. . . my statement is true, and . . . even those who disapprove of it must have sensed its truth to some extent' (p. 113). But, true or not, it calls for calm and uninhibited discussion. For years after 1958 it was my experience that Urdu speakers simply could not bring themselves to talk frankly and without embarrassment about illicit love, but I hope that by now this is no longer the case—or at any rate no longer the case with South Asian scholars working in the USA.

So it would be very good if they would tell us what they think, and I want hereby to invite them to do so.

NOTES AND REFERENCES

1. *The Pursuit of Urdu Literature: A Select History* (London and New Jersey: Zed Books, 1992).

2. *Nets of Awareness: Urdu Poetry and Its Critics* (Berkeley: University of California Press, 1994).

3. *Journal of South Asian and Middle Eastern Studies* 3(11) (Fall 1979): 60–77.

4. Ralph Russell and Khurshidul Islam, *Three Mughal Poets* (Cambridge: Harvard University Press and London: Allen and Unwin, 1968).

5. Ralph Russell, 'The Pursuit of the Urdu Ghazal', *The Journal of Asian Studies* XXIX(1)(1969): 107–24.

6. Two notes in passing: first that lesbian relationships also arise on the same social basis. I don't think anyone has yet worked out any far-fetched theory about some mythical, far distant origin of the existence in Urdu of the word *čapṭi*—delicately glossed by Platts in the Latin he deemed appropriate for such things as *'congressus libidinosus duarum mulierum'*—lustful congress of two women. Secondly, I do not suggest that homosexual relationships are a feature *only* of such societies or communities—still less that there is anything wrong with them.

7. Hanaway begins his review with a brief summary of the things he thinks I have got wrong and then proceeds to tell me what the Urdu ghazal owes to the Persian ghazal. Nothing to quarrel with there—except his apparent assumption that I did not know all that, whereas my writings, including, e.g. the first half of p. 24 of the book he is reviewing, make it clear that I do know it. (The same passage will show that Hanaway's suggestion that my treatment fails 'to show continuity rather than disjunction with the past' is quite unwarranted.)

8. See the essay 'Lives of the Poets', dated 1906, in his *Books and Characters, French and English* (London: Chatto and Windus, Phoenix Library Ed., 1928), p. 61.

9. Since her letter was not written for publication I wrote to ask whether she wished to send me a revised version of what she wrote. She replied: I've just looked over my letter to you, and although I'm not convinced it's as

lucid as I would have made it for the public, of course you have my permission to use it. I'm sure you'll identify it as being from a private letter, and then people will realize why the points in it aren't explicated more formally or at more length. And because I've thought so much about these points for so long, it certainly does represent my basic views. The only thing I didn't mention in it that I also would emphasize is the importance of wordplay and the value placed on it in the tradition.

10. 'The Urdu Ghazal in Muslim Society', *South Asian Review* 3(2) (1970): 141–9.

11. For a remarkable instance of this, see M. Mujeeb, *The Indian Muslims*, (London: George Allen Unwin, 1967), pp. 293–4.

12. Cf. *Three Mughal Poets*, pp. 174–6, where this is *directly* expressed, without recourse to symbols derived from Hinduism.

13. All the evidence of this is quoted in my and Khurshidul Islam's *Ghalib: Life and Letters* (London: George Allen and Unwin, 1969).

14. Cf. *The Pursuit of Urdu Literature*, p. 46, repeating what I had already written in 1969. But the same point holds good for *all* the themes of the ghazal.

❧5❧

LEADERSHIP IN THE ALL-INDIA
PROGRESSIVE WRITERS' MOVEMENT,
1935–1947

When I was invited to contribute to a seminar on 'leadership' I was hesitant about accepting. I am concerned with the study of literature; I was (and remain) sceptical about the usefulness of the concept of 'leadership' as applied to literature; and I was therefore inclined to refuse. But then it occurred to me that I might usefully contribute a paper on the All-India Progressive Writers' Association (PWA) which was initiated in 1936. For the PWA, besides being a literary movement, was also, in the broad sense of the words, a social and political movement—the kind of movement to which the concept of 'leadership' is obviously relevant—and it made an impact sufficiently significant to merit serious attention. My own interest in, and knowledge of, India dates roughly from the period when the movement began. My own political beliefs were, throughout the period of its existence which I shall cover (and indeed still are), broadly in harmony with those of the PWA. Its influence on writers of Urdu—the subject of my studies—was probably greater than on those of any other language. For the last twenty years or so I have been personally acquainted with many of its leading figures. And, finally, no very useful account of the PWA is available in English. For these reasons I decided to accept the invitation.[1]

* First published in B.N. Pandey, ed., *Leadership in South Asia* (Delhi: Vikas, 1977).

I must stress at the outset that it is not my aim to make any evaluation of the literature which the movement produced; nor shall I attempt, even in outline, a history of the PWA. My aim is simply to study important features of the way the movement was organized and led during the first period of its existence, from 1935 to 1947. After the partition of the subcontinent and the creation of the new independent states of India and Pakistan, a new period began, and subsequent developments would require separate analysis and treatment.

FIRST STEPS: THE POLITICAL CLIMATE OF 1935–6 INDIA

The first practical moves towards the formation of the Progressive Writers' Association seem to have been made in the Nanking Restaurant on Denmark Street, in November 1935, or perhaps in 1934: the date is not certain. It was here that a number of Indian students and intellectuals of political views ranging from the radical socialist nationalism of which Nehru was the main representative, to the communism of Sajjād Zahīr, met, discussed and formulated its original manifesto, and made plans to establish the movement in India. They included Mulk Raj Anand (at that time one of the very few Indian writers in English to have made an impact upon the English reading public), Sajjād Zahīr, Jyoti Ghosh, Promod Sen Gupta and M.D. Tāsīr. Through friends, who after completing their studies in London, Oxford, Cambridge, Paris and elsewhere had now returned home, contacts were made with sympathetic circles in India, and when Sajjād Zahīr returned to India shortly afterwards—he was the first of the London circle to return—he set about establishing the basis for an organized movement there. He landed at Bombay, spent only a few days there, and then went straight to Allahabad, where his parents (originally from Lucknow) were living at that time. It was here that the first substantial steps towards organizing the movement were taken.

The method was first to co-ordinate the efforts of all those who felt sufficiently committed to the formation of a movement to give a good deal of their time and energy to the practical work involved. At this stage these were for the most part communists and fairly close sympathizers of the communist movement. The next step was to seek the support of writers and intellectuals who had already established themselves on the Indian cultural scene, and if possible to get them to sign the draft manifesto of the movement. This was, presumbaly, identical with the 'Manifesto of the Indian Progressive Writers' Association, London' dated 'London, 1935'.[2] It is appropriate to quote this in full:

Radical changes are taking place in Indian society. Fixed ideas and old beliefs, social and political institutions are being challenged. Out of the present turmoil and conflict a new society is arising. The spirit of reaction, however, though moribund and doomed to ultimate decay, is still operative and is making desperate efforts to prolong itself.

It is the duty of Indian writers to give expression to the changes taking place in Indian life and to assist the spirit of progress in the country. Indian literature, since the breakdown of classical culture, has had the fatal tendency to escape from the actualities of life. It has tried to find a refuge from reality in spiritualism and idealism. The result has been that it has produced a rigid formalism and a banal and perverse ideology. Witness the mystical devotional obsession of our literature, its furtive and sentimental attitude towards sex, its emotional exhibitionism and its almost total lack of rationality. Such literature was produced particularly during the past two centuries, one of the most unhappy periods of our history, a period of disintegrating feudalism and of acute misery and degradation for the Indian people as a whole.

It is the object of our association to rescue literature and other arts from the priestly, academic and decadent classes in whose hands they have degenerated so long; to bring the arts into the closest touch with the people; and to make them the vital organs which will register the actualities of life, as well as lead us to the future.

While claiming to be the inheritors of the best traditions of Indian civilization, we shall criticize ruthlessly, in all its political, economic and cultural aspects, the spirit of reaction in our country; and we shall foster through interpretative and creative work (with both native and foreign resources) everything that will lead our country to the new life for which it is striving. We believe that the new literature of India must deal with the basic problems of our existence today—the problems of hunger and poverty, social backwardness and political subjugation, so that it may help us to understand these problems and through such understanding help us to act.

With the above aims in view, the following resolutions have been adopted:
(1) The establishment of organizations of writers to correspond to the various linguistic zones of India; the co-ordinations [*sic*] of these organizations by holding conferences, publishing of magazines, pamphlets, etc.

(2) To co-operate with those literary organizations whose aims do not conflict with the basic aims of the Association.

(3) To produce and to translate literature of a progressive nature and of a high technical standard; to fight cultural reaction; and in this way, to further to cause of Indian freedom and social regeneration.

(4) To strive for the acceptance of a common language (Hindustani) and a common script (Indo-Roman) for India.

(5) To protect the interests of authors; to help authors who require and deserve assistance for the publication of their works.

(6) To fight for the right of free expression of thought and opinion.

Within a matter of weeks it was clear that remarkably wide support for these aims would be forthcoming. Among those who expressed their sympathy were Pandit Amarnath Jha, then Vice-Chancellor of the University of Allahabad, and Dr Tara Chand, then secretary of the semi-official Hindustani Academy.[3] And though this is anticipating a little, it is worth saying at this point that within months some of the most prominent writers of verse, prose-fiction, and literary criticism had declared their sympathies for the movement, including not only those on the left, but Congressmen of predominantly Gandhian outlook, men who, though sympathetic to nationalist sentiment, had held aloof even from the Congress, and men of not very articulate political views at all. This wide support for a movement being formed by avowed communists looks more surprising in the 1970s than it did in the India of 1935. At that time a political climate was forming to which the nearest parallel that the West can offer is perhaps provided by the years from mid-1941 to the end of the Second World War. In those years the necessities of the war against fascist Germany, Italy, and Japan, fought in alliance with the Soviet Union and with a China in which nationalists and communists were formally in alliance, made communism respectable, and evoked ardent expressions of radical populism from even the most unlikely quarters. These were the days when *The Times* became what an incensed MP of the Tory rear-guard called (if I remember his words correctly), 'the fourpenny edition of the *Daily Worker*'—the daily paper of the Communist Party. (Those who are old enough to recall these years will recognize the correctness of this description; and those who aren't will discover its correctness if they turn back to the public speeches of British and American statesmen of the time.) India in the middle 1930s was in a situation where a fairly protracted, and on the whole inconclusive struggle with the British had produced among the politically articulate a dissatisfaction with Gandhian methods and a sympathy for more modern left-wing, Marxist-influenced political solutions. Nehru expressed these views very well, and his Harrow and Trinity education, and his closeness, through his father and through the now long-continued patronage of Gandhi, to the older established Congress leadership, further enhanced the range of his appeal. This was a period in which Congress, for good tactical reasons, committed itself to a programme of radical reforms, in which communists (including Sajjād Ẓahīr himself) became members of the All India Congress Committee,[4] and in which, in the elections of 1937, it gained victories which enabled it to take office in many of the Indian provinces. The British, in general, could not bring themselves to recognize the extent to which it was gaining ground, but by 1935–6 Indians, regardless of their own political persuasions, estimated the prospect more accurately, and to many of them a preparatory avowal of the radical sentiments of future governments must have seemed to be only prudent. On the international scene, the Soviet Union, with its declared policy of support for colonial liberation, attracted the sympathies of many who were far from being on the left, for in a country aspiring to win its independence, politics is understandably dominated by this one central issue (sometimes, one feels, to the almost total exclusion of all others) and sympathy or hostility to other countries is decided mainly by what is their attitude to this one central issue. Finally, the communist and near-communist pioneers of the PWA were able to take advantage, to some degree consciously and perhaps to an even greater degree unconsciously, of the remarkable class solidarity of the Indian privileged classes to which most of them belonged. I cannot speak for the rest of India, but the main organizers of the movement came from the Urdu-speaking intelligentsia of northern India; and in the vast region extending from Punjab in the west to Bihar in the east and from the Himalayas in the north to Hyderabad in the south, I think it is true to say that in those days if one was the son of a well-to-do family, distinguished by ownership of large landed estates and/or by eminence in the legal profession, if one spoke English well, and even more if one had completed one's education at a British university or in Paris, one was assured of an affable welcome from any other similar personage—no matter what one's political opinions might be. Besides, the pioneers of the PWA proposed to put their revolutionary beliefs into quite gentlemanly practice. This is quite clear from Sajjād Ẕahīr's statement of the revolutionary ambitions which the small group of progressives had formed during their stay in England. There is an engaging naivete in its tone. He writes, 'Most of the members of our small group wanted to become writers. What else could they do? We were incapable of manual labour, we had not learnt any craft, and our minds revolted against serving the imperialist government. What other field was left?'[5] I would add that since all of them knew very well that no writer in an Indian language could make a living by writing, they must all of them have known what they proposed to live on while pursuing their chosen course. But Sajjād Ẕahīr makes no reference to this sordid question.

Throughout the social stratum of which I am speaking the assertion of one's modernity was felt to be very important, and the outward and visible signs of that modernity commanded more attention than the necessarily less tangible things of the mind and the spirit. The wearer of a good English-style (or better still, English-made) suit showed his modernity through his suit. The expounder of Marxist doctrine showed his modernity through his Marxism—for what, in 1935 India, could be more modern than Marxism? The two differed only in the medium they had chosen to display their modernity, and this difference was of relatively minor importance to them.

There is of course an element of mockery in this description: let me hasten to add, therefore, that I do not take the view that Indian politics in general, and the Progressive Writers' Movement in particular, was the creation of people who were all shams. Periods like the late 1930s in India and the early 1940s in Britain saw a remarkable growth of radical sentiment, extending over an exceptionally wide social range; and in such periods one finds at all points on the spectrum men who are completely sincere, others who are the more or less willing victims of some degree of self-deception, others whose declared views are motivated by hard, cynical calculation, and yet others (perhaps a great majority) in whom all three of these things are mixed in infinitely differing proportions. All this is no doubt true of the political process in general—at all periods, and in all countries—but in periods like the late 1930s in India, at any rate when viewed in restrospect, it seems especially striking.

Sajjād Ẓahīr's quite detailed account of the building of the PWA—the developments of the four months from December 1935 to early April 1936 occupy nearly a quarter of the book—often illustrates the points I have made. When he and his fellow organizers reached Lahore[6] they went 'straight to the bungalow of Miyān Iftiḵẖār ud Dīn . . .' (Miyān Iftiḵẖār ud Dīn was a wealthy Punjab landlord and a prominent progressive, who later became well-known as the owner of the *Pakistan Times*.) 'There his servants received us: they told us that Miyān Sahib and his Begam Sahiba had gone to a party, but had said that they would be back shortly.' They felt rather put out at this, and were even more put out when on their return their hosts informed them that they were to spend the evening at an imposing dinner party in Civil Lines given by Sir 'Abdur Rashīd. (Sir 'Abdur Rashīd later became the first Chief Justice of the Federal Court of Pakistan.) Iftiḵẖār overcame their objections by arguing that he had already promised the host on their behalf, that anyway there would be important people there (including Begam Shāhnawāz) whom they could hope to influence favourably and whose influence would in turn be helpful to them in getting the PWA organized in the Punjab, and that they could leave early. Sajjād Ẓahīr describes the scene at the party:

> I soon noticed that Lahore's 'high society' was in some ways higher than the Lucknow and Allahabad 'high society' of the English-educated. People here were not only healthier than us but wore better suits than us and spoke English with more style than us. In UP in those days many people wore *sherwānīs* at such parties, but here everyone was wearing a suit. The women were perhaps no more beautiful than ours, but their complexions were fairer, and their saris more expensive: and they looked smarter than our women . . . But the mentality of this class was practically the same in the Punjab as it was in UP.

The friendly links with members of the big landlord class of UP are illustrated by the choice of Chaudhry Muhammad 'Alī Rudaulavī as president of the reception committee for the first PWA conference

in Lucknow in April 1936. Sajjād Ẓahīr devotes a page to describing
him.[7] He speaks of him as

> a *ta'lluqdār*, one of the aristocracy of Oudh, who observes the etiquette and
> manners of that class, and writes in the attractive Urdu style of Lucknow's
> old traditions, but can also discuss Nietzsche and Marx and Freud, Tagore
> and Iqbal. When he is with men of his own age he discusses the problems of
> life after death, and landed property, and family affairs, while in the company
> of younger men he will discourse on sexual problems in so a learned a manner
> that the eyes of even the most colourful among them open wider. Groups of
> beautiful young women attract him as surely as the magnet attracts iron. He
> has always looked upon progressive youngsters with a kindly and sympathetic
> eye.

I have gone into a measure of detail in order to make clear what at
this distance in time it is not always easy to get across—that the PWA
was not at all the disreputable movement which, had I not dwelt at
some length upon this, you might well have assumed it to be.

WINNING THE ESTABLISHED WRITERS

But the PWA was after all being organized as a movement of writers;
though in fact its membership was not to be rigidly confined to them.
And the main drive of the organizers was to win the support of the
most prominent writers of their day, including those of the very highest
reputation, whose association with the PWA would naturally attract
the support of many others. It was remarkably successful in this. Above
all it won the enthusiastic and active support of Premchand,
indisputably the most outstanding writer of novels and short stories,
both in Hindi and in Urdu, in the 1920s and 1930s. Some of the best
of his work is now available in good English translation. David Rubin's
The World of Premchand[8] presents some of his numerous short stories,
and Gordon Roadarmel has translated his last, and most mature, novel
Godān under the title of *The Gift of a Cow*.[9] Premchand's adherence
to the movement therefore brought it a great accession of strength.
His enormous prestige among both Urdu and Hindi speakers, his
simple style of living, his unassuming nature, his closeness to the people
of the villages, the pervasiveness of some of the most appealing of
already familiar Gandhian ideas in his work—all these things brought

strength to the new movement, and his death, only a few months after the Lucknow conference, was a heavy loss. Though assessment of the literature that the PWA produced is outside the scope of this essay, I may say in passing that just as Premchand brought strength to the movement, so did the movement bring strength to him; in his last work his realism is noticably less impaired by Gandhian preconceptions than it had been hitherto. An article which he wrote in Hindi at this time called 'Mahājanī Civilization'[10]—Moneylender's Civilization—throws light on the widely prevalent attitudes at that time. In it the detestable features of capitalist society, which exalts the greed for money above everything else, are sharply contrasted on the one hand with the more humane relationship between man and man which, he says, preceded the impact of capitalism, and on the other hand (and even more strongly) with the new socialist society which he believes has been established in the Soviet Union, though he nowhere mentions the country by name.

At this early stage, very few Hindi writers other than Premchand declared support for the movement, though quite a number had expressed sympathy with its aims.[11] It was amongst Urdu writers that the most striking headway was made. Iqbal was contacted, and his more active sympathy might perhaps have been won had a more prompt, persistent and tactful approach been made. Sajjād Zahīr describes the one occasion when he and Dr K.M. Ashraf visited Iqbal at the beginning of the summer of 1937.[12] The presence of another guest throughout this interview and Ashraf's sardonic loquacity had an inhibiting effect. Iqbal spoke of his interest in socialism, declared his general sympathy with the progressive writers' efforts, and asked them to keep in touch with him. Sajjād Zahīr says that he resolved to have a more complete discussion with him when he next visited the Punjab, but Iqbal died (on 20 April 1938) before this could happen.

This is perhaps the point at which to remark that one reason why the progressive writers' movement achieved such widespread support so rapidly was that its aim of harnessing literature to social and political aims was not at all startling to the Indian public. In the Indian and the Islamic tradition alike, literature had always been didactic in one way or another, and indeed its readers would have been puzzled and surprised by any suggestion that it ought not to be. Moreover, modern

Indian literature had come into being—about a hundred years earlier in Bengali and about sixty years earlier in Urdu—as the vehicle of modern, English-influenced ideas which it set itself to propagate, simultaneously conducting a polemic against traditional resistance to those ideas. By the 1920s themes of revolt against imperialism, of nationalism, and of radical social reform were already common in literature (for example, both in the poetry of Iqbal and in the prose of Premchand), and the PWA represented simply the continuation and development of such themes. All of which shows, incidentally, how false is the picture which the movement's manifesto had painted, of a literature which 'since the breakdown of classical culture' had 'become anaemic in body and mind'. These rather curious words were introduced into the 1938 revision of the manifesto. Quite the reverse is true. Since the emergence of new, western-inspired literary forms in the nineteenth century, Indian literatures had experienced a vigorous and healthy development, which the progressive writers were now to continue. Indeed, this continuity gave them an important advantage. It was the 'moderns' who developed somewhat in the wake of the 'progressives' rather than the 'progressives' themselves (I use terms which reflect the Urdu labels of the period) who represented a break with tradition, for it was they who insisted that literature harnessed to social and political ends must almost inevitably be inferior literature.

In Urdu poetry, the progressive movement won the allegiance of many of the big guns. They included Ḥasrat Mohānī, perhaps *the* greatest ghazal writer of the first two decades of this century, and one who had been from his earliest days a fiery worker for India's full independence, and had by the mid-1920s deduced from Islamic premises that communism was the answer to India's and the world's needs. It won also two of the most eminent of the poets who had made their name after Iqbal—Josh Malīhābādī, the self-styled 'Poet of Revolution' (*shā'ir i inqilāb*) and Firāq Gorakhpūrī, who, like Premchand, was a man of eminence in the Hindi, as well as in the Urdu literary world.

In literary criticism and literary scholarship 'Abdul Haq, secretary of the long-established Society for the Advancement of Urdu (Anjuman i Taraqqī i Urdū) was the figure whose adherence to the new movement most enhanced its appeal. Sajjād Zahīr quotes extracts from the presidential address which he sent to be read out to the conference of

Hindi and Urdu progressive writers held in Allahabad in 1937. (He was prevented by illness from coming in person.) In it he exhorts the progressives to do for Indian society what the Encyclopaedists had done for France in the eighteenth century.[13]

There are many more famous names that I could mention, but without annotation they would not mean anything except to those already acquainted with twentieth-century Urdu literature.[14]

FROM 1936 TO 1947

The movement continued to register this sort of success in the years that followed, notwithstanding weaknesses in organization and, here and there, a loss of direction of which I shall briefly speak later. Even a hostile press felt obliged to devote considerable attention to it, most notably in 1936, after the success of the first PWA conference in Lucknow, when the Calcutta *Statesman* published in two long instalments an article, widely believed to have been government-inspired, attacking the movement as the product of a sinister communist conspiracy to subvert all that was fine and spiritual in India's ancient civilization, etc. It is arguable that this attack, in the climate of 1936, did the movement more good than harm. Certainly defections from its ranks were negligible; some, like Amarnath Jha, who felt it necessary to withdraw public expression of support, continued to support it privately,[15] and any losses were more than counter-balanced by the advances it continued to make.

It made the most solid gains in the Hindi-Urdu-speaking area, where in 1937, 1938 and 1939 it organized joint conferences of Hindi and Urdu progressive writers.[16] The earlier aloofness of Hindi writers (other than Premchand) was to some extent overcome, and at the Allahabad Conference in 1938 one of the foremost poets of Hindi, Maithilī Sharan Gupta, attended and read a poem.[17] Nehru attended, and spoke at, this same conference,[18] and the movement scored an even greater triumph when Sajjād Ẓahīr succeeded in getting a declaration of support and a message to the conference from Rabindranath Tagore. His messsage is quoted at some length in *Raushnāī*[19] and shows a change in Tagore's outlook somewhat similar to that in Premchand which I have noted above, but even more striking. I re-translate from the Urdu:

To live in seclusion has become second nature to me, but it is a fact that the writer who holds himself aloof from society cannot get to know mankind. Remaining aloof, the writer deprives himself of the experience which comes from mingling with numbers of people. To know and understand society, and to show the path to progress, it is essential that we keep our finger on the pulse of society and listen to the beating of its heart. This is only possible when our sympathies are with humanity, and when we share its sorrows . . . New writers must mix with men, and recognize that if they live in seclusion as I do they will not achieve their aims. I understand now that in living apart from society for so long I have committed a grave mistake . . . This understanding burns in my heart like a lamp, and no argument can extinguish it.

He then goes on to express in his own words the same sentiments as the PWA manifesto had expressed, calling upon writers to dedicate themselves selflessly to the service of their country and their people.

The strong move to the left in Bengal at this time also helped the progress of the PWA there. (It was in 1938 that Subhas Chandra Bose, at that time regarded by many as more to the left than Nehru, was elected President of the Congress.) Calcutta was chosen as the venue of the second All-India PWA conference, and this was held there at the end of December 1938. This conference opened with an address by Tagore.[20] Among other things it approved plans for better and more regular organization, adopted a new constitution embodying these plans, and resolved to issue a quarterly journal (in English) from Lucknow, with the General Secretary (now 'Abdul 'Alīm as successor to Sajjād Ẓahīr) 'as *ex officio* Editor, and an Editorial Board consisting of representatives of all the important languages of India'. The journal, entitled *New Indian Literature,* duly appeared in 1939, with an editorial board consisting of representatives of 'Hindustani [i.e. Hindi and Urdu], Bengali, Gujerati, Maratthi [*sic*], Tamil, Telegu, Malayalam, Kannada' and finally of four names under the heading 'English and General', including Mulk Raj Anand and Raja Rao. The first issue carried most of the major materials of the Calcutta conference.

In practice the aims set forth in the new constitution soon proved to be too ambitious. Some were never realized at all, and others only partially and temporarily, with local branches being formed, disintegrating, and re-forming at intervals and few achieving any consistent pattern of activity for any great length of time. But the journal, even if it could not be brought out at regular quarterly intervals, could probably have continued to appear had not the outbreak of the Second World War in 1939 put insuperable obstacles in its way. Two issues did appear in 1939; then Mulk Raj Anand left for a visit to England and was stranded there when war broke out. And in 1940 'Abdul 'Alīm and others were put in jail and the journal never appeared again.[21]

The movement revived again in 1942, when the illegal Communist Party, after some months of internal discussion, finally took the line of support for the war, and the Government of India, after fairly lengthy secret discussions with its representatives, decided early in 1942 to grant it legality. With the arrest of the Congress leadership in August and the almost exclusive preoccupation of the Muslim League with the future of the Muslim community should the British transfer power, the communist and near-communist left had an unusually clear field, and its relative weight in the PWA increased. Accordingly the PWA in this period made its greatest advances in Bombay, where the Communist Party had its oldest industrial base, where its headquarters was situated, and from where its weekly journals were issued— including one in Urdu which was now in a position to employ some of the old PWA organizers. Bombay is itself a cosmopolitan city, with sizeable communities of, amongst others, Marathi, Gujarati, Hindi, Urdu and Malayalam speakers, and here the PWA developed in some degree, in a way which had not been possible while its headquarters had been in UP, into a sort of microcosm of its ideal all-India form. But Independence ended alike the broad united front climate in which the PWA had grown up and the abnormal near-monopoly of free political activity on current issues which the communists had enjoyed in the period from 1942. The vigorous anti-communist offensive launched by its one-time Congress allies (and not least by Nehru) in 1946–7, and the ultra-left line which the Communist Party itself adopted when Ranadive ousted Joshi from the leadership, radically changed the conditions in which the PWA must henceforth work, and initiated a new period which it is beyond the scope of this essay to discuss.

'Into the Closest Touch with the People . . . '

Even the shortest account of the PWA's activities would be incomplete without some reference to what it did to realize its aim, stated in its Manifesto, 'to bring the arts into the closest touch with the people'. During its heyday it scored some significant successes in this field. In the summer of 1937 the Punjab PWA had held its first provincial conference in Amritsar not only at the same time, but in the same meeting place—the historic Jaliānvālā Bāgh—as the Punjab Peasant Committee ('Committee' in the Indian left-wing political sense which comprehends 'association' and 'conference' as well). Sajjād Zahīr and K.M. Ashraf were there in the rather unlikely role of representatives of the peasants of UP. The decision of the PWA to meet there arose originally out of the refusal of halls to them—including a refusal by the authorities of Amritsar MAO College where one of them (Tāṣīr) was Principal and another (Faiz) a lecturer! The peasants were thereupon approached and gladly agreed to let them meet in the dais of the big pandal in Jaliānvālā Bāgh whenever it was not needed for the proceedings of their own conference; and this close contact was reckoned to be a great success.[22] More significantly, in the summer of 1938 a very successful conference of peasant poets was organized at Farīdābād, drawing in village poets from the area around Delhi and the easternmost regions of the (then) Punjab.[23] Later, in the post-1942 period, similar activities were successfully organized in the rural areas of other provinces where communist influence was strong,[24] very often (especially in Andhra)[25] in almost indistinguishable association with the Indian People's Theatre Association which was formed in those years on lines closely similar to the PWA but aiming at a much more predominantly plebeian audience, both in the towns and in the villages.[26] In the same period, side by side with the development of peasant movements in the Punjab, UP, Bihar and Bengal, there were developments of peasant poetry and folk song in these areas too.[27]

In this same post-1942 period the PWA made serious and successful efforts to organize activities which would appeal to the urban working class. In Bombay a working-class poet Annā Bhāo Sāthe (a *man's* name) took up the traditional Marathi folk form called (if I have correctly deciphered Sajjād Zahīr's Urdu script version of it) the *pavārā*, and used it for the expression of revolutionary working-class themes. His poems, Ẓahīr tells us, 'were recited before working-class audiences of thousands and were immensely popular. One on the Battle of Stalingrad was especially so.'[28]

Similar success was achieved in organizing 'revolutionary *mushā'iras*'—the *mushā'ira* is the traditional poetic symposium at which Urdu poets recite their verse—of the Urdu-speaking industrial workers of Bombay. The writers of sophisticated (as distinct from popular, plebeian) verse also took part in these, and one—Kaifī A'zmī—was very popular with these audiences.[29]

The ancient *mushā'ira* tradition was developed in another way too, when meetings were held at which not only poems but short stories and other writings were read, thus, as Sajjād Ẓahīr aptly says, reviving and developing the old tradition of *dāstān-goī*, the traditional institution of recitation by professional story-tellers of the long romances of Islamic chivalry, romances from which, as late as the 1860s, an important element in the modern Urdu novel derives.[30] The Urdu writers were particularly active in this period, and Sajjād Ẓahīr gives an interesting account of a successful 'Urdu literary conference and *mushā'ira*'[31] held in the town of Mālīgāon (in the heart of Maharashtra) two hundred miles from Bombay, where he says, the population consisted predominantly of Urdu-speaking weavers of homespun cloth, people who had originally come from the Banaras region of eastern UP.

THE PROCESSES OF LEADERSHIP IN THE PWA

The processes of leadership which become evident as one studies the PWA and its development are not peculiar to India. Those who seek to start a new movement anywhere are likely to do three things. At the ground level, so to speak, they will both try to win the allegiance of people not yet committed to any cause and to gain in whatever measure may be possible the support of those whose allegiance is indeed pledged elsewhere but is not felt to be inconsistent with support for the new movement. At a more exalted level it will seek to win over, or to ally itself with, men who are already established as leaders, who already have an important following and who can be expected to carry that following with them when they accept the claims, or some of the claims, of the new movement. As we have seen the PWA did all these things—the first two with the greatest success in the period when the left worked in the abnormally favourable conditions of the period from mid-1942, and the last in its early days, the period from the end of 1935 to 1939.

What does seem to me characteristically, though again not exclusively, Indian, is the extent to which its leaders went in the earlier period to accommodate themselves and their movement to a variety of social and political groups who already wielded influence in Indian society and the relatively great importance they attached to this method of building the movement as compared with the method of direct mass appeal for the support of the as yet uncommitted. A consequence of this was the blurring of the lines which, had they acted with greater consistency and in accordance with more sharply defined principles, would have demarcated them more clearly from other social, political and literary groups whose claim to be regarded as 'progressive' was at least somewhat dubious. Sajjād Z̤ahīr's method of handling this sort of situation is one of some refinement, well illustrated by the account of the descent of him and his colleagues on Lahore in January 1936 from which I quoted extracts above. You start by describing, bluntly enough, the undesirable qualities of the men and women who constitute 'high society', in general; but it soon emerges that you are quite at home in this society and consider it quite proper to enter into relationships, both personal and political, with individual members of this 'high society' of a kind which could be justified, by your own declared principles, only if these individuals could be shown to be markedly and significantly different from their fellows; but no such marked and significant difference appears.

In less sophisticated progressives this sort of free and easy opportunism is much more plain. The most amusing example in Sajjād Z̤ahīr's account is that of Krishan Chander's sterling efforts to organize the third All-India PWA Conference in Delhi early in 1942.[32] Krishan Chander has always been, and still remains, one of the staunchest supporters of the progressive cause, and Sajjād Z̤ahīr is clearly at pains in his account to let him off as lightly as possible. But it is pretty clear that he must have reasoned along something like the following lines: 'The PWA has suffered heavily from government policies since 1939, but now, with its leaders once more out of jail, we have the opportunity of really putting it on the map again. So let's get as many big names to our conference as possible.' The result was that he sent out invitations to people who could not, by any conceivable stretch of the imagination, be regarded as sympathetic to progressive causes. Many of these, on their side, seem to have reasoned that the Communist Party, now legalized, was now quite respectable, and association with communist writers in a conference which would demonstrate (as indeed it did) support for the war effort, would attract the favourable attention of the British authorities. So they accepted. When Sajjād Zahīr and 'Abdul 'Alīm arrived in Delhi on the eve of the conference, having gladly accepted Krishan Chander's offer to do most of the organizing, this was the situation which confronted them. 'Alīm solved it by organizing not one conference but two, running parallelly—a general 'Writers' Conference' and a Progressive Writers' Conference.

The same sort of ambivalence was often evident in the PWA's literary products too, and Krishan Chander again provides some of the clearest examples. He soon established himself as the most popular of the progressive Urdu short-story writers, and some of his work is extremely good. A great deal more would not rate very high by international standards, but has without any doubt served the progressive cause well and made a considerable impact on a wide readership. When in 1950 I criticized one of his most popular stories he was not in the least offended, named two other progressive writers (Ismat Chughtai and Rajindar Singh Bedi) whose stories he thought would be more worthwhile translating into English than his own, but said that he had read this and other stories like it to mass audiences, that they had been very popular, and that he wished to continue writing for such audiences. It seems to me that this stand is quite unobjectionable. During the terrible Hindu-Muslim riots he wrote many stories driving home the message that all decent men must abhor the communal killings and do their best to stop them. And if these stories are not great literature it is to be hoped nevertheless that no thoughtful and humane man will wish to deny that he performed a service to humanity in writing them. It is another matter when he goes a step beyond this and seems to reason, 'I will give my readers what they like. If they like it they will like me, and since I am a progressive that will mean that I am winning support for the progressive cause.' If you want to see what remarkable results such logic can produce you should read his *Seven Faces of London,* available under that title in an English translation in an Indian paperback series.[33] Marxists in the West who have close experience of their Indian counterparts must often have been struck by the very shallow quality of their internationalism at any rate where the nations of the West are concerned; and this, among other things, is evident in this book.[34] What apparently interests Krishan Chander most during his life in London is the discovery of an old Punjabi friend who is now a street-trader in Petticoat Lane, and visits to strip-tease joints in the company of Indians employed in the BBC. The climax of the book is a fantastic story (presented as fact, with himself as one of the characters) in which he is lured to the palatial residence of one of his old English flames (portrayed in a strictly one-dimensional way as a filthy-rich *femme fatale*) who receives him at the side of her private swimming pool and, having been given the false impression that he cannot swim, manages to make him fall into the pool and goes off leaving him to drown. This kind of stuff, too, continues the old tradition of *dāstān-goī* but not perhaps the best in that tradition, and not perhaps for any discernible progressive purpose. Krishan Chander also included in his two-volume selection of progressive literature *Naē Zāviye,*[35] a poem by N.M. Rāshid—a 'modern' rather than a 'progressive', but never mind—entitled *Intiqām* (Revenge) in which the Indian poet feels that he has taken revenge for India's subjection by having sexual intercourse with an English woman. The 'progressive' logic of this seems to be that the sovereign remedy for colonial slavery is mass copulation of the male slaves with the womenfolk of the enslavers. It was this same N.M. Rāshid whom the progressive poet Faiz chose to write the introduction for his first volume of verse,[36] perhaps in the calculation that the avowed progressives would buy it anyway, and an introduction by a 'modern' might help to bring in the 'moderns' too. And Krishan Chander had written the introduction of Rāshid's collection of verse *Māvara.*[37]

It is perhaps worth saying something of the problems which face the leadership of such a movement as the PWA set out to be, considered in general, or, if you will, objective terms—problems, in other words, to which the strengths and the weaknesses of the leadership of the actual historical PWA are irrelevant.

The ambitious aims set out in the constitution of December 1938 seem to me to be such that no voluntary movement, however well-led, could have hoped to realize them. At the all-Indian level it was forced to function in English—as, indeed, is still the case at that level with every countrywide organization. Yet it was concerned to promote the production of progressive literature not mainly in English (though, quite rightly, English was not excluded), but in the twelve to fifteen major Indian languages. For such a movement to retain any sort of continuing all-India coherence would have necessitated the prompt translation of at any rate the most representative work of every one of these languages into every other—a task of such formidable dimensions that only an organization financed from government funds could hope to make any headway with it. (In India this is what has happened. The Sahitya Akademi—Academy of Letters—now undertakes this task.) It may be thought that progressive writers in English from the various regions could have imparted some of this all-India coherence and perhaps in addition by translations from their mother tongues into English, mediate between the different language regions. But of the writers in English who were associated with the movement in the early days only Mulk Raj Anand stayed with it for more than a few years. The others, Ahmed Ali for example, soon realized that even if they wrote in an Indian language (and Ahmed Ali did—in Urdu) at any rate their English writing must be directed outside India, to the English-speaking world; and this turned their attention towards a field of interest which, for the PWA as a whole, could only be a subsidiary one; so that even if more of them had remained active in its ranks this could hardly have altered the pattern of events very significantly. As for acting as translators, quite apart from any natural (and reasonable) reluctance they might have felt to devote to translating the works of others, time which they could otherwise spend on writing works of their own, it is a fact that very few Indians who possess sufficient mastery of English to make it their medium of literary expression possess anything like a commensurate mastery of their own mother tongue, and adequate translation from its literature would have been beyond the powers of most of them.

The one section of the PWA to attain anything like an inter-regional range was that of the Urdu writers. But this was not because the PWA's Urdu writers and Urdu-speaking organizers were more able than the rest, but mainly because Urdu itself is not, for the most part, a regional language, but the language of the Muslims, and more especially of the urban Muslims, distributed in towns and cities throughout the north, the north-west and the centre of the subcontinent, and in those days the preferred literary medium of the majority of writers from Punjab—Muslim, Sikh and Hindu alike.

A further problem arose in pursuing the aim of bringing literature 'into the closest touch with the people'. The vast majority of the progressive writers were writers of sophisticated literature and wrote on themes, and in a tradition, and in a language, which was not very appealing to the uneducated, illiterate urban and rural poor. The languages themselves have not attained the degree of uniformity which compulsory education, a widely circulating popular press, radio and television have conferred upon English. Even in Urdu, where knowledge and appreciation of the sophisticated literary forms perhaps extend further into the mass of the language community than is the case with other languages, sophisticated poets had difficulty in getting across to the unsophisticated, and Sajjād Z̤ahīr's account rather suggests that only Kaifī A'z̤mī learned how to do this really successfully.

Bringing progressive literature to the peasants, and evoking progressive literature *from* the peasants, presented even greater problems, well illustrated by the two examples from the 1937–8 period which I gave earlier. When in 1937 force of circumstances brought the Punjab peasants and the Punjab progressive writers together to conduct simultaneous conferences in Jaliānvālā Bāgh, the revolutionary zeal which each inspired in the other derived in the main from simple physical proximity and Sajjād Z̤ahīr practically says as much.[38] Mere physical proximity cannot, I think, be regarded as a very advanced form of communication, but the progressive writers could not get much beyond that. As writers, they spoke a different language (both literally and metaphorically) from the peasants and were ignorant both of the language and the popular forms of peasant literature. The one outstanding peasant conference which was a success by literary standards was that of the peasant poets held in Farīdābād in the summer of 1938. But this success owed almost everything to the efforts of one very exceptional man, Sayyid Muṭallabī Farīdābādī,[39] an educated landlord who lived in the countryside and had a knowledge and understanding of the local peasants and of their language and traditional cultural forms which none of the writers of sophisticated Urdu literature possessed. In the communist-led cultural campaigns in the post-1942 period, in, for example, the Andhra region, it was song, dance and popular drama provided by the Indian People's Theatre Association that made the greatest impact.

With the best will and the greatest skill in the world it seems to me very doubtful whether the PWA could have made appreciably more headway than it did against these formidable objective obstacles that it faced. These are questions of really quite a different kind from those which arise about its methods of work in the areas in which it did achieve very notable successes. A full study of the history of the movement, pursued partly at least along the lines I have attempted to indicate in this essay, and based on a full study of the written materials supplemented by contact and discussion with its surviving leaders, would, I think, produce interesting and instructive results.

NOTES AND REFERENCES

1. There is a brief treatment of the PWA and of some of the Urdu writers associated with it in Mohammed Sadiq, *Twentieth-Century Urdu Literature* (Baroda: Padmaja Publications, 1947), chs. vii–x (pp. 60–93). A very partial account (in both senses of the word) is Hafeez Malik's 'The Marxist Literary Movement in India and Pakistan' (presented 6 April 1966, American Association of Asian Studies, New York, NY, and subsequently published in the *Journal of Asian Studies* XXVI (4) (August 1967): 649–64, which appears to have been written under the strong influence of the mythology of the cold war). I list the other relevant material in English of which I am aware. Though I have not been able to consult all of it in preparing this essay (and shall indicate what I have and what I have not seen), such a list may be of use to others wishing to study the subject. First comes *Towards Progressive Literature,* which I have not seen, but which *Raushnāī* (p. 135) (see below) tells us was published in 1936 and gives in English the main materials of the first Lucknow conference in April 1936—Premchand's presidential address, the Manifesto, Sajjād Ẓahīr's report, the conference

resolutions and other papers. *New Indian Literature* I, Lucknow (1939), similarly gives most of the documents of the second conference, held in Calcutta in December 1938. It is described as the 'Quarterly Journal of the Indian Progressive Writers' Association', but in fact only two issues ever appeared (cf. *Raushnāī*, pp. 216–17), and I have not seen the second. The files of the short-lived quarterly *Indian Writing*, London (1940–c. 1942), of which I have seen vol. I, nos. 1, 2 & 3, (issues dated Spring 1940, Summer 1940 and March 1941 respectively) and no. 5 ('Second Series, Summer 1942') also carry relevant materials, as do those of *Indian Literature*, published by the Central Cultural Commission of the Communist Party of India in 1952–3. Of this I have seen issues 1 and 2 of 1952 and 2 and 3 of 1953. I do not recall how many issues appeared in all, but it did not last long, and I think that the third issue of 1953 may well have been the last. I do not know of other materials of any importance in English.

In Urdu there are three substantial books covering the period with which the present paper deals. Sajjād Ẓahīr, *Raushnāī* (Lahore: Maktaba Urdu, November 1956) is a full-length (414 pp.) account of the movement up to 1947, and I have drawn mainly upon this for this essay. Its value is impaired a little by the fact that in the conditions in which it was written (its afterword is dated 'Central Jail, Much, Baluchistan, 17th January 1954') adequate reference materials were not available to the writer. Its scope is much the same as that of the present paper, in the sense that no evaluation of the literature the movement produced is attempted. 'Alī Sardār Ja'farī, *Taraqqī Pasand Adab*, vol. I, (Aligarh: Anjuman i Taraqqī i Urdū (Hind), 1951) discusses the 'theory'of progressive writing and its historical roots (in terms of Urdu literature). It gives the Urdu text of the PWA's first manifesto, adopted at the Lucknow conference of 1936 (pp. 13–14), and has a chapter which outlines the history of the PWA (Ch. 5, pp. 178–234). This book was the first of four volumes projected (cf. p. 275), but only the first volume ever appeared. References to materials covering developments in Pakistan may be found in Hafeez Malik's article. A study published after the present article was completed is Khalīl ur Raḥmān A'ẓmī, *Urdū meṅ Taraqqī Pasand Adabī Taḥrīk* (Aligarh: Anjuman i Taraqqī i Urdū (Hind), March 1972). It contains a survey of the historical development of the movement (pp. 19–120). A forthcoming study is Carlo Coppola's PhD dissertation. After completing this paper, I was able to read the second chapter of this in the form of a paper entitled 'Some European Aspects of the Progressive

Movement in Urdu' prepared for a congress in Lahore in March 1973 held to celebrate the centenary of the Oriental College of the University of Punjab. See also note 2 below.

2. Printed in the London *Left Review,* Vol. 2, 1936–7, p. 240. I am indebted to Carlo Coppola's article, referred to in note (1) above, for directing me to the *Left Review* text. Sajjād Ẓahīr tells us (*Raushnāī,* p. 115) that the draft was adopted with only minor modifications at the first, formatory conference of the PWA, held in Lucknow in April 1936. The second conference (Calcutta, December 1938) made further, but still not major, modifications. This 1938 text is given in *New Indian Literature* 1: 116–17.

At the time I wrote this paper I had not seen the April 1936 text, only the Urdu version of it reproduced in Ja'farī (1951)—a version, incidentally, which Urdu readers who are not acquainted with English would find difficult to understand. This does not include the last section of the 1935 draft (from 'With the above aims in view . . . '). Nor does the English version, reproduced in Walter Ruben, *Indische Romane, Eine ideologische Untersuchung,* Bd. I, (Berlin: Akademie-Verlag, 1964), p. 269, to which I am grateful to Dr Irene Zahra for having drawn my attention. Close comparison of the 1938 English text with the 1936 version shows that the only significant change made in 1938 was the introduction towards the end of words stating the need for progressive writers 'to act' and 'to organize'. Mohammed Sadiq (1947) on p. 62 of his book quotes the most important parts of the Manifesto, and the context suggests that he is quoting from the 1936 text. Comparison shows that this is not the case; indeed his text contains phrases not included in either the 1936 or the 1938 version—notably one about combating 'sexual libertinism'. A passage in *Raushnāī* (pp. 368–70) suggests that Sadiq has perhaps quoted from an amended draft which may have been prepared for submission to the All-India Urdu Progressive Writers' Conference in Hyderabad in October 1945. The organizers wanted this conference to resolve against 'obscenity', but in the end no motion was put, because Ḥasrat Mohānī insisted that if it were he would insist on proposing an amendment. He agreed that obscenity should be condemned, but wanted to add that there could be no objection to literary portrayal of 'refined sexual desire' (*laṭīf havasnākī*). The organizers then decided not to put forward any motion at all.

3. *Raushnāī,* p. 20.
4. Ibid., p. 186.
5. *Reminiscences,* tr. by Khalique Naqvi, in *Indian Literature* 2 (1952): 49.

6. The account which follows is condensed from *Raushnāī*, pp. 36–44.

7. Ibid., pp. 92–3.

8. London: Allen and Unwin, 1969.

9. London: Allen and Unwin, 1968.

10. Published under this title in English translation by Ravi Bakaya in *Indian Literature* 1 (1952): 26–33.

11. *Raushnāī*, pp. 96–7.

12. Ibid., pp. 168–72.

13. Ibid., p. 182.

14. Ja'farī, p. 196, lists the names of major Urdu writers who signed the Manifesto.

15. *Raushnāī*, pp. 122–3.

16. Ibid., pp. 175–97.

17. Ibid., p. 186.

18. Ibid., pp. 185–6.

19. Ibid., pp. 191–2.

20. Ibid., pp. 220–1. His advanced age and poor health prevented his attending in person, but he sent his opening address in writing, and this was read out.

21. Ibid., pp. 216–17.

22. This account is condensed from *Raushnāī*, pp. 165–8.

23. Ibid., pp. 232–9.

24. Ibid., pp. 313 ff.

25. Ibid., p. 316.

26. Ibid., pp. 313–16.

27. Ibid., pp. 304–5.

28. Ibid., pp. 303–4.

29. Ibid., p. 304.

30. Ibid., pp. 380–2.

31. Ibid., pp. 375 ff.

32. Ibid., pp. 283–7

33. *Seven Faces of London*, tr., L. Hayat Bouman (New Delhi: Paradise Publications, n.d.). One's enjoyment of this book is enhanced by the quality of the translation. For example, on p. 156 we have:

    Dorothy Gatmore answered the door . . . . For a moment I was taken aback, when I saw her standing there, in the doorway, completely naked.

    Of course, she cried out happily, when she saw me. It is you! My physiognomy was absolutely correct!

34. I hasten to add that this judgement does not imply any complacent assumptions about Marxists in the West. Their attitudes to their Indian counterparts have also left a lot to be desired.
35. Krishan Chander, ed. *Naē Zāviye*, 2 vols (Lahore: Maktaba Urdu, n.d.) The preface ('*ma'rūẓāt*') to vol. 2 is dated 1944, and the first sentence makes it clear that the first volume was first published before September 1939. The text of *Intiqām* can be found in vol. 1, p. 93.
36. Ja'farī, p. 196.
37. Ibid., p. 196.
38. See especially his summing up of the conference on pp. 167–8.
39. Ẓahīr gives a full account of him in *Raushnāī*, pp. 232 ff.

⚜6⚜

URDU IN INDEPENDENT INDIA
History and Prospects

To survey the whole period from independence to the present day is a formidable task. For the period up to 1965 I have first-hand experience of what was happening to Urdu, since I spent three separate years (1949–50, 1958 and 1964–5) on study leave from the School of Oriental and African Studies (SOAS), University of London, where I was teaching Urdu. I spent these years partly in Pakistan but mostly in India and on each occasion was in close personal contact with the leading figures of the Urdu world. Since then I have visited India for shorter periods, and have not had such continuing contact. What I shall write, therefore, will be based upon the numerous press cuttings supplied to me by the Maulana Azad Research and Educational Foundation and additional material (including copies of the Gujral, Suroor and Jafari reports)—which S.M.H. Burney was kind enough to send me.

Most readers of this article will be aware of what was happening to Urdu in the early years of independence. In the area which one might call the heartland of Urdu, Uttar Pradesh, and to a lesser extent Bihar, the state governments were doing everything possible to destroy

* The article is based upon a paper which I prepared for a projected seminar to be organized by the Maulana Azad Research and Educational Foundation (of Sikandrabad, Uttar Pradesh). The date of the seminar was repeatedly postponed, and it now seems unlikely that it will be held in the foreseeable future. The article includes a passage from an earlier one published in *The Indian Review of Books* v (1), 25 September–15 November 1995, to which due acknowledgement is hereby made.

it. This was achieved by an absurd interpretation of the 'three language formula' devised by the Government of India. This recommended that in every state three languages should be taught in the schools: (1) the language of the state (which would normally be the mother tongue of the majority of its inhabitants); (2) another modern Indian language (Hindi would often be chosen where the first language was not Hindi); and (3) one other language. A good deal of elasticity was envisaged in the implementation of this formula, and in UP, Urdu, the language of most inhabitants of UP after Hindi, could, and should, have been chosen as one of the three languages. The UP government, and I understand, the governments of the other states of the Hindi-Urdu-speaking area, decided instead to declare Sanskrit a modern language, and the teaching of Urdu in the schools—it had been taught in all UP schools before independence—was discontinued. On the whole that situation has continued ever since, at any rate until fairly recent times, when some minor changes have taken place in the situation.

In the first years of independence the main recourse of those people in the Urdu field who wanted to preserve Urdu as far as it could be preserved, to allow for its development, and to counter the policies being pursued against it, was to rely upon the sympathies for Urdu that existed at the level of the Government of India. Urdu speakers knew for example that Nehru, who spoke Urdu well, was in favour of doing something to support it and was opposed to the policies of the UP government; but the centre was not in any position to dictate the course which the state governments should follow, and the best it could do was to provide funds and other support for organizations manned by the protagonists of Urdu.

INDIVIDUAL AND SMALL COMMUNITY RESPONSIBILITIES

Obviously, in surveying developments since 1947 I shall be speaking of the activities—and/or lack of activities—of these organizations, bodies funded wholly or partly from government sources. But before I do so I want to speak of ways in which individual Urdu speakers or small voluntary organizations formed by them could and should have acted to combat the dangers that Urdu was facing.

One thing that they could have done was ensure that their own children learnt to read and write Urdu. If the schools were not providing for their education, the parents themselves could have provided it, and by and large they didn't. I recall two personal experiences of this kind, of how in Urdu-speaking families the children had not been taught to read and write it. Urdu for them was simply the language of the home. Many of them enjoyed Urdu poetry; they would go to *musha'iras* and most of them could understand what was being said, but when I visited a friend of mine, the late Habibur Rahman who lived in Moscow, I noticed that a young relative of his who had come to visit him was writing down Urdu verses which appealed to her in the Devanagari script. On another occasion I met Ismat Chughtai. She told me that her daughter could not read and write Urdu. So one asks oneself the question: Why not? Why didn't the parents make sure that their children could read and write Urdu? It seems to me that whatever the difficulties, it was, and is, primarily the responsibility of people who love Urdu and Urdu literature to arrange for the teaching of Urdu and Urdu literature themselves, with or without government support. They could and they should do that; and if I am not mistaken, in general they were not doing it then and are not doing it now.

It should be obvious that the basic thing that needs to be achieved for the defence of Urdu is a considerable increase in the numbers of people who have a command of it, and by that I mean not simply Urdu colloquial speech, but the Urdu which enables one to read and appreciate Urdu literature. I don't know how far the situation that I am about to describe as desirable already exists—perhaps it does in some areas—but I want to say first of all that anyone who is concerned with increasing the numbers of people who are competent in Urdu can do something practical about it without any external support at all. All that is needed is the willingness to do it and to spend your time and quite limited resources on it. There is a lesson to be learnt from what happens in many immigrant communities in countries like Britain where you have a situation similar to that which I have described about the children of Urdu speakers in India. Gujaratis, Punjabis, Urdu-speakers, Poles, Iranians and others who have settled in Britain want their children to acquire a much better knowledge of what some people call their heritage language than is provided for in any official provision in the schools and the educational system. They act accordingly. That is, they themselves set up classes, hire rooms or meet in suitably sized rooms in their own houses and impart some instruction to their children. And there is absolutely no reason in my opinion why Urdu speakers in India shouldn't do the same sort of thing.

That is only one step that could be taken. Another is the production of Urdu materials in the Devanagari script. I spoke earlier of young people who know Urdu but who cannot read the Urdu script; it would be extremely helpful to them and to the cause of Urdu generally if Urdu teaching materials and works of Urdu literature were published in the Devanagari script. I shall return to this proposal later.

THE ROLE OF LARGER ORGANIZATIONS

Obviously, there are some spheres in which nothing very substantial can be done by individuals or small-scale voluntary organizations. And this leads me on to speak first of the work of bodies established in the states and at the all-India level to promote the cause of Urdu.

It seems to me that in order to make a fair assessment of what these bodies have done one would need to know a great deal more about them. Accordingly I wrote on 4 June 1996 both to Anjuman i Taraqqi i Urdu and the Taraqqi Urdu Bureau asking for information. The letter to the Taraqqi Urdu Bureau included this passage:

Can you send me copies of the Gujral Commission report, and of the subsequent reports of the Suroor and Jafari committees? [I shall be saying more about these reports later.]

And, with regard to your own bureau, can you please send me materials that would supply the answers to the following questions?

1. Am I correct in thinking that the Taraqqi Urdu Bureau is financed entirely by government funding?
2. What is its constitution/terms of reference?
3. Who are the members of its governing body, and how are they chosen?
4. Does it issue regular reports of its activities? If so, how often? If not, are there informal accounts of its work available?

I should be most grateful if you can make an early response to this letter and send me by airmail all relevant materials. I shall of course pay for everything including packaging and postage.

I had no response to these letters, but in the meanwhile I contacted the former Chancellor of Jamia Millia Islamia, S.M.H. Burney, who kindly responded very promptly. He sent me copies of the Gujral, Suroor and Jafari reports, told me that he had contacted Khaliq Anjum of the Anjuman i Taraqqi i Urdu and Fahmida Begum of the Taraqqi Urdu Bureau, both of whom had promised to write to me ('soon', in Khaliq Anjum's case), and in the meanwhile told me something about both bodies. Of the Anjuman he wrote:

It is not entirely dependent on Government funding. It gets a Government grant of Rs 1.30 lakhs annually from the Delhi Administration. Its income from rent of its own multistoried 'Urdu-Ghar' is more than sufficient for its needs. It has a general body of 40 members and elections are held after 5 years. I doubt if they have any regular system of reporting to the Government.

Of the Bureau he wrote:

It is entirely dependent on Government funding. Reporting to the Government does not appear to be regular. The Bureau is passing through a 'retiring' phase.

A few days later he sent me some published reports of the work of both organizations—a nearly twenty-year-old special number of the Anjuman's weekly *Hamārī Zabān* (October–November 1977), and two pamphlets issued by the Bureau (*Khabarnāma*, January–July 1983 and January–June 1990).

At the time of writing (April 1997) I still have received no letter from either body. In the absence of further information I must say that my experience of the activities of the Anjuman i Taraqqi i Urdu in 1949–50 and again in 1964–5 and the years immediately following was not an encouraging one.

I wrote of this in an article and will quote from it here:

One of the most disappointing features (not to use a stronger word) of the picture of these years is the idleness and ineffectiveness displayed by those who have seen themselves as the,.so to speak, trustees and leaders of the Urdu-speaking community. This was already evident in 1949, when I first met many of them . . . From motives I shall not go into here (except to say that love of Urdu was, shall we say, not a major one) substantial resources were from very early days made available by the central government to organizations established to support and promote the interests of Urdu. But the record of these organizations is a far from impressive one. In 1949–50 I spoke personally to some of those who sat on the governing bodies of one of them (the Anjuman i Taraqqi i Urdu) and urged them to draw up a coherent plan of activity and proceed to implement it. One thing I drew attention to was the fact that we did not have good, accurate texts of even the greatest Urdu classics. I gave them the example of the Oxford Classical Texts of the great Latin and Greek authors, saying that the sole aim of those who prepared these texts was to publish as accurate a text of each author as it was possible to establish. If the Anjuman i Taraqqi i Urdu did nothing but that, it would be an enormously valuable service to the cause of Urdu. Twenty years later its total achievement in this field was the publication of one such text, Imtiyaz Ali Arshi's edition of Ghālib's Urdu verse. There were other ambitious projects allegedly started but never proceeded with, or, if proceeded with, never completed: and work done in connection with these projects which could and should have been published without impairing the success of the projects as a whole, never appeared.

I well remember a conversation I had with Professor Ale Ahmad Suroor in 1965. I urged that a plan to publish all of Ghālib's writings in good, reliable texts should be initiated at once so that these could appear in the centenary year, 1969. All that did appear was a disgracefully produced reissue of a volume of Ghālib's letters first published in the 1930s. In the same conversation he told me that he had received a glossary of the vocabulary of Nazir Akbarabadi, which he had asked Maikash Akbarabadi to prepare. I said, 'Publish it *now*. It can still be used as material for the full-scale Urdu dictionary you are planning.' He rejected the idea. And thirty years later we have neither a full-scale dictionary nor the glossary. (I was told in later years that Maikash's glossary had been lost.) I could quote a good many more examples of this kind of thing, but this will do as a sample.[1]

Rashid Hasan Khan, in the 'second and final instalment' of an interview with Athar Faruqi—(I have not seen any first instalment)—provides further information on this:

The Taraqqi Urdu Board long ago planned to produce a comprehensive Urdu dictionary in four or five volumes. Some extremely famous people . . . [Who?—RR] were chosen for this task and one volume was allotted to each. For years together regular payment was made to these people, and each was given an assistant [Who?—RR]. Years later it was learnt that work on the dictionary had not been completed. When the time came for them to render account of what they had done, these revered gentlemen (who were not only famous writers but well-publicized ones) returned their materials in the same state as they had received them. After that Dr Masud Husain Khan was entrusted with the task of compiling the Urdu dictionary. I once asked him what stage the work had reached. He said, 'I received some materials in sacks which it was difficult to keep properly, and work upon these materials had been done extremely inadequately.' On top of all that, twelve to eighteen months later this work was abandoned, and no work is now being done. There is an urgent need for an Urdu dictionary, but after ten years of continuous effort the Taraqqi Urdu Board has to this day not been able to compile one . . . Granted, a concise dictionary has been printed. I read it . . . and found not a single page in which there were not one or two mistakes of one kind or another.[2]

It seems that a projected Urdu-English (or English-Urdu?) dictionary suffered a similar fate. I myself was told years ago that one being prepared by Kalimuddin Ahmad was 'nearly complete' but I have heard nothing since then.

In the same interview Rashid Hasan Khan fills in the picture of another scandal of which I had known only the outlines:

The University Grants Commission made a plan for a history of Urdu literature in four substantial volumes. An appropriate grant for this purpose was given to Aligarh Muslim University. At first the University prepared an excellent plan, and the details they presented convinced me that this history of Urdu literature would be a work of really high quality. Nine writers [Who?—RR]—all of them very well known and highly regarded—were involved in the project [of which, he writes elsewhere, Ale Ahmad Suroor was Director and Majnun Gorakhpuri Assistant Director]. The first volume was to cover the period from the twelfth to the seventeenth century AD. When the first volume appeared I read it—and you cannot imagine my astonishment . . . All its references were completely unreliable, nor could one rely on the accuracy of the passages quoted. I wrote a detailed review of it at the time . . . This was reproduced in a number of periodicals and was much talked about. As a result all copies of this first volume were taken off the market and piled up in Aligarh, and a statement was issued that it would be corrected and then re-issued. To this day no corrected edition of the first volume has appeared, and neither have the remaining volumes.

It was only in relatively recent years—in 1969—that the Taraqqi Urdu Bureau was set up. It seems from Rashid Hasan Khan's account that it was the Bureau ('Board' as he calls it) and not, as I had thought, the Anjuman, that planned the comprehensive Urdu dictionary. With its other achievements I am less well acquainted, but Professor Atiq Ahmad Siddiqi informs us that the Bureau for the Promotion of Urdu set up by the central government has brought out about 700 useless books; most of them are translations. Similarly, Sahitya Akademi and National Book Trust, both government organizations, have brought out a large number of useless Urdu books.[3]

Later in the same article he is similarly critical of the Urdu academies that were established in many states:

In many states like UP, Bihar, West Bengal, Haryana, Maharashtra, Andhra Pradesh and Orissa, Urdu academies have been set up by the state governments. These academies have also been rendering so-called useful services e.g., publication of books, giving financial assistance to authors for publication, awarding stipends and scholarships to Urdu writers and students.

That is a harsh judgment, and I think that one can safely say that not all the books that have been brought out or financial assistance given by these government-sponsored organizations have been useless. However, I suspect that there is considerable force in what Professor Siddiqi said, and that the judgement that I formed in the periods in which I had personal experience of these things may well be valid for the more recent period as well.

Shamsur Rahman Faruqi in an interview with Athar Faruqi has this to say about the departments of Urdu in the universities:

. . . teachers at the university level started a retrograde strategy to save their jobs. They did not bother to save Urdu: the opportunistic strategy of Urdu teachers at that time led to the decline of the standard of Urdu in universities. Urdu teachers convinced university authorities that since enrolment in Urdu was dwindling seriously, it was necessary for the life of Urdu departments in universities that even those students who did not read Urdu at any level whatsoever, or inferior students, should be granted admission if they wished to study Urdu as a subject in BA or MA. This move by the university teachers, with a vested interest to save their jobs, proved very harmful for Urdu. It resulted in the intake of incompetent candidates as Urdu students. In due course, among students reading Urdu at BA or MA level, the majority came to be of those whose educational competence and general credibility were very low, and who would not have got admission into the university had they opted for any other subject. It was in the 1950s that these incompetent people, having obtained their degrees, joined the Urdu departments as teachers. Then followed the illiterate line of students taught by these illiterate teachers. It seems that now this phenomenon of generations of illiterates after illiterates will never come to an end.[4]

In short, not only did the champions of Urdu fail to do what they should have done on their own initiative, they also failed to do what they had promised (and what they had been paid) to do; and to crown it all they themselves took active steps which (in Shamsur Rahman Faruqi's words) 'proved very harmful for Urdu'. All of which surely justifies the harsh words Rashid Hasan Khan used of these standard-bearers of Urdu—that they are self-seeking (*bulhavas*) people, people without conscience (*bezamīr*), people in whom any sense of honest dealing is virtually dead (*un ke yahān īmāndārī ka tasavvur to taqrīban mar cukā hai*), seekers after worldly acclaim (*dunyadār*), place-seekers (*jāh-talab*), caught in a net of cheap group rivalries and intrigues (*ghatia grūpbāzī men giriftār*).[5]

Let me say in passing that I think it regrettable that Rashid Hasan Khan does not name all the distinguished people whom he characterizes in these harsh (and fully justified) words. These people do not deserve the protection of anonymity and should be thoroughly exposed. (But the veil of anonymity is in any case a pretty transparent one, since it would be quite easy in most cases to find out their identity from the circumstantial detail which he gives.)

At this stage it is relevant to go into a little more detail about the measures taken by the central government over the last two decades or so.

THE 1970S AND AFTER

From an article by Som Anand,[6] I learnt that the relationship between the Government of India and the state governments, and the divergence between their policies with regard to Urdu, had continued on much the same lines as I had experienced in a much earlier period. The Government of India, at any rate from Indira Gandhi's time onward, had its own reasons for doing something to support Urdu, and I needn't go into them here. There were political considerations motivating this, which didn't necessarily have much to do with sympathy for Urdu. From Som Anand's article I learnt that during the period when Indira Gandhi was in power a committee was set up in 1972, headed by I. K. Gujral, to consider how the cause of Urdu could be advanced. The report of the committee, which amounted to more than 250 pages, was presented in 1975, and 187 recommendations were made. According to Som Anand, this report was, so to speak, 'put on ice' and the main reason for this was the vigorous opposition of Jagjivan Ram to anything being done for the cause of Urdu and Mrs Gandhi's desire not to alienate him in the political situation which obtained at that time.

However in due course the Gujral report was laid before Parliament. Then, successively, two committees were set up to look once more at the situation of Urdu—one headed by Ale Ahmad Suroor, 'a sub-committee to examine the recommendations of the . . . Gujral Committee' (set up in 1979; reported in 1983) and one headed by Ali Sardar Jafari (set up in February 1990; reported, with unusual promptness, in September 1990). The Jafari committee discovered that 95 per cent of the recommendations made in the Gujral report had not been adopted, although in 1989 I think it was, the state government of Bihar, and shortly afterwards that of UP, recognized—on paper—Urdu as an official language of their respective states.

THE ROLE OF INDEPENDENT ORGANIZATIONS

I am well aware that dissatisfaction with the role played by bodies like the Anjuman i Taraqqi Urdu and the Taraqqi Urdu Bureau commonly leads people to wash their hands of them. In that this leads to the formation of organizations that make it a policy to refuse to accept government funding and so free themselves of all obligation to governments and their policies, this dissatisfaction is welcome. Such completely independent organizations are indeed necessary. I learnt in 1996 that the Maulana Azad Research and Educational Foundation is one such. Its vice-president, Amanullah Khalid, gave me information about it in a long letter to me in Urdu dated 14 May 1996. I summarize some of it here, occasionally quoting passages in English translation. He wrote:

The Maulana Azad Foundation was registered in 1989. Its patrons are all those gentlemen in Sikandrabad [District Bulandshahr, UP—a town of which the population is about 45 per cent Muslim] who, indifferent to any reward or recompense, have kept the candle of Urdu burning in the fiercest blasts of adverse winds . . . The executive council (*majlis i 'āmila*) of the Maulana Azad Foundation consists of seven of these gentlemen . . . From the very first day it has been our policy not to accept any kind of help from the Government of India, so that government policies cannot influence us either directly or indirectly. To continue the work of an organization run on these principles is extremely difficult, but we are confronting all such difficulties.

In a further letter to me dated 2 August 1996 he added:

From the very outset it was resolved that the members of the Foundation would not accept employment by the Government of India, would not accept membership of any governmental or non-governmental committee and would not establish any relationship, direct or indirect, with the Government of India. Members would not accept any financial assistance from the Government of India, or any grant or any prize. They would also as far as possible try to abstain from taking part in any seminar or *mushā'ira* connected in any way with the Government of India. As far as possible they would refrain from publishing anything they write in Urdu periodicals partly funded by the Government. I am happy to say that to this day all members of the Foundation have continued to observe this unwritten rule.

The earlier letter informed me:

In accordance with our objectives, for the last ten years two Urdu medium junior high schools have been running in Sikandrabad. Except for these two schools established by the Foundation there are only the Aligarh Muslim University's two junior high schools . . . in UP.

A third letter added that in the two Aligarh schools both Urdu and English are available as the medium of instruction, and that most parents choose the English medium for their children; this is even though the level of proficiency of these children in English is such that this is an intolerable burden for them. 'In short, Urdu medium is at its last gasp in both these schools and within a few years this so-called Urdu medium will cease to be used.' The 14 May letter continued: 'The Muslims of Sikandrabad are the sole source of our funding.'

I said earlier that dissatisfaction with government-sponsored organizations is justified, and that the setting up of independent bodies to defend Urdu and assert and campaign for its rights is a welcome development. But it should by no means follow that no further interest should be taken in government-sponsored initiatives. If associations and bureaus and academies set up to advance the cause of Urdu are not doing so satisfactorily, this needs to be said in organized public criticism of them, and, even more important, plans of activities which they should be carrying out need to be worked out, and widespread campaigning initiated and sustained to press these bodies to adopt these plans. The voluntary organizations should similarly have a coherent programme of activities which they should publicize, and for which they should enlist practical support on as large a scale as possible. There seems to be little evidence that as yet any of them has any such programme (and it must be said that this applies as much to the Maulana Azad Foundation as any other).

I would like to quote from the last two paragraphs of an article by Ahmad Rashid Sherwani, which relate both to the point I have just made and to the role of non-governmental organizations such as the Maulana Azad Foundation.

Finally I would say that basically it is the responsibility of the government to see that Muslim children are better educated. Are Muslims not the children of Bharat Mata [Mother India]? If many (yes, tens of millions) of these children of Bharat Mata are lagging behind in education, it is the fault of the government.

This does not, however, mean that we Muslims should just sit and wait for the government to do its duty. The education, the future of our children is involved and we have to do and go on doing whatever we can do, regardless of what the government does or does not do.[7]

Well, I don't disagree with either of his judgments, but the thing which strikes me immediately upon reading those two paragraphs is this: even if one accepts that basically it is the responsibility of the government to improve the standards of education of Muslim children, what is it that he wants the government to do? There isn't a single concrete proposal indicated there as to what the government should do in order to achieve this result. One would have thought that in an article like this he would have spelt out what measures he considers the government should take and what measures the Urdu-speaking community should press for. As for the final para- graph, 'This does not mean that we should just sit and wait for the government to do its duty' etc., of course that's true, but again there is absolutely no indication either of what the protagonists of Urdu have done or what they should do now in order to provide for the education of the children. 'We have to do and go on doing whatever we can do,' he says. Very well, what is it you have been doing? What is it you can do? What is it you want the protagonists of Urdu to do? He is silent about these things and this is something that needs more concrete consideration.

SHORTCOMINGS OF THE CHAMPIONS OF URDU

At this point I feel compelled to say that the protagonists of Urdu seem to me all too often to call upon somebody else to do something instead of doing it themselves, and that there is a historical background to this attitude, formed in the centuries when Muslims constituted the ruling élite of India. Shamsur Rahman Faruqi, who is himself a member of the UP Urdu-speaking élite strikes a rare—and welcome—note when he says in the interview (in English) with Athar Faruqi mentioned earlier: 'The Muslims of Uttar Pradesh . . . have a sense of superiority, which I consider quite stupid really.' To an outsider such as myself this quality is quite striking, and manifests itself, amongst other things, in an attitude of which I have written (rather sarcastically) in an unpublished article: 'The UP *sharīfzāda* will never do for himself anything that he can command, persuade or cajole anyone else to do for him.' Readers must excuse my frankness if I speak in this connection of a proposal which has recently found favour with, for example, Athar Faruqi and with Som Anand (although Som Anand is not a UP *sharīfzāda),* that the teaching of Urdu should be taken on as one of the main tasks of the religious foundations, the madrassas and so on, which are primarily established for the imparting of Islamic learning. I don't think that there is any point in this at all. In the first place, why do you want to hand over to other people what *you* should be doing? *You* should be doing it! In the second place, there never has been the least evidence that these organizations are interested in the teaching of Urdu, or at any rate in teaching it to any very worthwhile level. These madrassas have been functioning before independence and throughout the whole period since, and not one of them has ever shown as far as I am aware the least interest in teaching Urdu to the level which would introduce their students to Urdu literature. They are concerned with religious questions and only with religious questions. Well, that is their right, if that is what they want to concern themselves with. If they can be persuaded to undertake the teaching of Urdu to the point where their students can study and appreciate Urdu literature, by all means let that be done. And where they can be so persuaded, let them be given every material assistance in carrying out this task. But I don't think that it is in the least likely that they will undertake this task on anything like a large scale, and again it seems to me that the champions of Urdu are looking for someone else to do work which they ought to be doing themselves and which they are not doing.

As far as my experience goes there is no reason to assume that the attitude of the teachers in religious institutions has changed much since the time of Ashraf Ali Thanavi when, almost a hundred years ago now, he wrote *Bahishti Zevar*. He has a chapter in Part Ten in which he lists all the kinds of books which women should not read. Now it's true that here he is speaking particularly of women, but two things have to be said about that. Firstly, that we want women to be able to read everything that men can read. Secondly, the disapproval of the kind of literature which Ashraf Ali Thanavi censures obviously extends to the literature which men read. In *Bahishti Zevar*, he lists among other books that should not be read: '*dīvān aur ghazalon ki kitāben*' (divans and books of ghazals)—in other words, virtually the whole of Urdu poetry and certainly that part of Urdu poetry which is the most valuable: the *Indar Sabha;* the story of Badr i Munir (that is, the story of the *masnavi* of Mir Hasan); *Dāstān i Amir Hamza, Gul i Bakāvali* and other books. To expect people who are dedicated to religious teaching to teach people to read some of these best works of Urdu literature seems to me to be therefore quite unrealistic.

WHAT NEEDS TO BE DONE

I come therefore to what I think the protagonists of Urdu should do. I don't object to them saying that other people, like the Government of India, state governments and so on, ought to be doing this, that or the other, and should be pressed to do so; I don't object to them saying that one should try and get teachers in religious institutions to take up Urdu; but it is far more important that they should pay attention to what they themselves should do, regardless of what other people are or are not doing.

There are important activities in which all protagonists of Urdu need to engage themselves and all others whose support they can obtain.

A part of Som Anand's 1992 article highlights something of very great importance for those who are considering the prospects of Urdu in India. He says that quite substantial financial support was given to Urdu, but that the situation in the Urdu-speaking community is such that it has not been able to make proper use of the support which was given. A passage from his article illustrates this very well. I translate it freely, with some abridgement, from the Urdu. He says the Government of India makes considerable efforts to help the Urdu press, but the Urdu newspapers are in no position to derive any benefit from this. The news agency, United News of India (UNI), at the instance of the Government of India, decided to start an Urdu teleprinter service for the newspapers. In order to get this service started the government gave a grant of several lakhs of rupees to the UNI. But the Urdu press is in no position to take advantage of the opportunities thus offered. It is said that to get this scheme off the ground the UNI offered this service to forty Urdu newspapers, but this offer has not yet been taken up.

But this is not the only difficulty. To get such a service operating, you need good translators, and these are not available. The fact is that the new generation of Urdu speakers has grown up at a time when Urdu is not taught, so how could you expect to find young people who know Urdu well? And on top of that, in the so-called Hindi area of northern India, the standard of education in English has also declined very considerably. The result is that Urdu translators who are employed by the Urdu newspapers know neither good English nor good Urdu.

Meanwhile the government of UP has continued with its ancient policies. Som Anand writes in his 1992 article:

An example of the way in which Urdu is deliberately being finished in UP is this: About twenty years ago the centre advised the UP government that seven thousand Urdu teachers should be appointed for the primary schools . . . The expenses of hiring these teachers, the expenses of their salaries, would be borne by the central government. Well, the education department of the state took on these teachers but no time was allotted to them for the teaching of Urdu and they were told that any child who wished to read Urdu must read it outside school hours. And teachers who had been taken on to teach Urdu were ordered to teach other subjects.

(Amanullah Khalid told me in a letter written on 2 August 1996 that the facts about the appointment of teachers are not quite as Som Anand states them. He says that it was on Indira Gandhi's personal initiative that these teachers were appointed, but that their salaries were paid and their conditions of employment determined entirely by the UP department of education.)

In the light of what Som Anand has said about the inadequate numbers of people competent in Urdu and English I wondered how many of the seven thousand teachers would have been really competent to teach Urdu even if they had been allowed to do so. I found the answer to this unspoken question in an article by Athar Faruqi. He writes:

At a few places Urdu medium primary schools are run by local bodies where teachers were appointed . . . But in most of these schools Urdu is taught as an optional subject. Most of the people appointed . . . , the so-called Urdu teachers, generally do not even understand what is meant by the term Urdu medium.

Therefore, in UP, Urdu education means teaching Urdu as a subject. It is unfortunate that few of the so-called Urdu teachers in UP can even read the books in Urdu script meant for primary classes. It has also been observed that the Urdu teachers in UP are engaged in their family occupations like agriculture and milk dairies and go to the school once or twice a month . . . That was the time when even if a . . . . Muslim [was only a matriculate he] was recruited as an Urdu teacher. Later these people were imparted nominal training in teaching. They were also granted opportunities to appear in Oriental Urdu Examinations. Ironically, it was difficult to find Urdu-knowing youth matriculates from among the large Muslim population. Even today there are countless Urdu teachers recruited under that scheme who do not even recognize the alphabets of Urdu language.[8]

It seems too that there are other groups of people in the Urdu-speaking community—people of much more lowly status than the exalted figures whom Rashid Hasan Khan lambasts—who seem to be open to similar criticism. According to Ashfaq Muhammad Khan calligraphers (*kātib*) comprise one such group. He tells us that their performance is such that they drive writers to desperation. He writes,

'Calligraphers have caused me unending trouble. The story of these troubles is a long one and this is not the place to tell it, but I must say this much: proportionate to the numbers of centres that have been set up to train calligraphers, and the numbers of calligraphers who every year emerge from them after training and offer their services on the market, is the unending disgust and distress of the authors, editors and compilers [who employ them].'[9] (In his anger he goes on to make the totally unacceptable statement that 'When ignoramuses take up an honourable craft simply as a means of earning a livelihood and for no other reason then neither that craft nor the honour in which it is held survives.' There is nothing wrong with taking up calligraphy as a livelihood and there have been many professional calligraphers who have excelled at their craft.)

Nothing could illustrate more clearly than these facts the truth of what I have already said, that the basic thing that needs to be achieved is a considerable increase in the numbers of people who have a good command of Urdu. Classes, both for children and for adult learners, to impart such a command are one means of contributing to this end, but I want to speak now of another.

Urdu in Devanagari

All organizations—government-sponsored and voluntary—ought to consider the implications for them of the fact that many Urdu speakers know Urdu but do not know the Urdu script. They are anxious to read Urdu, but they can only read it if Urdu literature is presented in the Devanagari script. In my opinion it would be entirely within the remit of the government-funded organizations to produce texts of important and popular Urdu authors in Devanagari script. They should not wait for other people to do this.

Publications of Urdu works in the Devanagari script, of course, serve a wider audience than that which I have just described. They serve the audience of Hindi speakers who don't know Urdu but are interested in what Urdu literature has to offer. Hindi speakers offer the next most favourable audience for Urdu literature after that of Urdu speakers themselves. One knows that it is people—*some* people—in the Hindi-speaking community who are the most vociferous opponents of Urdu, but it would be a great mistake to think that all

Hindi speakers share their attitude, and it is quite evident that there are among them substantial numbers of people who don't want to make Urdu their first language, but are nevertheless interested in getting access to what Urdu literature has to offer. This is proved by the number of publications of Urdu works issued by Hindi publishers in the Devanagari script. I know that in her later years, according to what she herself told me, Ismat Chughtai could always find a publisher for her stories in Devanagari before any Urdu-script version was published. I also know that quite numerous selections from popular Urdu poets are being published by Hindi publishers. In February 1997 I visited a big Hindi bookshop in New Delhi and found twenty such selections, very moderately priced and in a format which presented the Urdu verse in the Urdu script on the left-hand page and the text in Devanagari script on the page facing it, with a gloss giving the meanings of Urdu words with which Hindi readers would not be familiar. In the same shop I saw two different editions of *Dīvān e Ghālib* in Devanagari, and I know that the Ghalib Institute has also produced one. I have also seen a multi-volume collection of all of Mantu's works in Devanagari script, beautifully produced—much more beautifully than any of the Urdu versions of any of his writings that I have seen—and was delighted to learn that this has already been reprinted more than once. My experience is that champions of Urdu are for the most part simply unaware that this is going on and even if they are aware they take an attitude towards it more or less of indifference—and they certainly shouldn't.

Already in the early 1950s a Hindi-speaking colleague of mine in the SOAS who also knew Urdu drew my attention to a multi-volume publication called *Sher-o-Sukhan*. This was a comprehensive selection of Urdu poetry presented in the Devanagari script with, at the bottom of the page, explanations in Hindi of the meanings of Urdu words which the editors thought their readers would not otherwise understand. Again, many years ago (in 1965) I encountered a periodical published in Allahabad called *Urdu Sahitya* (Urdu Literature).[10] This was a publication that presented contemporary writing in Urdu in the Devanagari script and with explanations of difficult words. Only recently my former colleague at the SOAS, David Matthews, who still teaches Urdu there, published an anthology of Urdu verse in English.[11] This is a bilingual book with the Urdu text on the left-hand page and the English translation on the right-hand page, and it was at the suggestion of the publishers that Matthews agreed to present the Urdu text in the Devanagari script. Again this is clear evidence that there is a bigger audience for people who want to read Urdu poetry if it's in Devanagari script than there is if it is presented in the Urdu script.

In a very stimulating article[12] Rahi Masum Raza asserted that unless the classics of Urdu literature were published in the Devanagari script they would cease to exist for future generations. I consider this forecast an entirely plausible one. It seems that he was also of the opinion (and here I differ from him) that Urdu speakers should discard their traditional script and adopt Devanagari instead.

In the same article, he reminds us that 'when Ale Ahmad Suroor was general secretary of the Anjuman i Taraqqi i Urdu ['in 1949–50'—but here Rahi is mistaken; Suroor did not become general secretary until 1956] the Anjuman issued a circular asking whether the Urdu script should be changed. Should it continue to use the same script, or the Roman script; or should it be written in Devanagari?' He goes on, 'I do not want to enter into discussion about the outcome of this'. Why not? Amanullah Khalid tells me that 'at his [Ale Ahmad Suroor's] instance the Anjuman planned to launch a movement for changing the Persian script of Urdu to Devanagari', but Rahi does not mention this.

My own view is that there should be no compulsion to adopt the Devanagari script, but equally there should be no opposition to those who choose to do so, and in any case every support should be given to publication of Urdu works in Devanagari as well as in Urdu-script editions. The protagonists of Urdu who are not doing this should be ashamed of themselves—and profoundly thankful that some of those people whom they are accustomed to think of as enemies *are* doing it.

It was only after writing the foregoing that I was able to read the Summary of Conclusions and Recommendations of the Gujral Committee Report. Paragraph 191 reads in part: 'There is a strong case for publishing Urdu books in Devanagari script . . . The *diwans* of Urdu poets and the anthologies of Urdu poetry in Devanagari script have sold in thousands. In our opinion, the experiment should be extended to cover fiction and humour also.' (As I have said above, 'the experiment' already has been 'extended'.) The Suroor Sub-Committee repeated this recommendation adding that 'the Government should earmark some funds' for this purpose (recommendation 84). And the Jafari Committee reiterated all this. These recommendations were very welcome ones. What one would like to know is how much notice the government, or the organizations established to promote Urdu, have taken of them. Ali Sardar Jafari, the chairman of the third of the three Committees, had already taken an admirable initiative many years ago in producing Devanagari editions of Ghālib and Mir, but I know of no other initiative in this respect taken by anyone else in the Urdu camp. (There may, of course, have been others of which I have no knowledge.)

Some years ago, K.C. Kanda's *Masterpieces of Urdu Ghazal from the Seventeenth to the Twentieth Century*[13] was published and it is quite clear that the editor of this book also was aware that not everybody could read the Urdu script. He adopted a rather different method from that of Matthews. In his book you have the Urdu text in the Urdu script on the left-hand page and on the right-hand page an English translation and then a transliteration or transcription of the Urdu text written in roman letters. He has also published two other collections—*Masterpieces of Urdu Rubaiyat*[14] and *Masterpieces of Urdu Nazam.*[15] All of this again makes the same point, that Urdu poetry has an appeal for people who cannot read the Urdu script but who are very glad to read it if it is presented to them in a script which they can read.

One important, and much to be desired, consequence of making as much Urdu literature as possible available in Devanagari is that it would do something to hinder the efforts of Hindi chauvinists to expel from contemporary Hindi what they falsely call 'un-Indian' elements. In an article Athar Faruqi commits himself to the quite untenable opinion that: 'If at any future point of time Urdu were to come to be written in the Devanagari script, the distinction between Urdu and Hindi will virtually disappear.'[16] This is certainly not the case. Far from it. Urdu in Devanagari will still be Urdu and Hindi will still be Hindi, for Urdu and Hindi had, at the literary level established themselves as in effect two distinct languages well before the First World War—that is, more than eighty years ago. (Premchand's turning from Urdu to Hindi at that time is ample proof of that.) But Urdu in Devanagari script will nevertheless help to maintain in Hindi too the use of much vocabulary which is still, despite all the efforts of the Hindi chauvinists, common to the two languages. Which is yet another reason why the champions of Urdu should be actively concerned with helping the production of Urdu works in the Devanagari script.

URDU AND ENGLISH

This leads me on naturally to the consideration of another constituency for Urdu literature, that of those who can only approach Urdu literature through the medium of English. Much of my own work in Urdu has been in this field; in collaboration with Khurshidul Islam I wrote two books, *Three Mughal Poets,*[17] presenting the poetry of Mir, Sauda and Mir Hasan, and *Ghālib, Life and Letters,*[18] which gives a representative selection of Ghālib's own writing, not only letters, and not only in Urdu but also in Persian, and substantial extracts from Hāli's *Yādgār i Ghālib.* These books were published in 1968 and 1969, a long time ago, and at the time when Khurshidul Islam and I wrote them we wrote with the consideration in mind that the audience for these books would be amongst people in the English-speaking world, that is Britain, North America, Australia and so on. It has become increasingly obvious in more recent years that there is a readership for these books far wider than that, and that within the subcontinent there are substantial numbers of people for whom the only approach to Urdu can be through English. This again I think is proved by the fact that Oxford University Press, Delhi, a year or two ago republished both of the books I have mentioned and that they have sold well enough to warrant a second printing. My claim is supported also by what David Matthews tells me about the publishing firm Rupa, that they are anxious to publish English translations of works of Urdu literature. They have already published in 1994 one such translation by David Matthews, *The Battle of Karbala,* of the famous *marsiya* of Mir Anis, '*jab qata kī musāfat i shab āftāb ne*'.

This is something of a digression but I want to say that it is not only publishers' realization of the existence of this wider audience for Urdu literature in English that has made them ready to publish books like these. Since the rise of the women's movement and since the emergence of a strong anti-racist movement in the West, respectable publishers are frightened of being seen as in any way conforming to the values of racism or anti-feminism and one of the interesting results of this has been that if you are an Asian woman and you know English well, and you can translate from Urdu, then you stand a very good chance of having your translations accepted for publication in the UK and in the USA, especially if it is women's writing that you have translated. A number of publishers have recently published works by Ismat Chughtai for example in English translation. However, that was in the nature of a digression. I simply wanted to make the point because even if there are quite fortuitous reasons which have not got anything to do with the value of Urdu literature, but which nevertheless make it possible for Urdu literature to be presented to a wider audience, the protagonists of Urdu should not hesitate to take advantage of such factors.

There is another, and increasingly important, audience for Urdu literature presented in English in the second and third generation immigrants from Urdu-speaking areas into the English-speaking and the English-knowing world. There are substantial numbers of such people both in North America and in Britain, and to a lesser extent in other European countries. In short, there is a much wider audience for books presenting Urdu literature in English than there was, say, thirty or forty years ago when Khurshidul Islam and I first started our work in this field. Books which have appeared in the 1980s and more recently include *The Penguin Book of Modern Urdu Poetry*,[19] *Ghalib, The Man, The Times*,[20] and a number of translations of Faiz including *The Rebel's Silhouette: Selected Poems*.[21]

The point I want to make in describing all these things is that in my opinion those organizations which are concerned with the promotion of Urdu need to be concerned with all these audiences and not simply, as they have been hitherto, with the audience of those who are already able to read the Urdu script. Bodies like the Anjuman i Taraqqi i Urdu and the Taraqqi Urdu Bureau need to go on doing what they have been doing, but also to give support, including if necessary financial support, to any of those bodies and individuals in India and in other countries, who are doing things which help the advancement of Urdu.

SOME CRITICISMS

I think it appropriate to conclude with some comments on the materials on which this article is based.[22]

Waheed-ud-Din Khan writes:

> My complaint is not against the national Press, but against the Muslim Press. At present all Muslim newspapers are trading in protests, complaints and the community suffering. It is a fact that the present Muslim journalism is protest journalism, not constructive journalism in any way. This is the main problem. I may be allowed to say that the Muslim intellectual class itself is devoid of any positive thinking. Then, how can they work to promote positive thinking among ordinary Muslims? What are the Muslim newspapers doing? They are indulging in convincing the Muslims that they are an oppressed and deprived minority for whom all avenues of living and progress are closed. The reality is that problems and opportunities are always there in the world. The correct approach, therefore, is to find out the opportunities lurking among the problems and urge the people to utilize them while overlooking the problems. The correct formula is to 'starve the problems, feed the opportunities'.[23]

The general tenor of the materials supplied to me certainly confirms the picture he has drawn, and his view of the matter commands support. The extracts from the English and Urdu press that have been sent to me are full of all the injustices done to Urdu, and there is very little else. The account they give is perfectly accurate, but that is not the full picture. There are factors which are working in favour of Urdu—I shall turn to them later—and these too need to be described if an accurate, full picture is to be presented.

The arguments of some of the leading protagonists of Urdu need to be radically modified. There are distortions—dishonesty, to be quite blunt—in the picture which some of them present of the historical context within which the problems facing Urdu have to be seen. I have read Athar Faruqi's (unpublished) Ph D thesis, 'Socio-Political Study of Urdu in Post-Independence India' (1995). This is the longest sustained treatment of the subject that I have read, and I find him more guilty of these distortions than most. His attacks on Hindu and Hindi chauvinists are fully warranted, but he greatly exaggerates the weight they carry on the Indian political and cultural scene. On the other hand he (and most other writers) are silent about the equally pernicious (and much more long-standing) Muslim chauvinism which is widely prevalent in the Urdu-speaking community. The impression is given that Muslims are thoughout completely innocent of the charges that are made against them. For example, one is given the impression that the Muslims who stayed in India after Partition did so because they had had no sympathy with the Pakistan demand and that Hindu hostility towards them was therefore unwarranted. In my experience that is only part of the picture. Many who stayed in India did so not because they did not want to go to Pakistan, but because for one reason or another they could not. This should not be concealed, and it in no way invalidates the argument that Indian Muslims are as fully entitled as others are to the rights which all Indian citizens enjoy. In the interview referred to earlier Shamsur Rahman Faruqi says of the influx of Biharis into India after the defeat of the Pakistan army in East Pakistan and the creation of Bangladesh that they had now firmly resolved that they would stay in India. He implies that this was because of a resurgence of Indian patriotic sentiment. This is a very inaccurate picture. The Biharis fled Bangladesh because the overwhelming majority of the population, fellow-Muslims but Bengalis, very justifiably hated them for their support of their West Pakistani oppressors, continued throughout the appalling atrocities committed by the Pakistan army. (Athar Faruqi is completely silent about these atrocities and speaks only of India's 'aggressiveness'.) And they did not go to West Pakistan (now simply Pakistan) not because they were now fervent Indian patriots but because Pakistan, to say the least of it, did not want them. Their fate was similar to that of the East African Indians. These allied themselves with the British oppressors of the African majority population, reaped their reward in African hostility, and when independence came found that their British patrons, having no further use for them, lost all interest in them and abandoned them to their fate. In what I have just written, substitute 'Bihari' for 'East African Indians', 'West Pakistani' for 'British' and 'Bengali' for 'African' and it fits the Biharis' case exactly.

Writers correctly assail the UP government for declaring Hindi the sole official language of the state. By exactly the same logic they should assail the government of Jammu and Kashmir for making Urdu its sole official language, when, as Syed Shahabuddin points out:

Urdu is the official language of the State and the medium of instruction and yet declared as mother tongue in 1971 or in 1981 as a household language by a very small proportion of the population who regard Kashmiri or Dogri or Hindi as their language.[24]

But I have never heard of any Muslim who takes the proper stand on this question.

In his articles Athar Faruqi argues, sometimes openly, and sometimes by implication, that Urdu speakers who have supported Congress or have consented to serve in government-financed organizations have 'sold out' to the enemies of Urdu. No doubt some of them have, but again this is much too simplified a picture. In particular his attacks on those Muslims who, long before independence was won, were with the Congress, are quite unwarranted. To describe Hayatullah Ansari as one 'who raised the slogan of Urdu but who in fact had no interest in the welfare of Urdu and Muslims',[25] is completely unjust. In the same article he writes, 'I consider the 20-lakh-signatures movement started by Dr Zakir Husain as an extremely unrealistic, escapist movement. Naturally, it did not yield any result.' In what way 'extremely unrealistic, escapist'? What does he mean? And why 'naturally'? It is quite fair to say that the signatures campaign did not achieve the result it aimed at, but this does not mean that it was of no significance.

Let me now return to the implications of the passage from Waheed-ud-Din Khan's article which I quoted earlier. His advice is to 'starve the problems, feed the opportunities', or, in other words, build upon the factors which help the cause of Urdu. Three of these have great significance. First, despite the efforts of the Hindi chauvinists the lingua franca, the 'link language' of everyday communication, continues to be, as it was before independence, one which is just as much Hindi as it is Urdu. This is evidenced by the recently published *Teach Yourself Hindi*, by R. Snell and S.C.R. Weightman.[26] On a typical page, of the vocabulary provided at the end of the book, out of 73 entries 54 are words of this kind and there are only 18 words at the most which would perhaps not be understood by Urdu speakers. Secondly, the immensely popular Hindi films could equally accurately be called Urdu films. The Gujral Committee in paragraph 140 of its summary of its conclusions rightly says: 'The major contribution of films is that they have not allowed any barriers to grow between Urdu and Hindi.' These two factors alone indicate that spoken Urdu is a language widely understood by millions of Indians, many of whom are not Muslims. Thirdly, interest in Urdu and its literature (especially its poetry) is widespread among very large numbers of people who do not know the Urdu script and have only a partial understanding of the literary language. I therefore quarrel with Athar Faruqi's constant stress on his view that Urdu is now essentially the language of the Muslims. (And this is nothing new; Urdu always was essentially the language of the Muslims, notwithstanding that before independence it was also the language of much greater numbers of non-Muslims than it is now.) I do not fundamentally disagree with Athar Faruqi on this point, but in the light of the positive factors I have spoken of, what is the point of constantly stressing that the Urdu-speaking community and the Muslim community are virtually one and the same? Such a stress obscures the important point that the defence of the rights of Muslims and the defence and promotion of Urdu are not the concern of Muslims alone. These things are the concern of all those who uphold the declared ideals of independent India, and one would hope that Urdu speakers would reach out to all of them and work in harmony with them for these common ideals.

NOTES AND REFERENCES

1. 'The Sad Decline', *Indian Review of Books* v(1) (15 September–15 November 1995): 7–8.
2. Rashid Hasan Khan's interview, *Akhbar i Nau* (Delhi), 2–8 December 1988.
3. 'Status of Urdu in India', *The Nation* (Lahore), 4 October 1993.
4. Shamsur Rahman Faruqi's interview, *The Nation* (Lahore), 8 July 1994.
5. Interview in *Akhbar i Nau*.
6. '*Dilli se ādāb arz*', *Ravi* (Bradford, UK), January 1992.
7. 'Educational Backwardness of Muslims in India', *The Nation* (Lahore), 25 December 1992.
8. *Economic and Political Weekly*, April 1994: 784.
9. *Mazhab, Musalman aur Sekularizam* (Religion, Muslims and Secularism) 1994, p.9.
10. The particular issue of *Urdu Sahitya* which I still have, tells us that the

editor was Balwant Singh, that this was the sixth year of publication, and was number 3 of volume VI.

11. *An Anthology of Urdu Verse* (Delhi: Oxford University Press, 1995).
12. Published in *Akhbar i Nau*, 9–15 February 1990.
13. Delhi: Sterling Publishers, 1990.
14. Delhi: Sterling Publishers, 1995.
15. Delhi: Sterling Publishers, 1996.
16. 'Future Prospects of Urdu in India', *Mainstream Annual*, 1992, p. 103.
17. Cambridge: Harvard University Press and London: Allen and Unwin, 1968.
18. Cambridge: Harvard University Press and London: Allen and Unwin, 1969.
19. Mahmood Jamal, tr. *The Penguin Book of Modern Urdu Poetry* (UK: Penguin, 1986).
20. Pavan K Varma, *Ghālib, The Man, The Times*, (New Delhi: Penguin, 1989).
21. Agha Shahid Ali, *The Rebel's Silhouette: Selected Poems* (New Delhi: Oxford University Press, 1991). This has also been published in the USA by the University of Massachusetts Press/Amherst.
22. I would add here that I would have wished to have been supplied with more. Thus *The Hindustan Times* reported on 10 January 1990 that an Urdu daily *Akhbar* was being published from Bhopal in the Devanagari script, but I have no further information about it. When did it start publication? Who are the publishers/editors? What is the circulation? Is it still being published? If not, when did it cease publication, and why? The *Akhbār i Nau*, published from Delhi, has carried very useful articles, but one wants to know the answers to these same questions.
23. 'Indian Press and the Muslims', *The Nation* (Lahore), 9 July 1993.
24. 'Status of Urdu in India', *Mainstream Annual* 1988: 57.
25. *The Nation* (Lahore), 15 July 1994.
26. UK: Hodder and Stoughton, 1989.

⚜7⚜

AZIZ AHMAD, SOUTH ASIA, ISLAM AND URDU

My acquaintance with Aziz Ahmad has a good deal to do with the other themes of this essay, and I hope that I may be forgiven therefore if I first write something about it. When in 1962 Aziz Ahmad moved from London to Canada to make his name in Islamic studies, he went as one who had already achieved distinction in several fields before that—as a university teacher of English literature, as a pioneer of new standards in the twentieth-century Urdu novel, as a talented translator from English into Urdu, and as an administrator in Pakistan government service.

I first made his acquaintance in the flesh (I had already read his novel *Gurez*) in 1957, when he left Pakistan to accept an overseas lectureship in Urdu at the School of Oriental and African Studies and thus became my colleague. We worked closely and, let it be said, not always amicably, together for five years and came to know each other pretty well. Our disagreements, which were sometimes sharp and vigorously pursued, arose nearly always from what I felt to be his inability to adequately comprehend the difficulties and the needs of foreign students of his native language, and since the teaching of such students was a major part of his assignment, such disagreements were not infrequent. That being so, it surprised and puzzled him when he found that this in no way inhibited my whole-hearted praise of his

* From Milton Israel and N.K. Wagle, eds. *Islamic Society and Culture, Essays in Honour of Professor Aziz Ahmad* (New Delhi: Manohar, 1983), pp. 59–68.

talents and of his published work. (He came from a milieu where it is indeed rare for these two things to go together.)

I have already said that I had read one of his novels. When we became colleagues we sat together one summer and translated another, *Aisi Bulandi, Aisi Pasti,* published some years later under the English title *The Shore and the Wave*.[1] He had written many more, and in his own country they had earned him in most quarters notoriety rather than fame, for they were very generally regarded as 'obscene' (of which, more in a moment) and felt to portray impermissibly and in only thin disguise, the private lives of men and women easily identifiable by those who knew him and his acquaintances. It is a pity that these views have predominated, because not only do they do him an injustice, they also impede the assessment of his novels at their true worth. They are 'obscene' only by the standards of conventional Indian society. Nirad Chaudhuri in his *Autobiography of an Unknown Indian* has provided a good illustration of the operation of these standards where he describes how 'one solitary scene of kissing within wedlock' in a novel of that eminently respectable writer Bankim Chandra Chatterji caused an outraged critic to describe it as 'in places . . . flooded with eroticism'.[2] And the second charge derives from the application of similar standards to a procedure which in the modern West would not have been regarded as exceptional.

What is the true assessment of his novels then? Aziz Ahmad was one of the very few native speakers of Urdu whose command of both his own language and English was such that he could speak and write both with facility. Most of those who acquire that sort of command of English do so at the price (which most of them willingly pay) of allowing their Urdu to rust. Not Aziz Ahmad. And so his novels show that he could express in fluent and effortless Urdu all that he learnt in his years of acquaintance with, and thorough study of, English and its literature. He also learnt to write frankly (as we have seen) on themes which most of his contemporaries still felt to be taboo. All the same, his novels do not really belong to the first rank. All the actions they portray are plausible enough, but the power to evoke deep human sympathies is somehow lacking. What is *not* lacking is a gallery of vivid pictures of many aspects of contemporary South Asian reality, painted by one who has absorbed the positive values of the West without losing touch with those of his own native tradition. And such a combination is rare.

The trouble is that hardly anyone in the West whose professional task it is to study these aspects can read what he has to tell them, while those in the West who can read Urdu well are for the most part lacking in the academic expertise of the professional historian and/or social scientist. And so important sources of study remain unutilized. For example, the problem of Kashmir is one of the major problems of the politics of the post-1945 period. An important element in the determining of the present situation was the internal political struggle of the 1930s and 1940s. Where can one find a vivid picture of Kashmir during those years? In Aziz Ahmad's novel *Āg*. But those who (if they knew about it) would like to read it for this purpose, can't. And those who *can* read it aren't for the most part interested in doing so for this purpose.

At this point a question that naturally arises is: What about historians and social scientists in Pakistan and India who write in English but know Urdu well? Don't *they* use these materials? The answer is: For the most part, no. Why not? For several reasons. First, numbers of them come in the category already described, of people who have acquired their English at the cost of letting their Urdu rust. Secondly, many of them are more English than the English, more royalist than the king. In a society where conventions have for centuries been more rigid than they are in the modern West, English-derived conventions (for example, that a novel cannot be a worthwhile source for academic studies of this kind) are observed with a rigidity which the Western world does not apply to them. Even where non-fictional writing is concerned they think (often, but not always, rightly) that works written in Urdu lack the scholarly qualities of works written in English, and that therefore no self-respecting scholar pays any attention to them. Even if the premiss were wholly correct (and it isn't) the conclusion doesn't follow from it. But there it is. They think that the premiss *is* correct, and that the conclusion *does* follow from it; and they act accordingly.

Where historians are concerned, another factor is at work. Indian history used to be divided into three periods, labelled the Hindu period, the Muslim period and the British period. Since independence a sense of propriety has re-labelled them the ancient, mediaeval and modern periods, but a good deal of the old content persists under the new labels, particularly where the modern period is concerned. There are still traces of the attitude sarcastically described by a historian colleague of mine, who said, 'Some historians think that for centuries Indians stood in the wings muttering the Urdu or Tamil equivalent of Rhubarb, Rhubarb! until such time as the British appeared on the stage and history could begin.' And there are many for whom the modern history of India means the history of what the British did here. There is, of course, a substantial measure of justification for this view in that from, say, the 1820s to, say, 1918, it was British policy that largely determined the course of historical development. From 1918 it could be argued that it was perhaps the Indians themselves who again made the running, and that major British policies were a response to their pressures. But even in the century or so of unchallenged British dominance one cannot put an equal sign between 'history of India' and 'history of the British in India'. What various classes and groups of Indians were doing is sufficiently important to merit much more study than it has yet received. And *this* aspect of Indian history cannot be adequately studied without a knowledge of Indian languages, among which Urdu perhaps has a wider spread than any other; by which I mean that materials in Urdu treat of the history and of the social and cultural life of a larger area, and over a longer period, than most other Indian languages do. In particular, there is material on the princely successor states to the old Mughal Empire (including those ruled by non-Muslims and/or inhabited by a majority of non-Muslims) and on the modern Muslim movements on a virtually all-India scale that arose in response to the impact of the British.

There are relevant materials in Persian too, and while in the caste system of languages Urdu is at best a vaiśya, Persian is a brahman. But historians competent in Persian are always assumed, not only by others, but also by themselves, to be naturally destined for the study of the mediaeval period. So both Persian and Urdu source materials for the study of the eighteenth century and after are generally unutilized.

I am not a professional historian, merely one who as a teacher and student of Urdu literature has an interest in all aspects of the history and the social and cultural life of the people who produced and still produce it. I am not therefore familiar with the whole field of relevant historical work; nor do I keep fully abreast of new contributions to that field. But unless I am out of date, it is still the case that whereas there is no substantial history of Avadh (Oudh) in English, there are two in Urdu—Najm ul Ghani Rampuri's *Tārīkh i Avadh* (1909–13) and Kamāl ud Din Haidar's two-volume *Qaisar ut Tavārīkh* (1896, written, as the author tells us, at the instance of Henry Elliot). Abdul Halīm Sharar's encyclopaedic work on old Lucknow *Guzashta Lakhnaū* appeared more than half a century ago and has only recently been made accessible to English readers.[3] There must surely also be volumes of Urdu material relating to the history of the Nizam's Dominions of Hyderabad. And in the modern history of India (as distinct from the history of the British in India) these two large areas, not to speak of others, surely deserve substantial study.

When one turns to Muslim movements in response to British rule, the picture is similar. In Shaikh Muhammad Ikram's 'kausar' trilogy, the third volume *Mauj i Kausar* is a clear account of Muslim movements from the so-called Wahhabi movement of the early nineteenth century up to 1947. Major materials for the study of the Wahhabis (and their successors) are in Urdu—for example, Abdul Hasan Nadvi's *Sīrat i Sayyid Ahmad Shahīd* (1939, and later editions) and Ghulām Rasūl Mehr's three volumes *Sayyid Ahmad Shahīd* (1954), *Jamā'at i Mujāhidīn* (1955) and *Sarguzasht i Mujāhidīn* (1956).

Moving on to the Aligarh movement that spans the second half of the nineteenth century almost *all* the essential source material is still in Urdu. Graham's sketchy life of Sir Sayyid Ahmad Khan has been reprinted,[4] but the major biography, Hāli's *Hayāt i Jāved*, completed within a year or two of Sir Sayyid's death in 1898 and first published in 1901, is in Urdu. The English translation, by my colleagues Dr David Matthews and Dr K.H. Qadiri, has only recently been published.[5] Of Sir Sayyid's own, very voluminous work in Urdu almost nothing has ever been translated into English. Of the work of his important younger contemporary (to name only one of them) Nazir Ahmad's didactic proto-novels (as one may call them), his collection of lectures, and his religious writings, only one novel, I think, has been fully translated into English.

Much the same picture could be presented for the period from 1900 right up to the present day, but I will give only the further example of Iqbal. Ignorance of Urdu, and of the South Asian background of Iqbal's development, has led to a curiously lopsided picture of him in the eyes of Western scholars. That he wrote in Persian the earliest sustained poetical account of his philosophical views, and that this aroused the enthusiasm of Nicholson to such a pitch that he asked, and received, the author's permission to translate it into English, enabled him to make a certain impression upon Western scholars of Islam. Ever since then it has been mainly through translations of his Persian work, and through his writings in English, that the world of Western scholarship knows him. But with all due respect to all concerned, it was not the fact that he so impressed Nicholson that made him a figure of major importance. What made him important was the sensational impact he made upon the Muslims of South Asia, and this impact owes relatively little to his Persian verse (which most of them could not and cannot read) and almost everything to his Urdu verse—to such poems as *Khizar i Rāh*, recited, we are told, to an audience of something like 20,000 people in an atmosphere so emotionally charged that both poet and audience were often in tears. Nicholson wrote of *Secrets of the Self* that it 'took the younger generation of Indian Moslems by storm',[6] and Arberry was to repeat this statement without comment years later (1966) in his introduction to his translation of *Jāvīd Nāma*.[7] Yet neither of them adduces any evidence that this was so, and the claim seems to me to be a highly implausible one.

What did take the Indian Muslims by storm was, as I have said, Iqbal's Urdu verse. Yet the overall significance and impact of his Urdu verse has not been the subject of any really first-rate substantial study in English—and for the same reason, that those in the West who would be competent to write such a study if they knew Urdu well, don't. Anne-Marie Schimmel's *Gabriel's Wing*[8] uses his Urdu as a source, but her book is confined to a study of his religious thought. And here a book of Aziz Ahmad's again comes into the picture. His *Iqbāl: Nai Tashkīl* (1950)—which may be roughly translated *Iqbal: A New Presentation*—is a book of 594 pages in the edition that I have, the best general study of Iqbal that I know of, and is, of course, in Urdu. It is true that in the second half he concentrates very much on exploring the socialist elements in Iqbal's thought, but the canvas of the first half is much broader, and illuminates the tradition which produced Iqbal, and to which he made his own contribution, modifying it as he did so, as does no other writing of which I have knowledge. During the last decade or so of his life I repeatedly urged Aziz to cover the same ground in English, and a few years before his tragic illness overtook him he had agreed to do so and to come to London for that purpose. Now, alas, someone else will have to take up this task.

This line of argument has already taken us towards a consideration not only of South Asian history but also of the specific features of South Asian Islam. Here the importance of Urdu source material is perhaps even more striking. From Sir Sayyid in the 1860s to Maududi in the present day almost all of the materials through which an analysis of South Asian interpretations and reinterpretations of Islam can be made is in Urdu. In the nineteenth century we have Sir Sayyid's writings, his contemporary Nazir Ahmad's comprehensive survey *Al Huqūq o Al Farāiz* and the writings of Shibli Numani. In the twentieth century there is Abul Kalam Azad. And so on to the present day. For what Islam meant to a much wider circle of Muslims one can study Ashraf Ali Thanavi's fascinating book *Bihishti Zewar*. In it the author sets out to tell the average Muslim woman everything she needs to know, from how to write, keep household accounts, make soap, and treat simple illnesses, to the doctrines of her faith, stories of pious Muslim women and lists of books which she should on no account read. (This last is especially interesting because it shows how widely these books *were* read and how great was their influence. They are still very popular and you can buy them, for example, in any small shop in Delhi in the region of the Jama Masjid.) At one time a copy of *Bihishti Zewar* commonly accompanied the Holy Quran as part of a young Urdu-speaking wife's dowry, and this gives some idea of the extent and depth of its influence.

In these pages I have been highly selective in naming both books and scholars. That is not because I am not aware of many others that might have been named, but because it was my object simply to illustrate, and not to give anything in the nature of a comprehensive review. I therefore feel that there is nothing to apologize for in this lack of comprehensiveness. But I have also concentrated on desiderata, and have spoken hardly at all of the modest, but welcome, advances that have been made to supply them; and here I do feel it would be regrettable if I did not conclude by making it clear that I am well aware of encouraging developments and ever hopeful that their exponents, in academic terms, may be fruitful and multiply. Aziz Ahmad was an example of a phenomenon of which we need many more—a man who united a thorough knowledge and a critical appreciation of his native traditions with the ability to view them through truly modern eyes and to a considerable extent to write frankly of what he saw and what he concluded. (I shall return to the qualification 'to a considerable extent' in a moment.) There are others on the other side—for example, Barbara Metcalf and Gail Minault in the USA, Peter Hardy, Simon Digby and Francis Robinson in Britain, and Peter Reeves in Australia (and here again I am being illustrative and not comprehensive) who come from a modern Western tradition and have learnt the value of Urdu source materials, the necessity of using them, and, with varying degrees of accomplishment, the ability to read them for themselves. Some of them, though not all, are in my view too timid in stating truths, and sometimes very important truths, that their knowledge of Urdu has taught them. I sometimes have the impression that in the field of Islamic studies more than most, scholars feel a need to be 'diplomatic' (which, let us face it, is only a polite way of saying 'less than completely honest') so that influential people will not be offended. Well, no sensible person would advocate giving offence unnecessarily or stating honest conclusions in deliberately offensive language, but neither should one forget what Hardy, quoting St Jerome, stressed in his Explanatory Note to *Tess*—that 'if an offence comes out of the truth, better is it that the offence come than that the truth be concealed'. Many writers on South Asian Islam know—and, because it is very important, should therefore *say*—that the viewpoint of nearly all Muslim thinkers about the position of Muslims in the subcontinent over the past three centuries has been that of Islamic chauvinism, which assumes that Muslims once occupied a privileged position among the inhabitants of the subcontinent, that they ought not to have lost it, and that they should do whatever historical circumstances allow them to do to regain it. That is a fact, and a very important fact, and whether you approve, disapprove, or are indifferent to it, it is impermissible not to state it as a fact. Aziz Ahmad himself (in my view) showed this all too common sense of diplomacy in his book *Islamic Modernism in India and Pakistan*.[10] In reviewing it I criticized him for his implied definition of 'Muslim' as one who is a Muslim believer and, moreover, to some extent competent in traditional Muslim learning instead of using W. Cantwell Smith's earlier and much more useful definition of a Muslim as 'any person who calls himself a Muslim'.[11] Further, I pointed out that nearly all modern Muslim thought has had, amongst others, a political aim, and that no study which does not give this aspect due prominence can be fully satisfactory. For modern Muslim thought both embraces and transcends the bounds of modern Muslim *religious* thought. It is not to belittle the religious rethinkers to acknowledge that they too shared a political aim; while on the other hand insufficient stress upon that aim makes impossible an adequate treatment of the enormously important figure of Jinnah, who, though he too may have been a Muslim in the sense of Aziz Ahmad's implied definition of the term, certainly sought the solution to Muslim problems not in a re-interpretation of traditional Muslim doctrine but in the study of modern politics. All of this Aziz Ahmad knew very well, and it was for diplomatic reasons that he refrained from making it clear that he knew it.

But this is a field in which it is—*al hamd ul illha!*—not only easier, but more immediately important and profitable to encourage a desire for greater knowledge than to inspire a greater courage. An important task for all those who wish to contribute to this greater knowledge is to learn Urdu really well. Let us hope that in increasing numbers they will.

NOTES AND REFERENCES

1. London: Allen and Unwin, 1971.
2. London: Macmillan, 1951, pp. 289–90.
3. *Lucknow: The Last Phase of an Oriental Culture,* trs. E.S. Harcourt and Fakhir Hussain (London: Paul Elek, 1975).
4. First edition, Edinburgh: Blackwood, 1885. Second Revised edition, London: Hodder and Stoughton, 1909. Reprinted, with a new introduction by Zaituna Y. Umer, Karachi: Oxford University Press, 1974.
5. New Delhi: Rupa, 1995.
6. Mohammed Iqbal, *The Secrets of the Self,* tr. R.A. Nicholson (London: Macmillan, 1920). Revised edition, Lahore: Sh Muhammad Ashraf, 1940), p. xxx.

7. Mohammed Iqbal, *Javid Nama*, tr. A.J. Arberry (London: Allen and Unwin, 1966), p. 11.

8. Leiden, 1963.

9. First published in instalments, from perhaps 1901–3, it later appeared in book form (the earliest edition in the British Museum Library is dated 1905), has been reprinted many times, and is still in print in Pakistan.

10. London, Bombay, Karachi: Oxford University Press, 1967.

11. *Modern Islam in India* (Lahore: Minerva Book Shop, 1943), p. 333.

⚛8⚛

SOME NOTES ON HINDI AND URDU

I read with interest the two pieces in *The Annual of Urdu Studies* 10 on Hindi and Urdu—Sushil Srivastava's review article on Christopher King's *One Language, Two Scripts*,[1] and David Lelyveld's review of the same book. King's is the second full-length book in recent years—the other being Amrit Rai's[2]—which deals with the emergence of modern Hindi and modern Urdu. I must confess that I can't summon up the interest to make a close study of either of them, because it seems to me that there are much more important issues to investigate and discuss than the polemics of past generations about the development and relationship between the two languages. (Yes, languages, as I shall argue below.)

It's not the historical survey that I object to; only the feeling I get that the writers feel a sort of continuing resentment of what people long dead once did. Present-day users, whether of Hindi or of Urdu, aren't to blame for whatever sins their ancestors committed, and the sustained recital of these real and/or imagined sins on either side serves no very useful purpose, to say the least of it. The sensible thing to do is to come to terms with the present situation, and the first step towards this, obviously, is to describe correctly what the present situation is.

It is remarkable how little serious attention seems to have been devoted to this obvious task and how much traditional mythology about it is being peddled.

Let us begin with Hindi. Lelyveld is right to describe the *One*

* Originally published in *The Annual of Urdu Studies* 11(1996). 203–9.

Language, Two Scripts of King's title as an 'unfortunate over-simplification'. King's description is valid only for one level of the language, the language of everyday conversation on mundane themes, and even there the correspondence is not quite a hundred per cent. The vocabulary used in Snell and Weightman's *Teach Yourself Hindi*[3] illustrates this very well. Pages 252 and 253—the first two pages of their Hindi-English vocabulary—have a total of 73 entries (counting such entries as *akelā, akele* and *akelāpan* as a single entry). Of these, 54 can equally well be called Urdu, and one, *amerikā*, would certainly be understood by Urdu speakers though they, in my experience, always say *amrīkā*. Another 18 are Hindi, and not Urdu, but one finds elsewhere in the vocabulary synonyms for some of them which are as current in Urdu as they are in Hindi. For example *adhik* on p. 252 is matched by *zyāda* on p. 270 and *ākāś* on p. 253 by *āsmān* on p. 255. And on the pattern of *amerikā/amrīkā* are *intazār/intiẓār*, and other words whose pronunciation is not the same in Hindi as it is in Urdu but which would nevertheless be immediately intelligible to Urdu speakers. Substantial random sampling of other pages suggests that a complete analysis of the whole vocabulary would yield similar results.

But to equate Hindi with just this range of Hindi would be absurd, and to do the same sort of thing with the comparable range of Urdu would be equally absurd. It is true that the Hindi equivalent of 'How far is the station from here?' is identical with the Urdu equivalent. And it is equally true that the Urdu for 'The eighteenth century was a period of social, economic and political decline' is '*athāravīṅ ṣadī samājī, iqtiṣādī aur siyāsī zavāl kā daur thī,*' while the Hindi equivalent is '*athāravīṅ sadī samājik, arthik, aur rājnitik girāv kī sadī thī*' (and in the Hindi version, Rupert Snell tells me, one could say '*satābdī*' instead of '*sadī*' and '*tathā*' instead of '*aur*'). He also tells me that instead of the second '*sadī*' (which simply repeats the word for 'century') one could say '*samay*' (which means simply 'time').

This is far from being a 'one language, two scripts' situation. Urdu speakers would not understand the Hindi version, and vice versa; and to find a version which could equally well be called Urdu and Hindi would be quite impossible. For all practical purposes, therefore, Urdu and Hindi are two separate languages and should be described as such, despite their almost completely common structure and less completely common stock of everyday words.

It seems to me that what I have written so far about the two languages is indisputable. But there is, of course, more to the question than this, and what I am about to say will be more controversial. There is no doubt that modern Hindi came into existence as the result of a widespread feeling amongst Hindus that Urdu was the product of centuries of Muslim domination and that Hindu self-respect demanded that 'Muslim' words should be expelled from their *khaṛī bōlī* base and replaced by words of pure Indian origin. (The first part of this assessment was entirely warranted, and the second part entirely *un*warranted. Words that come into general use in a language become part of that language and cease to be foreign, no matter where they have come from and why.) That this *was* the motive behind the creation of modern Hindi is clear from the common classification of Insha's *Rāni Kētki kī Kahānī* as a pioneering work of Hindi literature or, if you prefer, a milestone in the development of the language. Despite what the historians of Hindi literature may feel, this somewhat extraordinary view of it is the product of hindsight on the part of those who put it forward and has nothing to do with the actual genesis of the book. Insha wrote it as a *tour de force*, to demonstrate that he could do it, and for no other reason. If one can imagine a movement among modern Iranians to 'purify' Persian by expelling all words that came into it from Arabic one might find them discovering Ghālib's *Dastambū*, written in 1857, as a pioneering work of pure Persian. (*Dastambū* is Ghālib's journal of his experience of the momentous days of 1857, the occupation of Delhi by the rebel sepoys in May and its recapture by the British in September, days in which he was in Delhi throughout.) There is no reason to doubt that his reasons for writing it were what he said they were—to produce a work of 'pure' Persian free of all Arabic-derived words and by engaging in this difficult task to keep his mind off his troubles. There is no suggestion either in Insha or in Ghālib that the 'pure' languages they were writing should become standard languages.

So modern Hindi was, so to speak, invented—a statement to which I should at once add that 'invented' should not be regarded as a nasty word. All living languages experience a process of 'invention' all the time, in which not only are new words for new concepts coined but new words for concepts for which perfectly adequate words already exist. (This latter process is much beloved by modern academia.) What one has to see is whether these new words become generally current, and if they do it is pointless to raise objections to them. The new element in modern Hindi was perhaps an exceptionally large one, but that is neither here nor there. It took root with millions of people, and from that point onwards to deny it the status of a fully-fledged language was absurd. I do not know enough to date its achievement of this status, but it is certain that this was the position by the outbreak of the First World War in 1914. And here it becomes relevant to say something about Premchand, who at about this time decided that he should, without abandoning Urdu, start to write in Hindi. The fact that he took this decision is in itself conclusive proof that Hindi was now a living, flourishing language. And if at this point anyone jumps in to say, 'Oh, but Premchand's Hindi is simply Urdu in Devanagari script,' let me say at once, 'No, it isn't.' Premchand's Urdu is standard literary Urdu and his Hindi standard literary Hindi. I shall return to this point later. R.S. McGregor in his *Outline of Hindi Grammar*[4] was right to distinguish between the colloquial and literary forms of Hindi. He described modern Hindi clearly and generally accurately when he said, in effect, that there were words (many of them common to Hindi and Urdu) which you may speak but not write and others which you may write but not speak, and adopted the useful device of marking the former with a dagger and the latter with a star. To which one should add that the gap between colloquial and literary naturally tends to narrow in the case of speakers who have had a Hindi-medium education.

It is ironic that Premchand himself should have contributed to the myth that his Hindi is simply Urdu in Devanagari script, and conversely that his Urdu is simply Hindi in Urdu script. There is an easily discernible historical background to this. In the 1930s, with the approach of independence, the most influential leaders of the freedom movement, Gandhi and Nehru, saw that a major task before them was that of attempting to achieve Hindu–Muslim unity, and that another important task was to create a 'national language' spoken all over India and drawing its peoples into a closer national unity. Premchand took the same stand. Both of these aims influenced the language policies they advocated, but I think it is fair to say that at that stage the former one predominated. The policy which both Gandhi and Nehru advocated was to extend the common area between

Hindi and Urdu (which they called Hindustani), to make this the basis of a national language, and to recognize both the Urdu and Devanagari scripts as acceptable forms in which to write it. Premchand wrote an essay in Hindi[4] expressing this view—and wrote it in a Hindi which in no way exemplifies the language it is advocating! It is about as remote as it could be from 'Hindustani'. A key paragraph would read in English translation:

Everyone is agreed on the point that to make a *state firm* and *strong* it is very *necessary* that the country should have *cultural unity, and* the *language and script* of any state is a *special part* of this cultural unity. Miss Khalida Adib Khanam said in one of her speeches that the unity of the Turkish *nation* and state had come about *because* of the Turkish language alone. And it is an *undoubted* fact that without a national language the *existence* of a state cannot even be *imagined*. Until India has a language it cannot lay claim to *statehood*.

The words I have put in italics are, in the original Hindi, words which would probably not be understood by Urdu speakers, and I have (sparingly!) bolded words (including, believe it or not, his Hindi equivalent of English 'and') which exemplify totally unnecessary departures from the common Hindi–Urdu stock of words which are entirely acceptable even in written Hindi.

But let us for the moment put aside this remarkable contrast between Premchand's theories and his practice. The true relationship between his Hindi and his Urdu has not, to my knowledge, been adequately investigated in any published work; and I guess that the primary reason for this is that most of those who have written about his language have been fluent readers either of Hindi or of Urdu, but not of both. However, nearly twenty years ago Alison Barnsby (now Safadi), who graduated with first class honours in Urdu, with Hindi as her subsidiary subject, produced a valuable study in the form of her dissertation for her finals. (This in my opinion would be well worth publishing.) In it she made a detailed study of both the Hindi and the Urdu versions of ten of Premchand's short stories, representative of the whole period from 1910 to 1936. Her dissertation covers ninety handwritten pages and provides conclusive proof of the truth of my earlier assertion that Premchand's Urdu was standard literary Urdu and his Hindi standard literary Hindi, and that, by and large, he made no attempt to write in the 'Hindustani' he advocated.

(It is, I imagine, possible that the Hindi and Urdu versions of the stories are not all Premchand's own work, but even if that were the case it seems, to say the least of it, unlikely that either version would have been published without his approval.) Barnsby's study quotes numerous examples of sentences which could equally well be described as Hindi or Urdu but which are *not* used in both versions.

Premchand's example is clearly one of the greatest interest, but its main importance is that it proves that Hindi and Urdu already were by around 1915 two separate literary languages and should long ago have been classified as such.

The myth that they are not is only the most important of equally untenable ones that keep cropping up in Hindi–Urdu controversies. For example, those who advocate the view that the common stock of Hindi and Urdu vocabulary should be used as far as possible in the literary versions of both languages and attack the use of excessively Sanskritized Hindi, like to demonstrate their fairness by attacking with equal vigour an alleged form of Urdu so highly Persianized and Arabicized as to be the counterpart of the most highly Sanskritized form of Hindi. They generally add that a form of this kind is especially evident in Pakistan. This would be a very convenient argument if it had any basis in fact, but it hasn't. People who would like to think that Premchand wrote Hindustani therefore assume that he did; and he didn't. In the same way 'fair-minded' opponents of excessively Sanskritized Hindi assume that there is a parallel excessively Persianized/Arabicized form of Urdu; and there isn't. Urdu as written both in India and Pakistan is no more Persianized/Arabicized today than it ever was. Its Persianization, if one wants to use that term, was already accomplished when modern Hindi came into existence, and there is virtually no further scope for it. There has never been, is not now, and never can be any effective 'Muslim' movement to 'Muslimize' Urdu in the way that the creators of modern Hindi 'Indianized' it. To use the terminology of many of the advocates of Hindi, Urdu is a language with a large 'foreign', 'Muslim' element imposed upon its 'purely Indian' base, and the most 'Muslim' of Urdu speakers can't get away from the fact that Urdu is a partly 'Indian' and partly 'foreign' language. Hindi on the other hand can be to a great extent 'purely Indian' through and through.[6]

A good many other totally unsound propositions bandied about in controversy could (and should!) be examined. For instance, one could look at some of the nonsense said about the scripts of the two languages, with some Hindi enthusiasts (and even some Urdu writers) demanding, or at least urging, that Urdu 'must' henceforth be written only in the Devanagari script, while others at the other end of the spectrum resent the publication of Urdu classics in Devanagari. (One such person wrote to me a year or two ago saying that to publish Ghālib's verse in Devanagari was 'an insult to Ghālib'.) But the basic questions are those which I have tried to discuss in this essay and I hope (though well aware that I am not entitled to expect!) that the picture I have drawn will be widely recognized as being in all essentials an accurate one.

Notes and References

1. Bombay: Oxford University Press, 1994.
2. *A House Divided: The Origin and Development of Hindi / Hindavi* (Delhi: Oxford University Press, 1984).
3. London: Hodder and Stoughton, 1989.
4. Oxford: Clarendon Press, 1972.
5. 'Urdu, Hindi aur Hindustani', *Kuch Vicar* [Some Thoughts] (Allahabad: Sarasvati Press, 1965; originally published in 1939), pp. 101–113. The words I have quoted in translation are on p. 101.
6. In these last sentences I have used quotation marks to indicate that though I understand what those who use these terms mean by them I do not accept them as valid descriptions of the phenomena they purport to describe. For example, 'foreign' and 'Muslim' are considerable over-simplifications. Neither can even the most Sanskritized Hindi be accurately described as 'purely Indian'.

≈ PART THREE ≈

⊰9⊱

ISLAM IN A PAKISTAN VILLAGE
Some Impressions

In October 1976 I went to live for twelve days in the village of Kanyal, in the northern part of Punjab in Pakistan. My objective was to form a fairly comprehensive picture of what Islam means in the life of the villagers, and I was in a fairly good position to do this. First, I speak Urdu well, and this always evokes a warm response, partly because, despite the relative simplicity of the language, very few British people have ever taken the trouble to learn it, so that those who have, make a correspondingly greater impact. Urdu, and not the villagers' native Punjabi, is the 'prestige' language of Pakistan, and those who can speak it well command the admiration of those who cannot. (In Kanyal, which I believe is not untypical of the villages of Punjab in this respect, the great majority of the men can speak it reasonably fluently; the few men, and the very many women, who cannot, have no great difficulty in understanding it.) Secondly, it was a village where I was known. Before I even went there, I had become acquainted with Rashida, a Pakistani lady from Kanyal, a widow who has been settled in Britain since 1969; it was through her that I was introduced to the village when I visited it briefly in 1973, and it was her kinsmen who on both occasions were my hosts. Hence I was on intimate terms with the villagers, and I did not have the problem of breaking down the initial reserve which would have met me had I not

* Originally published in Robert Jackson, ed. *Perspectives on World Religions* (London: SOAS Extramural Division, 1978), pp. 221–35.

been in this advantageous position. From the very beginning I have looked upon the villagers of Kanyal as my friends; and from the very beginning it was clear that this was how they looked upon me. But it was for more than personal reasons that life in Kanyal interested me. Village society in Kanyal is typical in many ways of the society from which the great majority of Pakistanis now settled in Britain come. To understand it better is to understand better the background of the Pakistani immigrant population as a whole, and I think that there is an acute need for such understanding. True, more of them come from the adjacent area of Mirpur than from Punjab, but conditions in the two areas are closely comparable in most respects, so that most of what is true of Kanyal is also true of the whole region.

PATTERNS OF LIFE IN THE VILLAGE

For reasons which will emerge more clearly later, it will not be out of place to outline briefly what these conditions are.

The area is one of the least fertile in Pakistan. The ground is uneven, there seems to have been much wind erosion, and it has always been assumed (perhaps wrongly in recent years) that artificial irrigation is not possible. Kanyal is not much more than a mile from the great Upper Jhelum Canal, a broad, impressive, swift-running stream spanned, at the point nearest to Kanyal, by a brick bridge with ten arches. But none of this water reaches Kanyal, and the whole area depends entirely on rainfall. The villages are fairly small—Kanyal's population is about 600—and the land is the property of small farmers, with holdings ranging in size from about 5 acres to 25 acres. There is no road to the village. It lies some four miles from the main road from Lahore to Rawalpindi, on which long-distance buses run at frequent intervals, and the shortest way to it is to get off the bus at the point where the main road crosses the Upper Jhelum Canal, walk upstream along the bank for two and half miles and then turn right at the bridge, to Qasba. But you can follow this shortest route only if you walk, or go by bike, or motor-bike. In that case you can use the road belonging to the canal department that runs along the right bank (facing upstream). But this road is unmetalled, and is kept in reasonable condition by a prohibition on its use by cars, lorries and buses. A public road, also unmetalled, runs along the other bank, and this was still used by buses at the time of my first visit in April 1973. But this had so damaged the surface as to make it almost impassable, and at the time of my visit in October 1976 neither the buses nor even the *tongas*[1] used it any more. Instead they followed a longer but better road, brick-paved over most of its length, which issues onto the main road about a mile further up from the canal bridge. Qasba is a larger village than Kanyal, with several shops, a bank (to receive remittances from emigrants to Britian and elsewhere) and a Post Office—a room in the house of the man who carries out the duties of local postmaster. Once past Qasba, there is only a track running along the field boundaries (which, here, as in most villages of the subcontinent, consist of small strips of unploughed land about a foot wide, and raised a few inches above the level of the fields). If you are riding a bike, the depth of the dust sometimes compels you to dismount. A motor-bike gets through all right—I was taken there riding pillion on a Yamaha—and no doubt a jeep could too. But a car could not. As you approach the village you see the outer walls of the houses running along one boundary, and, rising above them, the minaret of the village mosque. Most of the flat-roofed houses are now built of brick which, with growing prosperity (and a growing sense of status) has replaced the old (and, in the hot season, more comfortable) thick walls of sun-dried mud. The houses cluster together, with narrow, unpaved lanes in between, and the village lands lie all around this central populated area of perhaps a hundred or so dwellings. There is no electricity (though it has come to Qasba), no sanitation (the 'lavatory' is the open fields round about, to which you go out first thing each morning), and the water supply is from wells. The village has one shop, situated not far from the mosque.

When I first visited Kanyal in April 1973 the wheat crop was being harvested. As I approached the village I asked my companions how the wheat was marketed. Did merchants come from the town to fetch it, or did they themselves take it to the town? They laughed and said, 'Neither! We eat it!' In other words, subsistence farming is the dominant pattern. Since the land is not fertile enough to support (in most cases) all the members of the family who own it, there has been for generations a tradition of people leaving the village to take employment elsewhere, and the wages they earn have helped to swell the income of the family as a whole. As a result, though the land is poor, the villagers are, if not exactly affluent, able to maintain a simple standard of·living that keeps them strong and healthy. (They have only one main meal a day, round about sunset, mainly of chapaties and vegetables. Meat is expensive by their standards: ten rupees a kilo for good quality meat and five for poorer quality, that is, about 70 pence and 35 pence a pound respectively. Fish costs eight rupees a kilo. So meat and fish are not a regular part of their diet.) At one time it was in the army that men sought employment outside the village— the great majority of the Pakistan army is recruited from these regions— and it still is a major outlet for the village's surplus manpower. About twenty to thirty Kanyal men are in the army. But in more recent years industries in the cities of Pakistan, especially the textile mills of Karachi and Hyderabad, have attracted increasing numbers, and more than one person told me that people now find this work more attractive than military service. Thirty to forty men from Kanyal are working in Karachi and sixteen work in Hyderabad. I met youngsters who had been employed in one or other of these two cities. I was struck by the evident youth of one of them and on enquiry was told in the most matter-of-fact way that the mills like 11–12 year olds because 'their fingers are more nimble'. I asked my host whether there was no law in Pakistan against child labour, and he said that he didn't think there was. A more highly educated man told me that he thought there was, but that he didn't suppose that it was enforced! Finally, in more recent years still, people have emigrated overseas. My host had worked for two years in Greece; a villager I had met in 1973 was currently working in Muscat; and Sharif, the more highly educated man I have just mentioned, had recently returned for a spell after working for five years in West Germany.

Within the village too there are occupations other than farming. The one shop in the village is run by a man who is one of four brothers. Only one works on the land; one is in Karachi, and the other in the army. My host's next-door neighbour is also from a similar family. He tills the land. One brother is in the police, and one owns a camel— there are several such in the village—and contributes to the family income the earnings he gains by the carrying trade. (Rates are two rupees a maund—roughly, 14 pence for 80 pounds—over short distances, going up to three, five, or seven rupees as the distances increase. They rarely go more than about five miles from Kanyal.) No one in the village works as a labourer on his fellow-villagers' lands.

A small number of people own no land at all. These are the *kammis*, to use the Punjabi term, that is, those who serve the village community as a whole and are paid (once wholly, and now partly) in kind, particularly at harvest times. Some of these are clearly the counterparts of the untouchables in rural Hindu society—the village shoemaker and leather worker being one of them and the barber another. Others are the blacksmith, the water-carrier, the *musalli*, the man who keeps the fires going when there is a big feast, and the *musāfir*, whose job it is to look after the mosque and keep it clean and tidy. Nowadays, their dependence upon the village community has greatly lessened. One of the shoemaker's sons works at the tobacco factory in Jhelum and both he and his brother have served in the army. The *musāfir's* son works part-time at a brick kiln, and the *musalli* works on piece rates at another brick kiln in a nearby village. Even with those who work within the old pattern, a proportion of their work is paid for, in cash, at the time it is done. All this has enhanced their standard of living, their status and their relative independence.

Finally, mention should be made of the women. They are strikingly unlike the stereotype mental picture of 'the Muslim woman' which many in the West have entertained. They play an active and important part in the everyday life of the village and, within the village, purdah is not observed. If my own experience is anything to go by, they are not noticeably shy, and they are on far more free and equal terms with the menfolk than their counterparts who live in the towns and/or belong to more well-to-do families. They are also much more free and independent than their counterparts in the Muslim villages of Uttar Pradesh in northern India which I have visited.

Two general features of village life which emerge from this pattern are worth stressing. The first is that though almost all the women and very many of the men are illiterate or semi-literate, it does not follow (as so many literate people thoughtlessly and quite illogically assume) that they are also ignorant. They don't read newspapers—I never saw one during the days I was there—and the few transistor radios (always, as far as I could see, the property of young people) are tuned almost continuously to film music. However, the villagers are not wholly unaware of what goes on in the country at large, or indeed of what happens on the international scene, because migrants from the village write to them and come home from time to time on visits.

The second is that the literacy rate is higher in this area than in the richer and more fertile parts of Punjab, because men have always had to seek employment outside the village, and a literate man can usually command a better-paid job than an illiterate one. It is significant that literacy is on the increase. Almost all the boys, and many of the girls, of school age now go to school.

ISLAM AND VILLAGE LIFE

Let me now turn to the more specifically Islamic features of Kanyal life.

Since the great communal massacres, and the huge movements of populations which accompanied independence and the partition of the Indian subcontinent in 1947, almost the whole population of Pakistan Punjab's villages has been Muslim. (The population of Kanyal was so even before 1947—a fact which I believe to be significant and to which I shall revert later.) Few will have realized as fully as it needs to be realized how much a part and parcel of the Pakistani villager his 'Muslimness' is. His Islam is, in a sense, all-embracing. The Pakistani villager takes his Muslim identity for granted, and he could no more conceive of his not being a Muslim than he could conceive of his not being a Pakistani. Islam is not a faith which at some stage of his life he adopts; it is something into which he is born and of which he acquires an ever fuller and more conscious knowledge as he grows into manhood. The child born in Kanyal grows up with religion all around him, and it would never enter anyone's head that his Islamic belief and observance is something that he may accept, modify or reject as his character and abilities develop. *Of course* he is a Muslim, and *of course* he will enter into the religious responsibilities which the village community expects of him and which he expects of himself. Islam is a religion whose observances are readily apparent on all sides. From infancy he will see the reverent care with which the Quran is kept, and the way in which his elders read it. The month-long fast of Ramzan (Ramadan) has an obvious impact on the whole household, and he will even in childhood be encouraged to keep, and be praised for his success in keeping, as many days of it as he feels able to manage. The mosque is (as in Islam it has traditionally always been), as obviously a centre of community life as it is a place of worship. For instance, it is to the mosque that the menfolk go to bathe. (My host and I used to make this trip every morning.) The village men will gather there to chat at the time of the sunset prayer, and the *muezzin* who gives the call to prayer will also announce from the minaret any piece of news of general interest to the village, for example that so and so has made a donation of such and such a sum to the mosque funds or to the local school. It is important to realize too that just as his Islam is a natural and integral part of the villager's life, so too is his life-pattern a natural and intergral part of his Islam. His life is all of a piece, and he is not accustomed to think in terms that would distinguish the things that make him a Muslim and the things that make him *him*, and define his place in the village community of which he is a part. Which does not mean that he does not see the explicit obligations of Islam as more important than the generality of his obligations.

Of course, human weakness is in evidence in the Kanyal community, as it is in every other human community anywhere else, and practice falls short of proclaimed ideals. Where this happens, it is not easy for a visitor to the village to get an accurate picture. It is part of the villagers' concept of courtesy to tell him what they think will please him, even if this means embroidering a little upon the strict truth. Thus at the time I was there everyone was very busy with the sowing of the wheat crop. People would be up at four in the morning and working hard in the fields until sundown—and even after; I saw people ploughing by moonlight while I was there. My host's brother-in-law was working in this way during these days, and I asked him whether he said his prayers at these busy times of the year, and whether he would stop work to say them in the fields when the appointed times came. He returned an unhesitating 'Yes' to both questions, but later when I reported this to Sharif, who has known him intimately since childhood, he laughed and said that this wasn't true, and that he wasn't *at all* regular about his prayers. I have referred to Sharif before. I found that conversation with him was often very illuminating. He is something of a loner in the village. In childhood and youth he was a close friend of my host and his brother-in-law, the late husband of Rashida, the Pakistani lady I spoke of at the beginning of this chapter. He is better educated than most, and is a graduate of the university of Karachi. He speaks English quite well and fluently, though with me he always preferred to speak in Urdu. Sharif left the village many years ago to work in Karachi, and later emigrated to West Germany, where he acquired a knowledge of German (better, he says than his English). During his sojourn overseas he re-acquired, under the influence of the Urdu writings of the celebrated (or notorious, according to taste) Pakistani divine Abul A'la Maududi, an intensity of devotion to Islam which had weakened over the years. I shall say a little more of Maududi later. One has to allow for a measure of consequent harshness in his judgements of his fellow-villagers, but by doing that, and checking them by conversations with others and by my own observation, I think I was able to get a fairly clear picture.

It is clear that even those who are lax in religious observance have a genuine and marked respect for those who are not. It is interesting that these latter are addressed as 'Sufi Sahib' and spoken of as 'Sufi so and so'. In the history of Islam the sufis were the mystics, those who stressed the essence of religion as love of the worshipper for his God and his fellow-men, counterposing this to the mechanical, and often hypocritical, insistence on the outward rituals of prayer, fasting, pilgrimage and the like. In Kanyal this contrast is no longer reflected very clearly, and it is those whose outward observances are most evident who receive the title of Sufi. At the same time I do not think it would be accorded to anyone who was not also, in the villagers' judgement, a good and upright man. I was myself very impressed by the character and personality of the most universally respected of these 'Sufi sahibs', and since he represents so well the villagers' concept of a good Muslim, I should say something about him. His name is Muhammad Aslam. I liked him very much, and had many conversations with him in which he told me, frankly and without inhibition, a lot about himself. He has no English, but his eight years in school, his excellent memory, his intelligence, and his fondness for preaching the message of Islam as he understands it have given him a good command of clear, lucid Urdu. He is a tall, good-looking man, with a fine, resonant voice, a forthright, plain-spoken manner, and a remarkable flow of articulate conversation, illustrated at every point by appropriate quotations from Urdu and Punjabi verse. He also excels all others in his recitation of the verses of *Saif ul Muluk*, the nineteenth-century poem of love and mysticism which belongs particularly to this area.

He prides himself on his knowledge of, and ability to expound, the history of Islam's golden age, of the life and character of the Prophet, of the pious Caliphs, and of the sufferings of Husain and his companions before their martyrdom at Karbala. I was struck by the absence from his conversation of any reference to the past glories of Islam in India and the chauvinist (one can only call it that) expression of superiority to the Hindus which are such commonplaces in the cultural equipment of the Pakistani townsman and the Muslim (townsman and villager alike) in India. I asked Sharif (among others) about this and asked whether he thought it was because Kanyal had always been a purely Muslim village and that there had been very few Hindus in the whole area even before Partition; so the impetus to make comparisons was lacking. He said he thought there might be something in that, but that a more obvious explanation was that the history of Muslim rule in India was something with which only those who had stayed on at school would have become familiar, and that Muhammad Aslam and most of his generation would not have had that much schooling. On the other hand, the knowledge of the early history of Islam was something that would be acquired from the Friday sermons preached in the mosque.

No doubt the deference accorded Muhammad Aslam springs partly from the fact that he is the largest landholder in the village, and is a hard-working and efficient farmer; but I think it is his other qualities which are decisive. The force of his moral authority is very evident, and is accepted as fully by the sophisticated Sharif as it is by his more traditional fellow-villagers. I asked Muhammad Aslam on one occasion whether everyone in Kanyal observes the Ramzan fast. He was emphatic that everyone does. I said, 'What would you think of one who didn't?' He said, 'We would beat him!' And I don't doubt that this is true. This conversation took place at Sharif's house, and I continued it after Muhammad Aslam left. Sharif confirmed his picture, and said that people who violated the fast would do so secretly in their own homes and take care that no one else knew of it. On the other hand he said that the obligation to say the five daily prayers was very generally not met, and my own observation supported the picture he gave. Sharif himself was the only one who ever excused himself when I was present in order to go and say his prayers; nor did I ever see anyone praying at prayer-time except on the occasions I was in the mosque at the time of the evening prayer. I had been struck by an incident that occurred on my first visit three and a half years earlier. I was accompanied on that occasion by a friend who had formerly been head of the department of Urdu in a Pakistani university. He was a devout man, though not in the least fanatical. We had arrived in the afternoon, and when the time for evening prayer came, he asked if he could be directed to the mosque so that he could say the evening prayer there. One of those present was sent to take him there, but no one else made any move to accompany him, nor did any of them retire to say the prayer in his own home. Sharif told me that if I went to the mosque at evening I would find relatively small numbers there, and that these would be mainly the older men who did not work full-time in the fields any more, and boys of school age. This latter group, he said, is influenced by the emphasis laid upon Islam at school, and also has the leisure, once school is over, to go to the mosque. My own observations on more than one occasion confirmed what he had told me.

One interesting theme that I should have liked to pursue further was that of the villagers' attitude to Maududi. Maududi is undoubtedly one of the most influential figures in Pakistan today. He argues that Pakistan cannot legitimately claim to be an Islamic state until it is a theocratic one, governed by the Holy Law of Islam, and he criticizes accordingly the secular standards of its rulers since independence, derived from the largely irreligious and immoral modern West. His organization, the Jama'at i Islami, functions as a political party too, and strongly influences the urban lower middle class and the university students.[2] Sharif had not mentioned Maududi to me, but one day while visiting his house I picked up a book lying on the table and saw it was one of Maududi's. I asked him about this, and it was then, when he saw that I knew of Maududi and his teachings, that he told me that it was Maududi's writings more than any others that had revived the intensity of his religious feeling. While we were talking about this my host came in. He smiled and said, 'If people here knew that you read Maududi, you would be refused water and the hookah.' This is a very strong expression, roughly equivalent to being sent to Coventry. (To refuse a request for a drink of water or for a smoke at the hookah is to deny the very minimum of hospitality that ordinary courtesy demands.) And though he spoke jokingly, there was obviously a serious meaning behind the words. When he had gone I asked Sharif why the villagers were so hostile to Maududi. He smiled and said, 'It's just their ignorance.' I could get nothing more specific out of him, nor did I have opportunity to question others about it. When I visited Kanyal again in 1977 I discovered that the hostility to Maududi is due to his attitude of disapproval towards those who believe in spiritual preceptors or *pīrs*.

People from Kanyal, like people everywhere else, tend to keep silent about such of their views and practices which they fear would provoke opposition or ridicule. I noticed more than once that my host, for all his genuine openness and friendliness, would introduce subjects by asking me what I thought about belief in such and such; and only when he felt sure that I would not ridicule his belief, whether I myself accepted it or not, would he then go on to speak of it. One such subject was belief in *pīrs*—and their powers. He opened up only when he was satisfied that I was familiar with the concept of the *pīr* and respected those who accepted their *pīrs'* spiritual guidance. Even so, it was not from him that I learnt about the *pīrs* of Kanyal.

Through the village runs a plateau, steep but not very high, overgrown with bushes. One evening as I walked round the village I got talking to a boy and asked him what this plateau was. He replied that it was the *darbār*—court—of the *pīrs*. I questioned him further, and he said that the tomb of the *pīrs* was on top of the hill. No one knew their names, but on Thursday evenings many villagers, including his own family, went up there to light a lamp by their graves. He also said that they could punish those who offended them. The next day I requested my host's young cousin, Salim, to take me to the tombs. He readily agreed, and told me what the villagers' beliefs about them were, gradually revealing, as he saw that my reaction was a respectful one, that he too shared these beliefs. As we approached the tomb we took off our shoes. It is a long tomb, and some villagers think it is that of a *pīr* of more than human stature while others think that two *pīrs* are buried there. He said that no one would cut firewood from the bushes on the hill for fear of punishment, though people from other villages could do so with impunity. He told me also that no one would sleep with their feet pointing towards the hill, as this would be disrespectful, and added that he himself had seen the displeasure of the *pīrs* one night when a guest from another village had stayed with him and had inadvertently slept with his feet towards the hill. He had groaned loudly in his sleep and it had been impossible to wake him until someone in the house had realized that he was sleeping with his feet towards the hill, and they had moved the bed, with the guest still sleeping on it, and turned its foot in the opposite direction. Then he awoke and told them how he had seen the *pīr*—a man of more than human stature—in a dream. Before we went down from the hill Salim asked if he should seek the *pīr's* blessing, and I said 'By all means' and stood respectfully silent as he did so. A day or two later I asked Sharif about it, and he confirmed all that Salim had said, adding, like Salim, that some Muslims believed it un-Islamic to seek the intercession of *pīrs* in their prayers to God. He said that he was not certain about this, and therefore (to be on the safe side, though he didn't put it in those words) went along with the prevailing belief.

The villagers in general are clearly at home with the idea of the *pīr* as a man of exceptional spiritual powers whose guidance is to be valued. It is very striking that the question of whether a *pīr* is dead or still living is of no importance to them. When you are told that a man follows a certain ritual 'because his *pīr* told him to' you do not know, until you ask, whether the *pīr* is a living person or one who died many years ago and appeared in a dream to give this instruction. Equally striking is the way in which this reverence for *pīrs* and holy men coexists with an entirely familiar, free and easy attitude towards them. One evening as I stood chatting outside the mosque to Akram, my host, and Muhammad Aslam, a middle-aged man dressed entirely in black ('at the command of his *pīr*', as I was subsequently told) approached us. Akram and Muhammad told me, in his presence, that he was a holy man, who never ate or drank during the hours of daylight and slept in the grave in which he would be buried when he died. He lived entirely upon what people gave him in charity. Yet with their obvious respect for him went a sense of humour, and an occasional dig at him which he too laughed at. I saw him again later—twice on the same evening; once at Sharif's, whose house he was entering as we left it. He spoke respectfully to Sharif, who replied that he was a sinner, and unworthy of such respect. Sharif's wife gave him some food and he left with us, accompanying us for some distance along our way and, perhaps for my benefit, praising the former British rulers of India and contrasting them with the allegedly more arrogant officials who now control Pakistan's destinies. Later he appeared in the doorway of the room in my host's house where people come and go at will after the day's work is done to chat and to smoke the hookah. He had food, but said he was afraid to move round the village now it was dark in case the dogs attacked him. The response was one of good-humoured mockery, in which both those who regarded him as a charlatan (and who subsequently told me so) and those who accepted his bona fides joined. He smiled (rather ruefully, I thought) and went on his way.

I don't know how far the villagers are accustomed to, and accept, the idea that people may legitimately differ about Islam and its interpretation. I should think that this is an unfamiliar concept and that the fierce hostility to Maududi's ideas would be matched by equally fierce hostility to other patterns of thought and action which deviated from the general norm. I had thought about my own position in these matters and had considered how far it would be wise to keep quiet about my own views on religion while I was in the village. I had decided that I would not seek controversy, but would not evade it if it arose naturally. It *did* arise naturally, and I responded accordingly. The villagers are nothing if not blunt, and on the very first evening I was there I was cross-questioned by one man, on the assumption that I was a Christian, about Christian beliefs and practices. He began by questioning, with fairly obvious scepticism, the alleged celibacy of priests and nuns, and passed on to explore the extent to which I observed the precepts of my own religion. I said I wasn't a Christian, and in fact was not a religious man at all. He was clearly taken aback, and the half-dozen others who were present (including my host) listened very attentively as I continued. I said I sincerely respected religious people, and *all* people who lived a good life and treated their fellow-men as they would wish to be treated themselves. To me it didn't matter if such people were Muslims or Christians or Hindus or Sikhs or atheists. I said that I whole-heartedly agreed with the great Persian poet Hafiz (a revered figure for all Muslims), who said:

So that you do not harm your fellow-men, do what you will
For in my Holy Law there is no other sin than this.

As for religious observances, obviously, if a man were a true Muslim, he should say the five daily prayers, keep the Ramzan fast, and so on. But a true Muslim was also one who did not lie, cheat, swindle and oppress his fellow-men or seek his own interests at the expense of the equally legitimate interests of others; and to me *these* were the important things. There were plenty of people who said their prayers and kept the fasts but who were liars and hypocrites, and to me, such people didn't deserve to be called Muslims at all, and I regarded them with contempt.

All this went down quite well. My host in particular seemed to feel that I had said things that needed saying, and on a number of occasions during the rest of my stay expressed similar sentiments himself. My original questioner was less readily convinced, though he saw the point and I think felt a quite genuine respect for my point of view. What *did* impress him was my action on the morning of my departure in giving a sum of money to the mosque. He was both very surprised and very pleased. He said 'You're not a religious man?' I said, 'No.' He said, 'Then why have you given money to the mosque?' I said, 'Everyone here has treated me like a close friend. The mosque is an institution that serves the needs of all of you, and there couldn't be a better way of showing you all how much I have enjoyed and appreciated your friendship. That I am not a Muslim doesn't matter. I wanted to contribute to something that *you* all value.'

I know very well that the fact that my expression of views like these was accepted and appreciated does not in the least mean that one of their own community would evoke the same reaction if he expressed them. All the same, it sheds light on the villagers' religious attitudes and may have a practical significance for readers, most of whom will not themselves be Muslims, but will be people who respect Muslim beliefs, and need to express that respect in ways which do not show them and their own different beliefs in a false light.[3]

CONCLUSION

The feature of Kanyal life which made (and, I trust, will again in the future make) participation in it so rewarding is the free and equal relationships that prevail there and the readiness with which I myself was accepted into the same sort of relationship. The fact that I know very well that this is not the total picture, and that the hostilities and cruelties which also characterize all peasant societies are there in Kanyal too, does not make it any the less real. In that sector of life in which I lived, everyone was, where *personal* relationships are concerned, everyone else's equal; all live much the same kind of life, at much the same standard of living, speak their mind freely and move in and out of one another's houses, sitting together to talk and smoke the hookah and laugh and joke with, and at, one another. The accepted, and in general, unresented, social subordination of the women to the men, and of the landless *kammi* to the peasant proprietor, does not contradict this, and the *kammi* neighbour of my host would sit with me and him, smoke his hookah and mock him to his face without him feeling any resentment. His womenfolk too behaved with the same freedom towards him in my presence, and the fact that men and women would pass their leisure hours separately—the women with other women, and the men with other men—does not invalidate this picture.

The question can be raised, how far is this situation a reflection of the egalitarian spirit of Islam, of the sense of Muslim brotherhood that enables the poorest Muslim worshipper in the mosque to stand shoulder to shoulder with the wealthiest as they say the congregational prayer? If this idea were suggested to them, I feel sure they would accept it with alacrity. I think myself that this is not the main explanation. The simpler and more obvious one is that they *are* more or less equal. None of them is individually dependent on any other. If some families have the prestige of owning sufficient land to keep them in modest affluence, others who do not can nevertheless match their life-style because the income they get from the land, from the camel transport trade, and from remittances of their brothers in the army, or in factory jobs in Karachi and elsewhere, adds up to much the same as that of the larger landholder. Similar questions arise about the relationship between the *kammis*—the landless servants of the village community—and the landholding villagers. That they are the counterparts of the village untouchables of Hindu society is obvious; and it is equally obvious that they enjoy a much higher status in their society than the Hindu untouchables do in theirs. How far this is a reflection of Islamic ideology is, again, difficult to assess. A Hindu friend of mine who grew up in Lahore and has many Muslim friends, insists that this is a major factor. I am less sure. An awareness of religious differences can sometimes lead to an unwarranted attribution to these differences things which relate to quite other causes, and one needs to be on one's guard against this tendency.

Be that as it may, the egalitarian values that Islam preaches are—whether because of that preaching or for other reasons—very evident in Kanyal life, and of all the pleasant impressions that I came away with, this has remained as the most pleasant and emotionally satisfying.

NOTES AND REFERENCES

1. The *tonga* is a light, two-wheeled horse-drawn passenger vehicle that plies for hire.
2. Cf. Peter Hardy, 'Modern Trends in Islam in India and Pakistan', in Robert Jackson, ed. *Perspectives on World Religions* (London: SOAS, 1978), pp. 209–20.
3. Cf. the discussion on the teaching of Islam in 'The World Religions Debate', Jackson, *Perspectives.*

⚓10⚓

A DAY IN A PAKISTANI VILLAGE

I want to record some impressions of a visit to Trikha, a village nine miles from Gujrat.[1] While in Trikha I spent most of the time with a young man called Chaudhri[2] Muhammad Arif[3] Zafar.[4] I was struck by the cleanliness of the houses and lanes: the only unclean feature was the open sewers—if one can dignify them by that name—running down the lanes. Many of the houses—about half, I think—are brick built. I asked him what the population of the village was and he said 1200 to 1300, from which it soon emerged, however, that he meant that this was the number of *voters* there—people above the age of twenty-one.

When we arrived two professional singers were singing, one of whom was also drumming and the other was playing a fiddle-like instrument called a *sārangī*. They were singing a song expressing the feelings of the wives and sisters and brothers of the Pakistani prisoners of war held in India—nine from this village alone. Another fifty or sixty of its men are in the army. Then they went on to another song celebrating the birthday of a small (about one-year-old) boy who was sitting happily on the drum and resting his back against the chest of the drummer. The population is mainly Sunni, but there are quite a few Shias too; and there is no discord between the two. The villagers have free education up to the eighth class—by law it's free and compulsory up to the sixth class—and have contributed their own labour and *some* money to build a small school building, the

---

* Extracts from a letter from Gujrat written in March 1973.

government providing Rs 4000 plus towards the cost. For the present, however the children study in the open under the shade of a huge tree. The master belongs to the village, and speaks simple English quite well.[5] There's almost no parda ('purdah') within the village, though the women have *burqas* which they put on to go to town. Arif said, 'The village is like a family: you don't observe purdah within a family.' I was surprised to discover that there is a regular branch of the Peoples' Party of Pakistan there, of which Arif is the secretary. I questioned him in detail about this. He says the party was founded in late 1967; he joined in March 1968 and has set up branches in four or five villages besides his own and in his own village there are twenty-one members. Other political views are also found there, but only the PPP has an organization. It has an annually elected organizing committee, meets every month, and in addition holds public meetings from time to time.

The village is a prosperous one—peasants generally holding their own land. Arif has 20 acres, and the largest landholder has 25. There are some landless labourers, some of whom work in the village, while others cycle into Gujrat town to work. The village labourers are paid yearly, and there is payment both in kind and in cash. Even labourers own a buffalo. The village has had electricity for the last fifteen years or so. This is exceptional. The village is very close to the canal, and to a small hydro-electric project. The level of political awareness is also exceptional, due, no doubt, partly to its nearness to Gujrat town, partly to the experience of the outside world which filters back from its serving soldiers and the odd emigrant to England, and partly I think due to Arif. He is really quite exceptional in that, although well educated (we could have conversed in English) and a trained welder (trained at a local institute of technology set up by the Swedes), he has not deserted the village even for the nearby town. Nor, though a veteran member of the now ruling party, does he want to enter government service. I asked him how he kept his welding skills in play, and he said he occasionally went 'for practice' to work at a local bus company. It's very rare, either in Pakistan or in India, for an educated man to bring his acquired skills back to the service of his village.

We had typical village food—yellow chapaties made of maize flour, spinach, and *makkhan*—butter made from curd (*dahī*). We also drank *lassī*—drink made from curd. Before the meal we listened to a group of four professional singers singing classical Panjabi folk (or semi-folk) poetry—Hīr Rānjhā, Saif ul Mulūk, Bulhe Shāh, etc.—and one Urdu ghazal and other folk forms. All of them also played some instrument in accompaniment—two-stringed fiddle-like things, one a drum, and one a sort of pair of tongs—two long (about 2 feet) flat iron strips joined by an iron ring. This is really a thing for getting the chapatis out of the oven, but is used to beat the time in singing too. One man came forward to take the money offered to them, and they would then sing a short poem in praise of the donor, mentioning him by name. 'Russell Sahib' was honoured three times in this way. The villagers' generosity is considerable. Last night a famous singer was invited, paid 200 rupees in advance, and in a session lasting from about 10 p.m. to 3 a.m. collected another 1000 rupees in donations from his audience. The songs are full of Sufi sentiment and I asked Arif afterwards how far these sentiments were expressed in the villagers' daily life. He was emphatic that they were. I asked him who was respected the most, the man who observed all the rituals, but cheated and lied and took advantage of his fellow-men, or the man who was lax in formal observances, but was honest and dealt fairly with his fellows. A loaded question, of course, but he was insistent that it was the latter who commanded respect. I asked about women. They don't come in large numbers to meetings. They *do* all vote. At big public meetings there are separate, purdah arrangements. Two local officials of the PPP are women: the president of the Gujrat town organization is one Surayya Malik and the president of the Gujrat district organization is also a woman—Samīya Fateh Usmān. (Fateh Usmān being her husband's name, which she uses as her surname. I gather she was already prominent in the PPP before her marriage.)

Men and women alike in the villages wear the *tahmad*–a long sheet-like thing reaching from the waist to the feet. You hold it round your waist, and when extended the two ends are each about an arm's length.[6] You gather these a bit and then cross them at the waist and tuck them in. (I don't *think* there's anything worn underneath.) Arif gave me a *khes*—a locally woven thing that can serve either as a bedcover or as a sort of blanket wrapped round you when it's cold—

and we promised to write to each other. We were there from about 12 to 4, and it was very enjoyable. At the end we had some political conversation. He agreed (reluctantly, I think) that Pakistan ought to recognize Bangladesh. *I* agreed that whether it did or not, India should release its Pakistani prisoners of war. I also expressed my belief that the British police killing the two Pakistani boys at the Indian High Commission was totally unjustified, spoke about colour prejudice in England and of my hatred of it, and a few other bits and pieces. I liked him, and we embraced warmly on parting. He pressed me to come again, accepted my explanation of why on this trip it would probably not be possible, and my (very genuine) assurance that when I next come on long study leave I will certainly come again. [In the event I never did.]

NOTES

1. The district town of Gujrat district, Panjab, Pakistan..
2. A man of some wealth—in this case 20 acres of good land—and social status in the village.
3. Personal name.
4. *Takhallus*—this necessarily means that he is a poet—an Urdu poet.
5. I met a man home on holiday from England. He hadn't decided whether to take his wife and family back with him.
6. The *shalvar* is the townsman's dress, and village people too wear it to go to town.

⊰11⊱

A DAY IN JHELUM, PAKISTAN

In October 1976, I went to stay for two weeks in the village of Kanyal in Gujrat district very near the boundary between Gujrat and Jhelum districts. Jhelum is the nearest big town. You get there via the smaller town of Sarai Alamgir. I have friends in both, including Ghulam Husain, who owns a cycle shop in Sarai Alamgir and Amanullah Khan, who lives in Sarai Alamgir but owns (or rather part-owns) a welding shop in Jhelum. During my stay I decided to take a day away from the village to visit Jhelum. I had it in mind to visit four houses there. The first two were the homes of relatives of Pakistanis in Nottingham to whom I had been introduced. Then I wanted to look up Amanullah Khan, since I had not been able to contact him in Sarai Alamgir. And finally I intended to call on a lady who after my visit to Pakistan in 1973 had seen an article about me in an Urdu weekly and had written to me.

The account that follows is taken mainly from one that I spoke onto tape two days later, but draws also on letters I wrote to England at the time, and on other written notes that I took.

I decided to go to Jhelum for the day and return to Sarai Alamgir in the evening, where I would have the evening meal and stay the night with Ghulam Husain at his house. When I first spoke of this in Kanyal, there was some discussion about how I should get to Sarai Alamgir, and further discussion about how I should get from there to Jhelum. When I spoke to Akram[1] about it he said, 'Salīm's[2] younger brother goes to college in Jhelum; you can fix up with him to go on the carrier of his bike.' However nothing was done about this and I discovered quite late at night that in fact that this was not going to be possible. Sharif[3] then offered to take me into Sarai Alamgir. He came about half-past eight, I suppose and we must have left before nine.

We walked across the fields the mile or so to the Qasba bridge. Sharif paused there to talk to one of the shopkeepers. They were talking in Punjabi, but at one point I became aware that the shopkeeper was saying something about me, and I worked it out that he was probably objecting to my rather long hair. I asked Sharif, who looked embarrassed and muttered something non-commital. So I laughed and asked the shopkeeper, in Urdu, whether he was objecting to my long hair. 'Yes,' he said with complete bluntness, and continued, in rhetorical style, '*Pucho kyon*? (ask why?) Because it's a woman's duty to look beautiful and a man's duty to look strong.' I said, 'Alright, but customs differ from country to country. Here in Pakistan men line their eyelashes with mascara and use perfume. In England a man who did that would be regarded as *very* effeminate.' He nodded sagely, and took the point. All of this was entirely friendly. The same man on another occasion stopped me and said, 'You come to Pakistan, and we don't stop you, do we?' 'No,' I said.

'So why is it you don't let us Pakistanis come to Britain? And what do you do about it?'

I said, 'I think you should be allowed to come, without any restriction,[4] and I say so publicly. But I don't make the laws.'

'Yes,' he said, 'What can one broken string of a *charpoy*[5] do?'

We took a tonga to Sarai Alamgir. When we got there we went straight to Ghulam Husain's shop and Sharif and he and I discussed how I should go to Jhelum. I'd thought that I would perhaps hire a bike or go by tonga[6] or by bus; these were the three alternatives. Ghulam Husain thought I ought to go by tonga and Sharif in fact went out to get a tonga after we had parted from Ghulam Husain. But then he said that he didn't like tongawallas;[7] in fact he was frightened of them; he said, 'They're very *harāmī*[8] people and it's difficult to make any proper arrangement with them.' So he thought it would be better if I hired a bike. I said, 'Where from?' and he said, 'We could get it from a different shop from Ghulam Husain's.' But I thought it would look very odd if I arrived back at Ghulam Husain's shop in the evening on a cycle hired from somewhere else, so I said,

'No, it's alright. If we can't get a tonga I'll go by bus. What's wrong with going by bus?' In the end we decided that I should go on the bus.

Sharif saw me onto the bus and I sat down next to a young chap whose name, I later learned, was Muhammad Zamān, and started a conversation with him. I asked him whether he knew Jhelum, he said yes, he knew it quite well. I asked him whether he knew where Shah Bhore Street was, and he said he didn't, but he would find out. I said, 'I have to go to the railway station first and make some enquiries. Would you please tell me when we get there?' He said he would. When we got there he called out to the bus-driver to stop, but he didn't, and went on a bit further. Zamān got off with me saying he would get off there as well. And just as Sharif had complained about the tonga drivers, he complained about the bus drivers and said, 'They're great *harāmīs*, they won't stop where you want them to.'

I said to him, 'Don't put yourself to any trouble. I can walk back to the station. I can see where the station is, so please don't bother.' He said, 'No, No, I'll come with you.' So we went to the station. I wanted to buy a timetable, and I discovered that the present timetable would expire at the end of this week and that a new one was in force from 1 November. Besides they hadn't got any copies of the old one, and of course, they hadn't yet got any copies of the new one, and in any case it didn't apply. So then I asked about the timing of trains; and Zamān stayed with me all this time. When we came out of the station I again said to him, 'Don't bother to stay with me any longer. I'll find my own way now.' But he said 'No, No, you stay with me.' We asked a young chap coming along the road where Shah Bhore Street was and to my pleasant surprise he said he knew; and he explained to Zamān in Punjabi how to get there. The quickest way was to go back into the station, cross the railway line, get under some trains and go out the other side. So that's what we did.

We walked along for a while and came to the point from which, according to our informant it should be easy to find Shah Bhore Street. There was a cafe there, so he took me in and insisted on giving me a cup of tea; and while we were there another young man came in whom Zamān knew. So he asked him about Shah Bhore Street and discovered that it was not at all in the area where our first informant had said. He told us how to get to a place from where we could find it easily. When we left him and came out of the shop Zaman said to me, 'This fellow is a great *harāmī*.' I thought to myself, 'The whole of Pakistan must be populated with *harāmīs*!' I said, 'Why do you say that?' He said, 'He worked in the . . . Bank and he's embezzled something like Rs 1500-1600 by forging papers.' I said, 'Have they caught him, then?' He said, 'Yes, he's being tried at the moment.' 'He'll presumably get a very heavy punishment if he's found guilty,' I said, and he answered yes, he would. I said, 'Well, if he's such a *harāmī* why did you ask him the way? And how do you know that he'll have told us the right way? And how do you know him?' He said, 'I know him well, and he knows Jhelum, so he'll know where the place is.' So we walked along and came to a fruit market where the commission agents sit. They get the fruit in and then distribute it to wholesalers and take a commission on it. I sat there and talked a while to one of these chaps, who said that his elder brother had done an MA in English from London and was a teacher of English in Government College, Lahore.

Then we walked through various streets and bazars and came to a road that runs along the side of the Jhelum river. We turned left there and walked upstream, following the road along the river bank. A bit further on we asked and found out where Shah Bhore Street was. It was a turning off that road. We went along it and asked two people in a shop if they could direct us to Major B's house. I was interested to note that people didn't know Major B as well as they knew his brother N, who was not a Major or anything exalted at all, but had settled in England. Anyway a man ultimately took us to the Major Sahib's house. We found he wasn't there and nobody invited us in. Presumably only the women were at home and in purdah. But a woman next door said that she thought he might be supervising the building of his new house, and directed us to where we might find this new house.

So we walked off and went from site to site, but couldn't find any trace of a new house being built by Major B. By this time it was after twelve o' clock and my companion said, 'Well, we don't seem to be able to trace him. So what shall we do?' I said, 'I'd better try this second address I've got on my list which is in Naya Muhalla. Presumably people will know where Naya Muhalla is, so I can get a tonga there. Please don't bother any further.' He said, 'No, no, I'll find this address for you too.' It turned out that we were practically in Naya Muhalla at that time—I didn't know it was so near—and he went to a shopkeeper and asked whether he could tell him where Muhammad Sadiq was. The shopkeeper gave a call to a man standing at the shop next door and that turned out to be Muhammad Sadiq himself. At that point Zamān took leave of me. He gave me his address and I gave him mine and promised to correspond with him if he wrote to me. The address was in standard South Asian form—so and so, son of so and so, village so and so, etc. The 'son of so and so' is often necessary because many South Asian names are very common, and you can distinguish one from the other only by giving the father's name as well; and also because in the villages the houses are not numbered and the roads are not named. Zamān lived in a village not far from Jhelum. I wrote of him later that he was 'endlessly helpful, in the way that is so common in Pakistan, and so unthinkable in England'.

Muhammad Sadiq took me home. He is the father of Rafiq, who works on the buses in Nottingham. (My friend Jill Evans took me one day with Ian (my son) to meet him and his family.) I liked him; he was a very nice old man, and we sat and talked a long time. He said that he'd spent all his life as a driver of cars and trucks and buses, and had driven cars for British officers in Quetta before the earthquake in 1935. He retired from his job only three years ago. He's sixty-three now, so he must have been driving for near enough forty years and had seen different parts of Pakistan. He spoke very freely and informally. He was wearing a white skull cap, and when it was time for the midday prayer he asked me to take my meal by myself while he would go off and say his prayers and then come back and join me. I'd already been fed on peanuts, *chīlgozas*[9], walnuts, and raisins; and now the proper meal was brought in—goat's foot, savoury omelette, and chapatis. Sadiq's wife served me, and sat and talked with me as I ate. She too was very friendly and informal. She speaks Punjabi, can speak Urdu at a pinch and understands Urdu perfectly well.

I also met their youngest daughter, a girl of about 15–16 who had just passed her matric, and also two small children—Sadiq's grandchildren. Sadiq returned before I'd finished eating. (By that time I was on to tea, samosas and sweet cake!) We all went on talking together and I learnt about the rest of their family. Rafiq, the eldest, is in Nottingham, as I have already said. He'd worked as a Post Office clerk in Jhelum for eleven years before he went to England. The second son, Nazīr, came in from work while I was eating. Of the others, one son and one son-in-law were working in Saudi Arabia, and I think he said another son-in-law was, like Rafiq, in England, though, unlike Rafiq, he hadn't got his wife (Rafiq's sister) with him. The Major Sahib whom I'd sought in vain in the morning is Sadiq's *bhānjā*—sister's son, and Rafiq's wife is his *bhānjī*—sister's daughter. (Cousin marriage is the general rule among Pakistani Muslims.)

When I'd finished eating and drinking I said I'd better be moving on, as I still had to find my friend Amanullah at the Asia Engineering Works. Nazīr asked further details about his address, but the only address I had was GT Road, Jhelum. (The GT Road is the Grand Trunk Road, the historic road that runs all the way from Peshawar to Calcutta.) So he went off to make enquiries, and returned after discovering precisely where it was, and announced that he would take me there—and to the other places where I had to go. I protested that he shouldn't interrupt his work, but he said, 'That's alright. I work in my own office. I can shut it up at any time and go off when I like. So I'll come with you.' So I very gladly accepted his offer. Our first port of call was to be the telegraph office, where I wanted to send a telegram to India, and then we were to go to the GT Road to find Amanullah's welding shop. As we walked towards the tonga stand I noticed, as I'd noticed elsewhere in Jhelum that morning, the slogan *'Haq i chār yār'* stencilled on the walls. This means 'The right of the four friends'—meaning the first four caliphs,[10] the Pious Caliphs, as they are commonly called—and is an anti-Shia slogan, because the Shias regard the first three of them as usurpers. I asked Nazīr whether there was much Shia-Sunni conflict in Jhelum. (Pakistan is overwhelmingly Sunni.) He said 'Yes, there's quite a lot, and there have even been Sunni-Shia riots here.'

We got to the tonga stand, and he spoke to a tongawalla, but he said he wouldn't go to Amanullah's shop. Nazir said to me, 'Never mind, we'll find another one who will go, and I'll hire a cycle and follow you on the tonga.' I agreed and then he hesitated a bit and looked at me and said 'Would you ride on the crossbar?' I said 'Yes, by all means.' So he hired a bike, and I sat on the crossbar and off we went. We went to the telegraph office and I sent a very expensive telegram to India costing Rs 36.30; then I posted some letters; and then we set off along the Grand Trunk Road.

The Asian Engineering Works turned out (characteristically!) to be quite a small place, on the Grand Trunk Road going north from Jhelum towards Rawalpindi. When we got there Amanullah wasn't there. They said 'He'll be coming', but I know from long experience that 'He'll be coming' means either in five minutes, or one hour, or five hours, or tomorrow morning; so it didn't surprise me when we sat there for quite a long time and nobody came. I said to Nazīr, 'Look, there's another place I want to go to. If you think we've got time let's go there and then come back.' I told him about the letter I had had from this girl called S nearly three years ago, in December 1973. In fact I gave it to him to read. She had written that she had read an account of an interview with me in an Urdu weekly in June 1973, and went on to say, in very effusive terms, how fervently she desired to correspond with me and, one day, to meet me. At that time she was in the final year of her BA course. I hadn't written to her but I'd kept the letter because I knew I should be going to Jhelum one day and I thought I might look her up. He said 'Have you got the address?' I said 'Yes', and he noted it. Then he said, 'She doesn't give her father's name?' I said 'No'. He commented that this might make it a bit difficult to find the place. 'This was written three years ago, and she was in her final year then, and God knows what she's done since. And perhaps she's married.' I said, 'Do you think that anybody would think it improper for me to go there simply on the basis of this letter?' He said, 'No, I don't think so, but we might not find her; but anyway let's go and look.' We set off again on the bike. Turning the corner we fell off because the handlebars had knocked against me, and I got a large bruise on my thigh, but otherwise I didn't suffer any ill effects, and I think he was alright too; and we went on to the *muhalla*[11] where she lived. There was a chap sitting at the shop where we stopped and I showed him the letter and the address. He at once said that he knew the house and he would take us there. When we got there he said, 'You wait outside a moment,' and went in. He was out in a moment and ushered us in. When we were seated, he said, 'S is my sister; you know our eastern etiquette; I didn't like to say this outside in front of everybody else, when I was sitting in the shop. But she is my sister.' It later turned out that she wasn't in fact his sister but his sister-in-law; he was the husband of her elder sister. S's mother was there, a very strongly built woman who apparently had been a teacher in a mission school for a long, long time. She stressed to me how she had grown up in this mission school, that she was very interested in Christianity and that she knew all about the Psalms and the Bible and the Old Testament and the New Testament, emphasizing the closeness between Christianity and Islam for my benefit, no doubt under the mistaken impression that I was a Christian and would be duly impressed. She also pointed to a young boy sitting on a bench and said, 'He goes to an English medium school too.' Anyway we chatted a bit and she said that her daughter was still unmarried and that she worked in an office. I said, 'Oh dear, she'll be at work now, and I can't stay very long.' She said, 'No, no, she'll be coming back very soon,' and so she did. We sat and chatted there quite a long time and they gave us sweets and tea once again and then we took leave and went off back to the welding shop.

Amanullah had still rot returned, and we sat there talking to an old man sitting there in the verandah, facing the road, whose name was Raja[12] Afzal Khan, the same as his more illustrious namesake in Sarai Alamgir.[13] I was surprised to discover that he knew Rafiq—the Nottingham Rafiq—and had been at school with him. Nazīr left soon after this, and I think it was after he had gone that Raja Afzal Khan said, 'I think I know that family you've just visited.' He asked me to describe the man who'd shown us to the house, and at once identified him from my description. He said, 'They're a very dubious sort of family. There's bad feeling between that chap and his wife and in fact he's left her, and the children have grown up and she's working as a nurse in . . . and he's taken up with somebody else.' I said, 'With another woman?' He grinned and said, 'No, with a man.' I smiled and said, 'There are all sorts of people in the world, aren't there?' and he laughed and slapped my hand in a sort of open handshake in the way an Urdu speaker does when he thinks that you (or he!) has said something witty or amusing. (The following morning I met Amanullah and was sitting with his young friend Fyāz (outside Punjab, he would be called Fayyāz, but in the characteristically Punjabi pronunciation calls himself Fyāz, pronounced as a monosyllable). He was looking at the list of addresses I had, and I had been saying what a coincidence it was that Raja Afzal Khan had known both Rafiq, that is the family I'd visited before coming to the shop, and the family whom I was next going to visit, although as far as I knew there was no connection between any of these people. He laughed and said, 'You've been talking about coincidences. Shah Bhore Street is the street where my in-laws live!' We laughed about that too, and then I said what difficulty we'd had in finding the place and asked him how I should direct anybody to it. He drew me a little map and said that people should first ask for the mosque by the river. Everyone knew where that was, and the map would show how to go on from there. Then he said, 'I also know about this family that you went to visit yesterday. The mother too is a woman of very bad character. She married a *chowkidar*[14] and because she was a teacher in a school she earned much more money than he did.' He didn't say it was a love marriage, but I would think it must have been a love marriage; because a school teacher doesn't normally marry a *chowkidar*. He said, 'She liked to have a good time [in the bad sense of the word] and she virtually starved her husband to death.' I said, 'How so?' He replied, 'Because she was a teacher and got good money and he was only a chowkidar and got very poor wages. She never let him forget this, and fed him on what was left over after she and her children had had their meals, and he only had the scraps to eat. He died in a very deplorable state. She brought up her daughters in the same way. This daughter who is married to the man who took you to the house—this was a love marriage. The poor fellow didn't know it, but she'd already had affairs with other men and continued to have affairs with other men. He thought that she loved him, and he broke off with all his relatives and everybody else in order to marry her; and then she treated him in the same way. One day when he came home she wasn't there; she'd disappeared taking their young daughter with her, and he didn't know what to do about it. Anyway he made enquiries around and ultimately found out that she was in Rawalpindi. He went to Rawalpindi, and there he found her in bed with another man. He of course raised a hue and cry, and neighbours came in, and she tried to make out that the man she was in bed with was her husband and that she didn't know anything about this other fellow who'd come alleging that he was her husband; and the neighbours were going to beat him up when the child said to the man, 'Daddy, give me a drink of water.' Then they realized that since this little girl called him daddy he must be her father. This convinced people that it was she who was in the wrong and that this man was her real husband.' I seem to have got in touch with a very colourful family! Fyāz too said that the abandoned husband was now in some homosexual relationship with someone. I don't know how much of this is true; anyway, this is what they said.

We'd got back to the shop I suppose about five in the evening. Amanullah had still not come back. I waited there chatting with people about things of not very much consequence until 6.20 and then said, 'I'll leave here at 6.30. When Amanullah comes tell him that I've gone to Ghulam Husain's.' I'd discovered in the meanwhile that although Amanullah worked in Jhelum at the shop, he still lived in Sarai Alamgir. I knew he knew Ghulam Husain's home well, and was an old friend of his; and therefore was quite confident that if I left a message saying I was at Ghulam Husain's he could quite easily come and find me there if he wanted to. Anyway about five minutes later someone in the shop brought me a message that Amanullah was already at Ghulam Husain's cycle shop and would be there when I got there. So Fayyāz ('Fyāz') then sat me on the pillion of his motorbike and took me off to Sarai Alamgir. We found that Amanullah had left. We waited for a while for him to come back, but he didn't, and Ghulam Husain said, 'He'll be coming to my house this evening and will eat and spend the evening with us. So let's go.' So we went. He lives in a house the other side of the railway line. Quite a big impressive house which he built, I think, two to three years ago. It has an upper storey with rooms and is on the usual plan—rooms round a courtyard opening into it, and a big outer gate enclosing the whole place. He also has another house, his older house, which is two houses away. I discovered the next day to my amusement that the house has no lavatory and that like everybody else in these parts you sally forth and go into the fields or to some open land first thing in the morning. I also discovered something else. When I wanted to go out I asked him, 'Have you got a *lotā*?'[15] He said, 'No, there isn't one here, I'll get one from the other house.' From which I deduced that they don't use a

lotā for this purpose, and I wondered what they did use.[16] I went out
and came back, and then we went off to the shop. I spent that morning
in Jhelum too, talking with Fyāz and with Amanullah, and got back
to Kanyal early that afternoon.

NOTES

1. My host in Kanyal, and brother of a Pakistani lady in Burton-on-Trent
   who, so to speak, sent me there.
2. Akram's young cousin (paternal uncle's son).
3. There are at least two Sharifs in Kanyal. This one was the village's only
   graduate. He had just returned (temporarily) to Kanyal after working
   five years in West Germany.
4. I had better make it clear that this is my view. I was not saying it just to
   placate him.
5. The light-weight bed used everywhere in Pakistan and India, and
   consisting simply of a wooden frame standing on four legs, and with a
   criss-cross of strings made of tough springy grass forming the base on
   which you lie.
6. A light horse-drawn vehicle—the rural and small-town equivalent of a
   taxi.
7. Tonga drivers.
8. Literally, 'bastard'—but it means little more than 'awkward customer'.
9. A kind of nut.
10. Temporal and spiritual heads of the Muslims after the Prophet's death.
    Sunnis and Shias are the two main sects of Muslims.
11. The ward, or quarter, of a city. Formerly each muhalla would often be
    the quarter in which a particular craft—e.g., metal-work—would be
    practised, and would be named accordingly.
12. Raja is the title by which people of Rajput origin or caste are called. It
    doesn't necessarily imply anything exalted.
13. A very popular local leader of the Tahrik i Istiqlal, and a vigorous
    opponent of Bhutto.
14. Caretaker, watchman.
15. South Asians don't use toilet paper; they use water. You fill a *lotā* with
    water and take it with you. When you've finished you pour some water
    from it onto your left hand and continue pouring, cleaning your bottom
    as you do so. The Muslims' *lotā* is the size and shape of a metal coffee-
    pot without a lid. The Hindu one is an open, round-bottomed vessel,

smaller than the Muslim one. In immigrant households in Britain you often find in the lavatory a milk bottle used for the same purpose.

16. Later on I asked Amanullah. He seemed puzzled and said that everyone uses a *lotā*. Actually I'd already noticed in Kanyal that I was the only one that took a *lotā* out with me into the fields, but had forgotten to ask about it. My son Ian asked Akram when *he* visited Kanyal. Akram said, 'We wash our hands when we get back.' Presumably they use earth to clean themselves while they're out there.

⚜ 12 ⚜

MEETING A *PĪR'S* DISCIPLE

O n 1 October 1981, I reached Lahore airport at 10 in the morning though checking-in time for my flight was not till 11. Still, I had nothing more to do in Lahore, so I thought I might as well be off, thinking that there might be interesting people to talk to at the airport. There were.

I got talking to a tall, rather ugly man (by which I intend no disrespect to him) with a curly black beard, dressed in white *shalvar-qamis* and a white hat of the same material. He had noticed me speaking in Urdu with an old man sitting on the seat next to me, and when we'd finished, I noticed him quietly talking to the same old man. It seemed that he was satisfying himself that I could cope with a simple Urdu conversation, and, having done so he began to talk to me. It took him a little while, when he was first speaking, to convince himself that I really did know Urdu. When he first said *'haqīqat'* (fact, reality) he asked me if I knew what it meant. Also did I know what *'mītha'* (sweet) meant (!). But then he got into his stride.

He began talking about *dīn* (religion) and I thought, 'Here we go. I'm about to receive the usual spiel on Islam.' But it quickly became evident that he wanted to talk about his *pīr*.[1] I used the word first, which clearly encouraged him. He said if I wanted to go and meet his *pīr* now (in Gujranwala!) there might be just enough time before my flight, because Gujranwala was only an hour's journey from Lahore, and my flight didn't leave until 12.30! I'll give the rest of what he told me in more logical order than he gave it.

He comes from a village (he used the English word, pronouncing it vilj!) in Multan district. He studied up to the eight class, but is obviously not very strong on reading and writing because when I asked him to dictate his name—Muhammad Sarvar—he said *sin, re, vao, alif, re,* and only when he saw it in writing realized that there was no *alif* in it. He said that before becoming the disciple of his *pīr* he had been a very bad man, and had done things that it would be improper even to mention. A friend of his, against his urgings, had gone to this *pīr,* and had come back a changed man. When he asked him why he had gone, the friend had replied that he himself didn't know why, but that the desire to go had been irresistible. So he went too, and experienced the same irresistible influence. This was in 1971. He said that all his evil actions, and all desire to do wrong, simply ceased. I asked him his *pīr's* name and address, because I was going (perhaps) to Gujranwala and might visit him. (He'd already urged me to do so—'whether you feel his influence or not, you should meet him.') He'd said his *pīr's* name was Hazrat Khaja Sufi Karamat Husain Sahib but when I began to write it down he amended it and told me to write 'Munir' instead of 'Karamat' because Karamat was now dead and his son Munir was his successor. He also gave me the address.

He says his *pīr* has never told him, 'Say your prayers' or anything like that. He just said *'mujh ko milte raho'*—continue to see me. (He should have said *'mujh se . . .'*; and perhaps he did; but this is Md. Sarvar's version.) I said, 'How often do you go?' and he said when in Pakistan he went every month or at least every two months, but he had just returned from four and a half years in Dubai and had not been to see his *pīr* during that time. He was now going straight there, before going home.

He had gone to Dubai as a labourer, but now has a small business making aluminium door and window frames. (He was very emphatic that Islam in no way interferes with business activities. I suggested there'd be problems over *sūd*—taking interest on loans, etc.—but he ducked that one and made no comment.) He employs three or four fellow-Pakistanis. ('The Arabs don't work.') Any difficulties in setting up his business? No. But he had to wait a long time for a licence. Did he have to bribe anyone? No, there's no bribery there.

He has a younger brother. I forgot to ask if he has a wife and family. See what interesting conversations you can have if you know Urdu!

NOTES

1. A *pīr*—the word originally means 'old man'; hence 'elder'; hence one whom you revere—is a man believed by his disciples to possess exceptional spiritual powers, so much so that one should follow and obey his directions implicitly. *Pīrs* play a very important part in the religious life of Pakistan.

≈13≈

STRANDS OF MUSLIM IDENTITY
IN SOUTH ASIA

Since the break-up of Pakistan in 1971 questions have been raised as to how far there still is, or indeed ever was, any justification for the existence of a separate Muslim state or states on the South Asian subcontinent. In my view the study of so large a question would be of rather limited value. The emergence of the separate Muslim state of Pakistan was a fact of history, and so too is the emergence of the separate Muslim (or predominantly Muslim) state of Bangladesh; and the separate existence of both is likely to be maintained for at any rate long enough to make any speculation about their ultimate destiny premature. This article therefore confines itself to a more limited field of study, and seeks to identify the major strands in the South Asian Muslims' sense of identity which have been and will continue to be relevant to the study of their history and political development. As we shall see, some of them are complementary to, and some in conflict with one another, and in different periods and different regions now one, and now another, has emerged as dominant. There is no reason to think that these shifts and interplays will not continue.

Islam's impact upon India—that is, upon the mainstream of Indian history—dates from about AD 1200; and from then on for five centuries until the decline of the Mughal Empire in the eighteenth century Muslim rulers dominated the north and centre of India. The Muslims

* Originally published in *South Asian Review,* 6(I): 21–32.

of South Asia have never forgotten this, and it would be a mistake to underestimate the strength and pervasiveness of this memory. There is a very general feeling, both in Pakistan and in India, that for centuries 'we Muslims' ruled the whole country; bearers of the true faith prevailing by sheer superior dynamism; and if the poor illiterate Muslim villager feels it as strongly as the actual descendant of the old Muslim ruling élite, this should cause no surprise, at any rate to readers in Britain, where a very similar feeling prevails about Britain's imperial past.

The decline of this Muslim ascendancy becomes clearly evident from the end of the seventeenth century, and from the eighteenth century onwards there has been serious thinking among the Muslims about the causes of the decline and the measures needed to restore their fallen fortunes. There have been several phases and several trends, and since all of them still have their influence today it is appropriate to summarize them here.

1. Up to 1857, the year of what the British have generally called the Mutiny and Indians and Pakistanis now call the First War of Independence—but which was in fact something more than the one and something less than the other—prevailing Muslim feeling was quite straightforward. It regarded the British as the usurpers of Muslim power; and it aimed to break that power and restore Muslim ascendancy.

2. From 1857—alongside this uncompromising trend, which continued bloody but unbowed—there emerged a new one, led by Sir Sayyid Aḥmad Khan. His essential aims were to restore Muslim ascendancy in the only way and to the only degree now practicable, by complete identification of the Muslims with the British. This was to be achieved first by dissociation from all political activities not approved by the British; secondly by education to implant the values of Victorian Britain in the educated, articulate sections of the Muslim community; and thirdly by a reinterpretation of Islam along modern lines with the same end in view. This trend has continued in one form or another—indeed, as the *dominant* trend, taking the period as a whole—right up to our time.

3. With the rise of Indian nationalism, the old anti-British trend

began again to make headway, to the extent, in the period from about 1910 to 1922, where it became strong enough to prevail over the modernist, pro-British trend. The ultimate aim, perhaps, was in alliance with the non-Muslim majority of the population to break the British power and so in a free India create the conditions in which the inherent superiority of Islam could not fail to raise its adherents to positions of influence out of proportion to their mere numerical strength. The break-up of Hindu–Muslim unity in the early 1920s resulted in some years of confusion, but from the late 1930s, as the prospect of independence won by a predominantly Hindu nationalist movement drew closer, conviction grew that Muslim fortunes could be restored only if they could win a separate, independent new state, based upon the Muslim majority areas in the north-west and north-east of the subcontinent—in short, in the areas that in 1947 became Pakistan.

What is common to all these trends is the sense of the separateness of the Muslims. No movement which did not appeal to them *as Muslims* ever gained significant Muslim support. And to this extent Jinnah's concept of a separate Indian Muslim 'nation' had several centuries of history on its side. The words 'to this extent' are important, however. Acceptance of the concept of a 'Muslim nation', even if one now limits its application to the surviving western half of Pakistan, can be seriously misleading, unless in this context one defines 'nation' in a quite unique way—which there seems little point in doing. On the other hand it is not much more helpful here to define the Muslims as a religious community. Jinnah was right in insisting on the inadequacy of such a description. For 'Muslim' in this context includes everyone who calls himself a Muslim, including those who are indifferent to religion, and the community of Muslims so defined has been for generations a social and political entity, with a consciousness dominated by political aims, and led by men whose goal was the preservation and enhancement of the community's political, social and cultural power. It is not relevant to my purpose here either to vindicate or to condemn the policies which were pursued to this end, but simply to note the historical fact that they culminated in the creation, with the consent of the Indian National Congress, of Pakistan.

The development which I have sketched in these paragraphs gives, I think, a valid picture of the Muslim sense of identity looked at on an all-India scale. But if it was not clear before, it has been made abundantly clear now by the break-up of Pakistan, that within this overall unity there were different, and often conflicting, trends. I shall outline a number sufficiently distinct from one another to call for separate treatment. The need to be concise will make some degree of over-simplification unavoidable, but so long as this is borne in mind I think a reasonably accurate picture will emerge.

What I may call the all-India outlook was always strongest in Delhi, the old Mughal capital, and, after the disintegration of the Mughal Empire, in the areas centred upon Lucknow and Hyderabad (Deccan), the capitals respectively of the state of Oudh and of the Nizam's dominions, both of which saw themselves as heirs to whatever could be preserved of the old imperial tradition. When S. Abid Husain, in his *The Destiny of Indian Muslims* remarks with satisfaction on the absence among the Muslims of any feelings of what he calls 'linguistic communalism' or 'linguistic separatism'[1] he is claiming for them more credit than they deserve, for this 'all-India' feeling derives mainly from the all-India imperial tradition, which takes it for granted that Delhi and UP provide the leadership for the country as a whole and ignores to a quite indefensible degree the legitimate aspirations of India's fairly numerous nationalities.

In the rest of this essay I shall be dealing mainly with the areas that became Pakistan. Let me therefore just remark at this point that in India (in the post-1947 sense) Muslim feeling has in general continued to be divided between the trends described above. In the former category come those of whom S. Abid Husain and Muhammad Mujeeb are the most effective spokesmen, men who remained true to their alliance with the Congress even after the general Muslim disillusionment of the mid-1920s. They have been joined now by others who, though originally supporters of Pakistan, found for one reason or another that they could best serve their own interests by staying in India, and so now speak and behave as though they had all along been Indian nationalists. And in the second and much more numerous category come many who, having experienced the disadvantages of living in India and *not* having experienced the disadvantages of living in Pakistan, still have some of the rosy illusions about Pakistan which prevailed more widely when it was still only an ideal and not yet a reality. It is only fair to add that between them stand the educated, secular, radical-to-left Muslims who, unlike the veteran Muslim supporters of the Congress, have forsaken Islam as a religion and are Muslims only in the cultural sense of the term. But these would (in private at any rate) make no bones about admitting that their political influence is extremely limited.

In the Muslim areas of the subcontinent which now lie outside the boundaries of India the old 'all-India' feeling which I have described jostles with other sentiments to which it often takes second place. It has always been in Bengal, the area of the largest single concentration of Muslims, that Muslim feeling has been most clearly distinguishable from that of other Muslim communities elsewhere. In Bengal, from the very earliest days of continuous Muslim impact on the sub-continent, there developed a close interpenetration of Islamic sentiment with what one may call Bengali proto-nationalism, and it has followed that while in the north and the north-west Indian Muslim sentiment has always been markedly aristocratic in the values it reflects, in Bengal it has for centuries been no less markedly plebeian. I can do no more here than indicate very briefly some of the factors that brought this situation about, but reference even to such summary accounts as those of M. Mujeeb[2] and Aziz Ahmad[3] will make abundantly clear the specifically Bengali element in Muslim consciousness in the north-east. There are good historical reasons for this. The Muslim conquerors of Bengal were not exceptional in seeking the maximum *de facto* independence from central control, but geographical remoteness enabled them to realize this aim more often and more easily than most others could. The same remoteness deprived them of the opportunity to draw constantly in the way their counterparts in the north and north-west did on the reservoirs of manpower existing in Iran and Central Asia, and impelled them to strengthen their position by an appeal to local feeling; and in this they were helped by the juncture of circumstances which prevailed when they arrived on the scene. A popular dynasty of Buddhist kings had comparatively recently been overthrown by an orthodox Hindu one, hostile to the plebeian values and culture to which Buddhism had been sympathetic and correspondingly unpopular with the people of Bengal. Islam with its egalitarian doctrines made a ready appeal, and the new Muslim rulers took full advantage of this, for instance by coming forward as the patrons of Bengali literature where their Hindu predecessors had patronized only the aristocratic Sanskrit.

In the days when Mughal power was at its height this close identification of the Muslim aristocracy in Bengal with Bengali national feeling ceased. The Bengal-based Muslim nobles were, in the main, exponents of the same Persian (and, later, Urdu) culture as their counterparts in the north and north-west; and with such of them as survived the heavy losses which British rule inflicted upon their class as a whole in Bengal this has perhaps continued to be the case to the present day. (For example, this is the situation in the Suhrawardy family.)

But from the days of the Permanent Settlement the power of Muslim aristocracy in Bengal declined rapidly, and the over-whelmingly plebeian character of Muslim Bengal again asserted itself, though in a new historical context. A new feature that now—from about 1800—appeared and grew ever more marked was the estrangement of the Muslim from the Hindu Bengali. The articulate leaders of the so-called Bengali Renaissance were all Hindu, and well into the latter half of the nineteenth century they took the general view that the British had liberated them from the Muslim yoke. (Whether or not this view was a correct one is a question irrelevant to the present discussion, but clearly it was one which Muslims were unlikely to share.) Furthermore, the Hindus took to British ways far more readily than the Muslims did, and a time came when, under the British, an overwhelmingly Hindu upper stratum directed the economic, social, political and administrative life of a more-than-half Muslim people. All of this maintained Muslim separatism, but made it necessary for would-be leaders to reflect plebeian aspirations too in their political stand. It is significant that Fazlul Huq, the most influential Muslim leader of Bengal in the late 1930s and early 1940s, and winner in the 1937 elections of much the largest section of the Muslim vote, called his party the Krishak Praja Party—Peasant People's Party—a name which makes no overt reference to Islam. The Bengali Muslim intelligentsia too found themselves in an ambivalent position.

They had long clung to Persian, and then to Urdu, as their literary language (though making no very remarkable contribution to either), and when they did turn to Bengali, modern Bengali literature had been not only created but developed to a very high level by their Hindu compatriots. Understandably, it was in practice quite impossible to reject this enormous contribution to Bengali literature and strike out on a new and different path, and even the most firm Bengali supporters of a united Pakistan ideology have had to accept this as a fact. Thus a writer in the semi-official book *The Cultural Heritage of Pakistan*[4] says of the successive periods covering the years from the First World War to the present day that 'the Muslim contribution is immeasurably small in comparison' (with that of the Hindus); 'not even five per cent of the whole'; 'a hopelessly minority group'.[4] (He stresses in contrast that 'strange and paradoxical as it may seem, the illiterate Muslim peasants of Bengal have an overwhelming superiority in the field of ballads'.[5])

This is the background to the virtual annihilation of the Muslim League in the East Bengal (then East Pakistan, and now Bangladesh) elections of March 1954, less than seven years after the creation of Pakistan; and it is clear now, even if it was not already clear at the time, that there was thenceforth no likelihood of a united Pakistan surviving any longer than its unity could be sustained by the decisive bringing to bear of the superior force of West Pakistan.

In the north-west—the area that became West Pakistan—the differences between the 'all-India' outlook and local sentiments were less marked. The Frontier, Sind and Baluchistan all exhibited nationalist strivings, but the long near-fusion of Islamic and proto-nationalist feeling which characterized Bengal was never in evidence in the north-west. One clear indication of this is that none of the regional languages here ever developed the status that Bengali did. Bengali has long been *the* language of its region, the language not only of everyday speech, but also of a substantial modern, sophisticated literature and of journalism, with a range of themes approaching comparability with that of the more developed modern languages of other countries. Pushtu, Sindhi and Baluchi, on the other hand, despite the efforts of academies to develop them, have remained by and large the languages of the home and of folk or near-folk literature. In these regions the language of sophisticated literature and of journalism is Urdu.

In the Punjab the situation is much the same, with the difference that the position of Punjabi relative to Urdu is even weaker. Three main reasons for this, interrelated but worth stating separately, suggest themselves. The first is the early emergence of the Sikhs as the main spokesmen of Punjabi national feeling, a role which has been intensified with the passage of time, and naturally lowered the temperature of Punjabi fervour in Punjabi Muslims and Punjabi Hindus. The second is the remarkable phenomenon—still not adequately examined, so far as I know—of the almost universal adoption of Urdu from the mid-nineteenth century up to 1947 as the language of almost every field of social life outside the home, by Muslims, Hindus and Sikhs alike. (Two of the most famous contemporary Urdu short story writers are Krishan Chander, a Punjabi Hindu, and Rajindar Singh Bedi, a Sikh.) And the third reason is the enormously greater strength, in population, prosperity, economic development and mobility of inhabitants, of the Punjab than of the other predominantly Muslim nationalities of the Frontier, Baluchistan and Sind; a strength which has given rise to Punjabi ambitions to dominate the whole region, and to a corresponding indifference to national feeling, including Punjabi national feeling.

All the differences which I have outlined were well in evidence long before the subcontinent reached the final stage, from about 1937 onwards, of its advance to independence. Looking at the development of Muslim politics in this period one cannot help seeing that Muslim leadership had two major tasks to accomplish. First it had to effect a stable marriage of convenience between an all-Indian leadership with negligible support in the Muslim majority regions and leaderships strong in regional support but with negligible all-Indian influence. And secondly it had to create on an all-India scale the mass sanctions which alone could compel acceptance of its demands.

The processes by which the first aim was achieved cannot even be summarized in an essay of this length.[6] Nor perhaps would there have been much point in attempting a summary even had it been possible; for the one area—East Bengal—where regional sentiment was so strong as to be a major factor in Pakistan politics has irrevocably departed from Pakistan, and similar strivings in the residual Pakistan are not likely to develop such strength as would make it impossible for them to be contained. And the realization of the second aim, of building mass sanctions to back the demands of the all-India Muslim leadership, is in any case more deserving of study, for its legacy to West Pakistan has been one of the most intractable of its problems.

The sophisticated Muslim case underlying the separatist demands that ultimately became the demand for Pakistan rested on the secular or quasi-secular concept of the Muslims of the subcontinent as a separate nationality; in the years preceding independence it was this concept that was always stressed by the authoritative spokesmen of the movement for the creation of Pakistan. To such a concept religious orthodoxy was irrelevant. 'Muslim' meant anyone who called himself a Muslim, anyone who was born into the Muslim community, even if he were a militant atheist. Jinnah himself, the *Qāid e Azam* (Great Leader) of the Muslim League, was anything but an orthodox Muslim of the old-fashioned kind. For him, the concept of a Muslim *nationhood* implied even an onslaught on the conservative Muslim divines, and an effort, as he wrote in 1942, 'to free our people from the most undesirable reactionary elements'. But such sophisticated concepts could not arouse the mass Muslim enthusiasm which the leadership needed if acceptance of its demands were to be enforced. With the illiterate and half-literate Muslim masses, what carried weight was precisely the ideas of 'the most undesirable reactionary elements'— the prejudices which told them: 'One Muslim is worth ten Hindus. We Muslims ruled over these people for centuries. We are a fine, manly people: the Hindus are slaves and cowards. Our type is the warrior, bold and generous: theirs is the *baniya*, the cowardly, extortionate, hypocritical moneylender. Islam is a fine faith, the acme of all religious development: Hinduism is an inhuman and revolting system which sanctifies human degradation.' And so on and so forth. An appeal to the Muslim masses to come into the political arena could, in the late 1930s and 1940s, hardly have had any other result than to fan this sort of Muslim chauvinism. The response to Jinnah's call in December 1939, to celebrate a 'Day of Deliverance' when the Congress ministries resigned, already showed this; still more horrifying was the response to his Direct Action Day of 16 August 1946.

It hardly needs to be said that if appeal to sentiments of this kind helped to mobilize the mass support without which Pakistan could not have been won, it also strengthened the religious (or pseudo-religious) fanaticism which Jinnah had opposed.

Once Pakistan had come into being, this force, which the new country's rulers had themselves done so much to foster, confronted them with a challenge. It has done so ever since. Committed to making their Pakistan an Islamic state, they have not been able to show the average Pakistani that their politics are distinctively and recognizably Islamic in any way. Their obscurantist opponents, of whom Maududi has been the most coherent spokesman, have laboured under no such disadvantage. Maududi's declared aims have been fairly summed up by Wilber and his collaborators in their book *Pakistan*: 'He holds that in Islam all rights of legislation and all power to give commands rest not in humans, individually or collectively, but in Allah alone. Society is to be regulated and the government administered by the Quran and Sunna [conventions established by reference to the traditions of the Prophet] with only devout Muslims in the administrative posts of the state. The head of state would be an amir ('leader') who would be Allah's vice-regent on earth . . . the amir . . . would be a sort of philosopher-king.'[7] Such views may be horrifying to the modern man (including the modern educated Muslims of Pakistan, who rule over the vast uneducated majority of the population), but few would deny that they are based on clearly recognizable Islamic premises.

In the face of this powerful, widespread feeling, the moderns—and in Pakistani terms this embraces the spokesmen of a wide spectrum of views, ranging from those of Queen Victoria to those of Mao Ze Dong!—have generally felt themselves acutely embarrassed. The plain fact is that their policies, unlike those of Maududi and his followers, are not derived from Islamic premises at all; and that being so, it is no wonder that they have not been able to present them as if they were. Those who have held power have doubtless been sincere in regarding themselves as Muslims and in their assumption that their policies do not conflict with the principles of Islam as they understand it. But neither they nor their ideologists have the kind of proficiency in Islamic learning which would have enabled them to meet their more obviously Islamic obscurantist opponents on their own ground, arguing their case from Islamic premisses and, from these same Islamic premisses, demolishing the arguments of the Maududis. To which it must be added that politicians, being politicians, have always felt that, faced with so powerful a sentiment, discretion was the better part of valour, and that they must seek to minimize the differences between the two positions. Their more radical Marxist-influenced opponents have, for the same reasons, in general displayed the same moral cowardice; and the welcome large-scale rejection of the Maududi-type candidates in the elections of December 1970 (a rejection which will not necessarily be continued indefinitely), speaks much more for the common sense of the average elector than it does for the courage of the moderns of all parties. It may be remarked in passing that this cowardice in the face of obscurantism is not the only thing the radicals have in common with their fellow moderns. For a century now all sections of the modern sophisticated élite have continued the traditions of their medieval forebears (in regarding it as the whole duty of the unsophisticated masses to do as the élite tells them) and the traditions of Sir Sayyid Ahmad Khan (of looking for essential support—even if, in some cases, only moral support—to more powerful forces based outside their own country, be it the British or the Americans, the Russians or the Chinese).

This brings me to the last strand of Muslim identity which I want to consider. Ex-President Ayub Khan once (in 1959) wrote of the urgent need to find a concept which would 'weld the people into unity'—'an answer which is comprehensive, tangible, arouses spontaneous and consistent enthusiasm, and is workable in the light of the requirements of modern life'—and added that he had 'not been able to find an effective answer so far'. Since such an answer is not to be found either in conventional Islam or in Sandhurst, his helplessness was perhaps not surprising. But it seems to me that Islam in the subcontinent possesses a still living tradition which is at once authentically and recognizably Islamic, intelligible to the mass of the people and a more than adequate sanction for policies 'workable in the light of the requirements of modern life'. This is the tradition of sufism, of Muslim mysticism, which finds such powerful expression in the poetry both of Urdu and of the regional languages such as Punjabi and Sindhi, and which is as familiar to the illiterate peasants as it is to the sophisticated Urdu-speaking literati. It proclaims values which are no less authentically Islamic than those proclaimed by Maududi and his supporters, but which have little else in common with them. Among these values are a cordial, and bluntly declared, hatred and contempt for religious bigotry, and a passionate dedication to humanist ideals which inculcates, among other things, a proper respect for the rights of *all* men, whether they be Muslim or not. Values like these are expressed very forcefully and with an extreme of exaggeration quite acceptable to the conventions of Islamic poetry. They express implacable hostility to Muslim chauvinism, love and respect for every man, whether Muslim or non-Muslim, who loves his God (whether he knows him as Allah, or as Ram, or as Jesus) and serves his fellow men, and one which sanctions and approves every measure, whether it bears the explicit Islamic stamp or not, which tends to the welfare and the dignity of man. I have written more or less extensively on this Muslim mystic theme elsewhere, and it is one that makes a strong appeal to me; but I do not think that this leads me to exaggerate its potential importance in the social and political setting of which I am speaking. Poetry is important to the South Asian Muslim. He has not yet acquired (and one hopes he never will acquire) that 'successfully cultivated distaste for poetry' which the late Edward Thompson noted in the English.[8] And while he himself often feels that poetry is poetry and life is life, he is also heir to a still living tradition which reveres the exceptional man who practises in daily life the values which the poetry proclaims. At all events this strand too is an important one in Muslim consciousness, and no account which fails to speak of it can be regarded as complete.

It has not been my purpose in this essay to make any prophecies, and I do not intend to conclude with one. But one may perhaps point to this last-named strand in Muslim consciousness as one which could provide even the most modern and progressive of Pakistani politicians with the authentically Islamic sanction for their policies which they seem to feel that they need. I had better add that I do not mean that modern politicians have to pose as Muslim mystics, only that there is, to say the least of it, nothing either foolish or unprincipled in appealing to those traditions in the religion and culture of their people which they believe to be valid and which they can harness to the support of modern, progressive policies. None of them has tried to do this; nor is there much sign that anyone intends to try. But if there *is* a hope for the development of Pakistani politics and Pakistani society along modern, progressive lines, it surely lies partly in the reviving of this old tradition, in bringing it more fully to bear in political and social life, and in making it the basis for future advance.

NOTES AND REFERENCES

1. London: Asia Publishing House, 1965, pp. 2–6.
2. *The Indian Muslims* (London: Allen and Unwin, 1967), pp. 316–20.
3. *An Intellectual History of Islam in India* (Edinburgh: Edinburgh University Press, 1969), pp. 112–16.
4. S.M. Ikram and Percival Spear, eds. *The Cultural Heritage of Pakistan* (London: Oxford University Press, 1955), p. 144.
5. Ibid., p. 145.
6. Ram Gopal's *Indian Muslims* (London: Asia Publishing House, 1959), ch. XXXI gives a useful account of them.
7. Wilber et al, *Pakistan* (Connecticut: HRAF Press, 1964), p. 206.
8. *A History of India* (London: Benn, 1927), pp. 32–33.

⚜14⚜

THE CONCEPT OF ISLAM IN
URDU POETRY

I n 1980, the beginning of the fifteenth century *hijri* (of
the Muslim calendar) was being celebrated. In this connection
the University of London's School of Oriental and African Studies
(SOAS) arranged a series of lectures, and I was asked to give one
lecture in the series. I accepted the invitation, and entitled my lecture
'The Concept of Islam in Urdu Poetry'. A report of this lecture, with
a photograph of me, was printed in an Urdu newspaper[1] under these
headlines:

> Ralph Russell's lecture in London University
> The Concept of Islam in Urdu Poetry
> is different from the beliefs of those who interpret
> 'religion' according to the letter.

The report included these sentences:

Mr. Ralph Russell . . . is acknowledged to be Britain's *Baba e Urdu* [roughly
'Grand Old Man of Urdu'].
  Urdu poetry bears the very deep imprint of the belief 'Drink wine, and
burn the Holy Quran, but do good to your fellow man'.

One gentleman took strong objection to my lecture. Here is his
letter, and my reply to the letter, which was printed in three instalments.

---

* Translated by Russell from a series of letters originally written in Urdu.

He wrote:

In the issue of your newspaper of 25th November I have seen a report of a lecture by Britain's *Baba e Urdu* Professor Ralph Russell. This report is unsatisfactory in that general readers like the present writer have been denied those verses of Mir, Ghālib and Iqbal with the aid of which Ralph Russell revealed to your reporter that the verse of these three great poets shows the very deep imprint of the 'belief' (theory?), 'Drink wine, and burn the Holy Quran—but do good to your fellow man'. In addition it has not been made clear whose belief (theory?) this is, and where it has been expounded. If Ghālib or Iqbal have anywhere spoken of burning the Holy Quran, it would have been better if the reference had been given. After reading the whole report it is also not clear what new concept of Islam Urdu poetry has put forward which is different from the 'generally current' beliefs and theories of Islam. Suppose there is some new concept of this kind in Urdu poetry, should one call it a concept of 'Islam'? In the present writer's opinion it is impossible to conceive of any concept of Islam which is at variance with Islamic beliefs. If Mr Russell, or, through Mr Russell's agency, your reporter, has discovered some new concept in Urdu poetry then he should be good enough not on any account to call it a 'concept of Islam'. I confess my ignorance, but I was extremely distressed to see published in so great a newspaper a headline to the report which is wrong not only in its content but also in its wording. The headline tells us that the concept of Islam in Urdu poetry differs from the beliefs of 'people who interpret religion according to the letter'.

First what does 'religion according to the letter' mean? And secondly, how is this being 'interpreted'? . . . If you are good enough to publish these lines in your paper perhaps Professor Russell in his role of *Baba e Urdu* will feel the need to turn his attention to extending the knowledge of your humble servant. At all events your reporter has conferred great lustre upon him.

Yours etc.

Abul Arshan, London, N.I.[2]

FIRST INSTALMENT OF THE REPLY

Some days ago you published a report of my lecture in the School of Oriental and African Studies on the concept of Islam in Urdu poetry. Abul Arshan Sahib has written a letter raising objections to it. I am very pleased that he has expressed his views, and will gladly reply to those objections where I do not agree with them—from which you will gather that I myself consider some of his objections to be sound.

The trouble is that to give a full reply I need both the leisure to write it and space of not less than half a page in *Jang*, and at present I cannot afford the time, and *Jang* cannot give so much space. So I shall have to reply in instalments. Here is the first instalment.

I agree with Abul Arshan Sahib that to deny your readers the verses I quoted was unfair both to them and to me. The couplet of which your report gave a free Urdu translation is in fact by a Persian poet. The verse is:

Drink wine, and burn the Quran, and throw fire into the Kaba
Dwell in the house of idols—and do not harm your fellow men.

The verse calls for some explanation, and in my lecture I gave that explanation. In brief, there is a lot of poetic hyperbole in this verse. It certainly does not mean that the poet really wants you to do these reprehensible things. I first met the verse in Mirza Rusva's famous novel *Umrao Jan Ada*, where he says that it is by Hafiz. I suspected that it was probably *not* by Hafiz; I looked for it in his *divan* [collected verse] and could not find it. However, the verse does not contradict in the least degree the famous verse which *is* by Hafiz:

Do not distress your fellow men, and do what else you will
For in my Holy Law there is no other sin than this.

I have still not been able to discover who wrote the first verse. (A Pakistani friend tells me it is Khaqani's.) But people in Iran are well acquainted with it. I asked my Iranian colleague [at SOAS] whose verse it was, and had got no further than 'Drink wine . . . ' when he at once completed the rest. But he too did not know whose verse it was.

This is enough for a first instalment. In further instalments—if *Jang* can give me the opportunity—I will (1) explain what in my opinion is the real concept which lies behind this verse, (2) give a few examples of the countless Urdu verses which express approximately the same thought, (3) explain why I like this concept and (4) explain why I am not prepared to accept anyone as a Muslim in the true sense of the word who does not accept this concept. If *Jang* cannot afford the space for all this, and if Abul Arshan Sahib would like to meet me and hear what I have to say, I shall be glad to meet him. I am ready to reply to all of his objections, whether in private or publicly.

Two more points. (1) 'Those who interpret religion according to the letter.' These were not my words. Probably they were the reporter's translation of 'fundamentalists'. (2) The title of *Bāba e Urdu*, obviously, is not one that I invented myself. Probably it was the unwarranted high opinion of me which the editor of *Jang* holds that impelled him to confer this title upon me. Generally before conferring a title upon anyone you ask him whether he is ready to accept it, but I was not granted this opportunity: otherwise I would certainly have refused it. Granted that I serve the cause of Urdu, but I in no way deserve to be called *Bāba e Urdu*. Anyway, it's a free country, as the English say, and if Asif Jilani Sahib [editor of *Jang*] wants to give me this title, who can stop him? And at any rate it has afforded people an occasion for laughter and cracking jokes.[3]

Second Instalment of the Reply

In my last letter I quoted two Persian verses. Literally translated, they say:

1) Khaqani's(?) : Drink wine, burn the Quran, and throw fire into the Kaba. Live in the idol-temple, and do not distress [your fellow] men.

2) Hafiz's : Do not attempt to cause distress to [your fellow] men, and do what [else] you like. Because in our Holy Law (Shariat) there is no other sin than this [i.e. than the sin of distressing your fellow men].

There is a lot of hyperbole in both these verses, and especially in the first one. They mean that the worst sin is to cause distress to others. The poet is aware that very few people realize what a grave sin causing distress to others is. He knows that if you tell a Muslim to burn the Quran he will be deeply shocked; and yet that same Muslim will very readily cause distress to his fellow men and think that if he has committed a sin, well, it is only a very ordinary one. The poet tells him that it is not an ordinary sin but a very grave one, and in order to impress this upon him thoroughly he uses hyperbole and tells him that, compared to this, burning the Quran, drinking wine and so on are sins of no importance. Obviously the poet does not want you really to do those things; he uses hyperbole solely in order to impress a very important point upon you. He means to tell you that every

Muslim must refrain from drinking wine, revere the Quran, and if possible perform the Pilgrimage. But if along with all these things he distresses his fellow men then all these virtuous deeds cannot atone for the single sin of causing distress to his fellow men. His vices will weigh more heavily on the scale than his virtues. On the other hand, if he drinks wine and disobeys the other commandments of Islam but at the same time always behaves well towards his fellow men, then notwithstanding all his sins his virtue will weigh more heavily in the scale than his vices.

This concept and others closely related to it are extremely common in the Urdu ghazal too. In the next instalment I shall quote some verses by way of example.[4]

THIRD INSTALMENT OF THE REPLY

In my last letter I quoted and commented on a famous couplet of Hafiz. There are two linked couplets of Mir Taqi Mir which are clearly inspired by this couplet of Hafiz. One of them reads:

Stand knocking at the door of the mosque
Or go and sit in the tavern
Do whatever you like my friend
But don't attempt to harm others.

Consider too these couplets of Mir:

I am a Muslim. I love these idols. There is no god but God.

Come Shaikh ji, pawn your prayer mat for a cup of wine
Spend all your stock of piety on wine.

Today Mir again led the prayers in the Great Mosque—
—that Mir who yesterday was washing the wine-stains from his prayer mat.

Does anyone practise submission [to the laws of Islam] when the clouds sway mightily in the sky?
Ascetic, now is the time, if you can, to sin.

Why do you ask now what Mir's religion is? He has
Put on the caste-mark, sat himself down in the temple, and long ago abandoned Islam.

Linked to this concept is another very important one—that if, for example, you say your prayers and perform the Pilgrimage, these actions in themselves have absolutely no importance. They matter only if you love God, and this love obliges you to worship God by these means. If saying your prayers means no more than repeating Arabic words you have learnt by rote and performing certain movements of your body, or if you say your prayers to show that you are a much better Muslim than others, then your prayers are not only useless but harmful, and have nothing whatsoever to do with true Islam. This is the idea behind these verses of Mir:

He went to Mecca, and to Medina and to Karbala
—and came back just the same as he had gone.

Don't be deceived by the shaikh ji's prayers
He is just setting down a burden he's been carrying on his head.

Let me again stress at this point that the poet certainly does not mean that you should really not say your prayers or not really go on the Pilgrimage. He means that only those prayers are prayers in the true sense of the word in which the worshipper is engrossed heart and soul in the worship of God.

In this letter I have quoted verses only from Mir, but lovers of literature know that verses like these will be found in abundance in the work of every good poet.

If you are a Muslim then clearly you are obliged to do all the things which, in the Islamic term, are *farz* for [binding upon] every Muslim. You should say the five daily prayers, keep the fast every day in the month of Ramzan, and so on. But the value of your prayers and your fasting depends upon the emotion you feel when you do these things. There is prayer in which you are in all sincerity engrossed in the worship of God; and there is prayer which you perform merely in order to show off to others. I am not a Muslim, but I think every Muslim who is not just a Muslim in name but a Muslim in the true sense of the word, will agree with me when I say that this second kind of prayer is of absolutely no value. Indeed, the 'Muslim' who prays with this feeling [of superiority to others] is, in a way, insulting God, because his outward observance of the rules of Islam conceals a feeling which can in no way be regarded as justified by Islam. And now the question arises of how can one tell the difference between the true worshipper and the false. When you see someone praying, how can you know what is in his heart? Only the worshipper himself and God can know this. You cannot.

In my opinion there is only one reliable way of recognizing a true Muslim, and that is to see all the time how he behaves towards his fellow men. In Islamic terminology there are several kinds of rights (*huqūq*). Two of these are the rights of God (i.e. what is due to God)—(*huqūq ullāh*)—and the rights of God's servants (i.e. humankind)—(*huqūq ul ibād*). God's rights include prayer, fasting, pilgrimage and so on. But you are giving God his due only if love of God and worship of God alone occupy your mind and no other feeling has a place in it. And only you and God know what is in your mind. No one else can know.

On the other hand the case with the rights of God's servants (i.e. humankind) is this. A little experience can tell you at once who is giving people their due and who is not, and since it is just as binding on every Muslim to give what is due to God's servants as it is to deliver what is due to God, it follows that the mark of a true Muslim is that he performs what is due to his fellow men—and this includes everyone—Muslims, Christians, Jews, Hindus, Sikhs and atheists—that is, that he treats others exactly as he expects them to treat him. Only about such a Muslim can you make a reliable estimate that he also performs what is due to God. In fact I have been told that it is orthodox Islamic doctrine that God will forgive shortcomings in giving Him His due, but will not forgive shortcomings in giving His servants their due until they whose rights have been violated grant *their* forgiveness.

And that is why in my opinion the concept of Islam which one finds so forcefully expressed in Urdu poetry is an absolutely correct one; and I strongly approve of this concept because it is one which every good human being can and should accept, whether he professes the religion of Islam or any other, or indeed even if he is an atheist.

Finally I express my thanks both to Abul Arshan Sahib and to *Jang* for raising these very important questions and giving me the opportunity to express some of my thoughts about them.[5]

REFERENCES

1. *Jang* (London), 25 November 1980.
2. *Jang* (London), 15 December, 1980.
3. *Jang* (London), 24 December, 1980.
4. *Jang* (London), 10 January 1981.
5. *Jang* (London), 12 January 1981.

≈15≈

SALMAN RUSHDIE, ISLAM AND MULTICULTURALISM

Someone said recently that since the Salman Rushdie affair multiculturalism is dead. It isn't, of course, and never will be. But there is no denying that the publication of *Satanic Verses* and its aftermath poses, very bluntly, some very difficult questions for those of us who want to maintain and extend the ground on which people of different cultures can encounter one another and learn from one another on terms of mutual respect. I want to discuss some of these questions here, concentrating on those which have barely been touched upon since the uproar began, and proceeding from the anti-Rushdie agitation to a discussion of the Islamic viewpoints involved, and thence to the bearing of all this upon multiculturalism.

I should first say something about my own reactions to Salman Rushdie's writing. *Midnight's Children* made little or no appeal to me and I gave up after reading about a hundred pages. I have not read his subsequent books and feel no desire to do so. This is not because I do not respect him. On the contrary, some of his comments on public affairs (notably his critique of the 'British heritage' myths assiduously cultivated at the time of the Falklands war) have been perceptive, hard-hitting and true; and the theme of his second novel *Shame* with its exposure of the repulsiveness of regimes like that of the late Zia ul

* Originally published in instalments in the English section of the London Urdu daily *Jang*, 12–16 August 1989 and subsequently in *Yad-nāma, In Memoria di Alessandro Bausani*, vol. 1, Rome, 1991, pp. 429–36.

Haq is one that I think admirable. It is, if you like, a matter of personal literary taste that his fiction does not appeal to me. The merging of fantasy with realism and of realism with fantasy which characterizes his work is something I find profoundly unsatisfying, the more so because I feel that straightforward realism would be a much more effective way of combating the evils he seeks to combat. However, he and his publishers and his readers clearly do not share my taste in this; and of course, they have a perfect right to proceed accordingly. About *Satanic Verses* other questions need to be raised. Is it desirable to write things which will be deeply offensive to millions of people? And is it permissible to do so? My answer to the first question is: perhaps not. And my answer to the second question is: yes; desirable or not, it is most certainly permissible. No one, and no group of people, however large, has any right to demand that no one be permitted to write things that are deeply offensive to them. They may express their anger and outrage at such writing, and organize others to do so, as vigorously as they like; they have no right to it banned. And the archaic blasphemy laws, far from having their scope extended, should be abolished.

So much by way of prelude. I want now to look at the character of the movement of protest. All those who participate in it are united in their abhorrence of the book (which, it is safe to say, most of them have, like myself, never read), and all declare that they are motivated solely by devotion to Islam and to the Prophet.

Let us assume that this is so. I know very well that, as in every movement of this kind, there will be those for whom it is not so. But, as Muslims would say, only God knows which of them are sincere and which are not. There is no denying that, for example, Khomeini's death sentence on Rushdie strengthened his position both in the internal politics of Iran and in the Muslim world at large, but nobody knows for certain to what extent, if any, this formed a part of his motive. Similarly there is no denying that my friend Maqsood Elahi Sheikh, the editor of the Urdu weekly *Ravi* to which I am a regular subscriber and occasional contributor, in sustaining a campaign against Rushdie has enhanced the influence of his paper. But again, nobody knows for certain how far this consideration has motivated him. And anyway it is not necessary to impute unworthy motives; so let us examine the protesters' stand on the assumption that it is entirely sincere.

The demands of the participants in the protest movement are not all the same. Most would call for the banning of *Satanic Verses;* fewer would approve of Khomeini's sentence of death on its author. But all would claim that their stand is consistent with the teachings of Islam, and this claim has hitherto been accepted by their supporters and by most of their opponents alike. I propose to challenge that claim. Muslims turn for guidance first to the Quran and then to the *hadīth*—the duly authenticated accounts of the words and deeds of Muhammad in various situations which indicate to true believers how they should feel and act in similar circumstances. In my view, nothing in either justifies the protesters' stand.

The common arguments advanced against Rushdie are two. First, that he is an apostate—one who has rejected the religion which once he accepted—and that the punishment for apostasy is death. And secondly, that whether he is an apostate or not, the punishment to be meted out to anyone, whoever he may be, who insults the Prophet, is death. The first proposition is commonly accepted by Muslims and non-Muslims alike. The second is, to me at any rate, a less familiar one, but I have been assured that it is so by a close and valued Muslim friend of more than twenty years' standing. With all due respect to all concerned I question these assertions. As far as I can discover there is nothing in the Quran or the *hadīth* which supports them. Quite the contrary. The much-quoted verse of the Quran (II, 256), 'Let there be no compulsion in religion' surely rules out any such punishment for apostasy. As for insults to the Prophet, Muhammad himself felt quite differently from his present-day devotees. (Not having read *Satanic Verses* I cannot say whether the charge that it insults Muhammad is a valid one. But for the sake of argument, let us assume that it is). The Prophet's own response to insult is clear from a *hadīth* that tells us how a party of Jews asked, and was granted, permission to visit him. On being admitted they greeted him not with *as salāmu 'alaykum*—peace be upon you —but with *as sāmu 'alaykum*—death be upon you. The Prophet's wife 'Āisha, who was present, angrily replied, 'And death be upon you too', whereupon Muhammad rebuked her, telling her that God is kind and loves kindness in all things. She, thinking perhaps that he had not registered that they had said *sāmu* (death) and not *salāmu* (peace), asked if he had heard what they said. He replied that he had. I may remark at this point that Islam exhorts its followers to create in themselves, as far as is humanly possible, the attributes of God. God's attributes are many but it is surely significant that those which have always been most stressed are His compassion and His mercy. Muslims all over the world begin their letters, and indeed any important task on which they embark, with the words, 'In the name of God, the Compassionate, the Merciful'. It would seem to follow that it is above all these qualities that they should try to implant in their own character. The anti-Rushdie campaigners can hardly claim that these qualities are much in evidence in their campaign.

In short, without suggesting that the campaigners are deliberately deceiving either themselves or anyone else, I deny that their stand is authentically an Islamic one. If Yusuf Islam (the former Cat Stevens) or anyone else tells us that it is, let him produce his authority. I do not believe that he can produce any which can stand against the message of the Quran and of the *ḥadīth* I have quoted.

I am aware that many Muslim readers will at this stage want to know what are my own credentials for taking this stand. Many of them in my experience declare as if it were a self-evident truth that only Muslims are qualified to make statements about Islamic doctrines, and many non-Muslims seem to think this too. The obvious unsoundness of this view should not need stating. If I quote a verse from the Quran and argue that certain logical consequences follow from it, the question of whether I am myself a Muslim or not is irrelevant. The consequences I state either do follow from it or they don't. If they do, accept them. If they don't, prove to me that they don't by rational argument that Muslims and non-Muslims alike accept as a proper means of arriving at the truth. Muslim resentment against non-Muslim polemics against their beliefs is understandable, because it was for centuries engaged in by bigoted, self-styled Christians who vigorously supported every imperialist act of aggression against Muslim peoples; and it cannot be denied that such motives, even if far less crudely expressed, are still in evidence. But I, although not a Muslim, condemn such attacks as wholeheartedly as Muslims do, and my own standpoint is a very different one—one which I think every sincere Muslim can respect whether he agrees with it or not.

I am not a Muslim, but I have spent long periods of my life living amongst Muslims in India and Pakistan and the greater part of my life studying Urdu, the vehicle of one of the greatest branches of their literature. In the course of it I developed a great love and regard for its poetry and for the major values—authentically Islamic values—which that poetry expresses. Those values derive from the tradition of Sufism—Islamic mysticism—a tradition almost as old as Islam itself. Sufism preaches the religion of love, of which love of God and love of His human creation are two facets of the same thing.

Sufism is an Islamic tradition with which the mainstream orthodox always have been, and still are, uncomfortable. (One Hesham El Essawy, reviewing *The Concise Encyclopaedia of Islam*[1] frankly says as much.) This despite the fact that it is not in the least incompatible with the basic doctrines of Islam—a fact which the theologian al-Ghazālī (AD1058–1111) demonstrated to the satisfaction of most Muslims centuries ago. Sufism merely stresses, and very strongly too, that the formal observances of Islam, like prayer and fasting, are worthless unless they are inspired by love of God, a love which necessarily involves love for God's creation, humankind—*all* humankind; not just the Muslim section of it—and not by a selfseeking desire for human approval. There is nothing unorthodox about this. A very forceful *ḥadīth* says the same thing. It says that on Judgement Day the first three men to be summoned to answer to God will be one who knows the Quran by heart, one who has been killed while waging holy war and one whose abundant wealth has been given in charity. God will question them and they will in every case declare that they did what they did in a spirit of sincere devotion to Islam. God will reject their claims, telling them that their real motive was to win men's praise. The *ḥadīth* ends: 'These are the three men who of all creatures shall first be sent to hell.'

Not only in Persian poetry, but in the poetry of all the major languages of South Asia in which Muslim life and culture is reflected—Urdu, Pushtu, Sindhi and Panjabi—this mystic, humanist concept of Islam is all-pervasive, and millions upon millions of people, literate and illiterate alike, are familiar with it and influenced by it. To which one must unfortunately add that the majority of them can be compared with the millions of their Christian counterparts who happily praise God because He has 'put down the mighty from their seats' and 'exalted the humble and meek' and equally happily live their lives supporting the mighty in their seats and despising the humble and meek. All the same, the concept of Islam which pervades Persian and South Asian poetry is one to which all progressive people, of any religion and (like myself) none can and should appeal, and on which they should seek to build. The fact that its strongly humanist, anti-establishment principles are expressed in religious form should be no obstacle to this. Dedication to the welfare of humankind and to the high ideals of conduct which this necessarily involves, can be something common to religious and irreligious people alike.

Once again there is mainstream Islamic doctrine too to be enlisted to the same end. Some years ago I made the point in a series of letters published in *Jang*.[2] On that occasion numbers of my Muslim acquaintances, some of them in quite influential positions in their community, congratulated me on these letters and declared their complete agreement with them. To which I must regretfully add that not one of them was willing to declare this publicly, in print.

The argument has another important implication. If Muslims are shocked and angered by non-Muslims' offences against the principles of Islam, should they not be doubly shocked by even greater offences committed by people who proclaim themselves to be Muslims? If a non-Muslim offends against these principles that may be reprehensible, but it is hardly surprising. If one who himself claims to be a Muslim does so one might legitimately expect true Muslims to react with a redoubled sense of outrage and anger. But that does not happen. It seems that it is enough for any Muslim potentate to declare loudly his devotion to Islam for his fellow Muslims to approve, or at least condone, any crime he may care to commit. So the Pakistan army could invade what was then East Pakistan and is now Bangladesh, killing, looting and raping, and Muslim opinion at large was unmoved. Idi Amin could commit his bloody atrocities and his fellow Muslim rulers of Libya and Saudi Arabia, far from condemning him, gave him support and protection. Iraqi Muslims use poison gas, and there is no Muslim protest. Turkish Muslims, Iraqi Muslims, and Iranian

Muslims all pursue a policy of virtual genocide against the Kurds and, again, the organs of Muslim opinion voice no disapproval. True Muslims should regard the perpetrators of these crimes as a disgrace to Islam. A brief but forceful *ḥadīth* tells us that the greatest *jihād* (holy war) is to speak the truth to the tyrant's face, and another says that there are three kinds of *jihād;* the first is action to prevent wrong-doing; the second (if you haven't the courage to undertake the first) is the public censure of wrong doing; and the third (if you haven't the courage to undertake the second) is to silently, in your heart, condemn wrong-doing. And the third is the weakest *jihād.* For Muslims living in Britain, rather than, say, Iran, the second kind of *jihād* should not require much courage. When substantial numbers of them can bring themselves to wage even this second kind of *jihād* their anger against relatively powerless and insignificant offenders against Islamic principles will perhaps command rather more sympathy than it currently receives.

To return to my main theme. I contend that unassailable Islamic arguments refute the stand of the anti-Rushdie campaigners. I think that many Muslims will agree with me, as they did when I wrote my letters to *Jang.* I also think that, as on that occasion, and equally regrettably, few if any of them will have the courage to say so publicly. The question again arises as to whether if they do not, I, a non-Muslim, am entitled to advance these arguments. I think that I am not only entitled to do so but that I have a duty to do so. Which brings me to the alleged death of multiculturalism.

Those who believe that Britain has now become, and will henceforth remain, a multicultural society, and who welcome the opportunity this brings for different communities to get to know one another's cultural traditions and to learn from one another, need to follow through the logic of their stand in a way which all too few of them yet do. None of us will get very far if our response to, for example, the anti-Rushdie campaigners is simply to say, 'Yes, we recognize that this is the expression of your culture, and we respect it.' If the interplay of cultures is to get us anywhere it must be one in which mutual respect and mutual criticism go hand in hand. You don't learn much unless you criticize and assess the worth of the things you are studying. Everyone has the right to criticize everyone, and if the primary need is a willingness to be constantly critical of one's own values and constantly re-assess them, that in no way implies that we may not apply the same critical approach to the cultures of others or that they may not do the same to ours. Further, we need to recognize that there is no such thing in any community as a single, uniform, unchanging, conflict-free set of values. True, there are some values in every culture which, in a given period, people of that culture almost universally accept. For example, nearly all South Asians (and not just Muslims) have a far more generous concept of hospitality, a far greater sense of responsibility for the care of the aged, and a far greater respect for patriarchal values than the white British have. I think that the white British should reject those of their own traditional values which make them less hospitable and less caring than the South Asians, accept that spirit of South Asian values in this area, declare that they are doing so, and acknowledge their debt to the South Asians for the model they have provided. On the other hand, I think that they should, equally avowedly, maintain their rejection of authoritarian patriarchal values. But if these are examples of values which a community may hold almost unanimously, it is no less true that all cultures of all communities are in a constant process of change and embrace conflicting values, different outlooks which contend all the time for general acceptance. Within Islamic communities the strongly humanist Sufi trend contends with the bigoted fundamentalist trend. Within the white British community the narrow-minded national chauvinism sometimes exalted as 'the Falklands spirit' is an authentically British cultural trait. But so also, thank God, is the detestation of flag-wagging jingoism. And people of all communities are fully entitled to express their opinion on these two tendencies. True multiculturalism not only permits them to do so: it demands that they should. A spurious 'respect' for what the most vociferous, in all communities, declare to be the one authentic expression of their distinctive values is positively harmful to all of us. What is needed is the open, vigorous interplay of diverse values, both within and between communities, and the emergence from this not only of a willing tolerance of diversity but also of values which were once those of a particular section of our multicultural society but have become the common values of us all.

Notes and References

1. *The Independent,* 3 May 1989.
2. 24 December 1980, 10 and 12 January 1981. See chapter 14, 'The Concept of Islam in Urdu Poetry', of this volume.

⊰16⊱

MAUDUDI AND ISLAMIC
OBSCURANTISM

No one who wants to study seriously what is going on in the Islamic world today can afford to neglect the writings and activities of Abul Ala Maududi and his supporters. Bolstered by Saudi approval and finance his message has been conveyed to the world through the activities of well-resourced organizations such as, in Britain, the Islamic Foundation.

His most widely circulated book is, in English, entitled *Towards Understanding Islam*. I have the nicely produced edition published by the Islamic Foundation in 1980, and we learn from it that it derives from a booklet in Urdu published in 1932, fifteen years before the creation of Pakistan, by which he had already made his name in his native India as a well-known propagandist for Islam. An English version first appeared in 1940, but additions and amendments made by Maududi himself from that time onwards made it desirable to produce a new revised translation, and a 1959 edition, approved by Maududi himself, was the result. The editor's introduction tells us that 'over a million copies of this book have appeared in different languages of the world including English, Arabic, Hindi, Persian, German, French, Italian, Turkish, Portuguese, Swahili, Indonesian, Japanese, Malayalam, Tamil, Pushto, Bengali, Gujrati and Sindhi'. The 1980 edition is a further revised one (and we are not told whether Maududi saw and approved it). It was produced with 'the encouragement and help' of Salem Azzam, Secretary-General, Islamic Council of

Europe and Dr Abdullah Nasif, Secretary-General, King Abdul Aziz University.

To say the least of it, its approach is unsophisticated, and only readers who are ready to accept unthinkingly that Islam is the one true and universally valid system of beliefs are likely to respond favourably to it. Not only non-Muslims, but Muslims too who think deeply about all that the teachings of Islam imply, will find little of value in it.

Thus the 'argument' of the book begins from a virtual assumption that the existence of God is obvious and that any sane person is bound to see that God exists and that He rules the universe. It is the argument with which most people have been familiar from their childhood, namely that you only have to observe the universe, the wonderful universe, and the motion of the stars and the sun and the moon to realize that it is quite obvious that they could not have come there on their own, and must have been created. I am happy to say that a very important Muslim thinker of the nineteenth century—Nazir Ahmad, in his novel *Ibn ul Vaqt*—saw the flaw in this argument. If you argue that something is so wonderful that it could not have come here without a creator then obviously the creator of that something was even more wonderful and it's even more obvious that he must have had a creator who was even more wonderful, and he, on the same logic, must have had a creator who was even more wonderful and so on, right the way back as far as you like to go. So if it's an argument for the existence of God that the universe is wonderful and works according to laws, then it's also an argument for the existence of God behind God behind God behind God. Nazir Ahmad believed in God but rightly argued that this argument is no argument for that belief.

The rest of the book too consists of statements which will appeal only to the unthinking, and all the difficult problems which necessarily engage the attention of all who think deeply about their religion are simply bypassed. Thus there is no reference to the problem of evil, for example. We been told from our childhood that God is wonderful because He gave us eyes to see and ears to hear, and, in the words of the Christian hymn, created 'all things bright and beautiful'. But He created everything else too, for example, the malarial mosquito and the louse. He is, in both Muslim and Christian belief, all-merciful and all-powerful. So why does He allow millions of people to die of starvation? Maududi doesn't make any reference to this problem. Nor has he anything worthwhile to say about a standing problem in Islamic as well as other theologies, the apparent clash between the doctrine of predestination and the doctrine of free will.

He not only assumes the existence of God, he also assumes that to any human being who has studied them the correctness of basic Islamic beliefs is obvious. In an earlier edition of *Towards Understanding Islam* he writes: 'Any human being, who studies without bias his [Muhammad's] life and teachings will testify that verily he was the true Prophet of God and Quran—the Book he gave to mankind— the true Book of God. No unbiased and serious seeker after truth can escape this conclusion.' In the 1980 edition he tones this down a little, but the effect is the same. 'Any human being who studies his [Muhammad's] life and teachings without bias will testify that he was the true Prophet of God and the Quran—the Book he gave to mankind—the true Book of God. No serious seeker after truth can come to any other conclusion.' It hardly needs pointing out that this belief releases him from any obligation to attempt strenuous argument. People who don't conclude after studying Islam that the Quran is the word of God and Muhammad God's true prophet, are not 'serious seekers after truth'. So why present the truth to people who aren't interested in it?

To learn what relevance Maududi's teachings have to the world in which we live, one must turn from this somewhat anodyne book and study some of his other writings. And I should say at this point that his insistence that Islam provides comprehensive guidance for human conduct in absolutely every department of life is one which strikes a chord with me. I share his belief that any system of values which does not provide such guidance is, to say the least of it, of very limited value. It is another matter that his system of values is Islam and mine is atheistic humanism. Despite this he and I agree on some very important points, for instance, on the perniciousness of nationalism.

At the most basic level political, social and economic systems are founded upon a concept of human rights, and Maududi's pamphlet *Human Rights in Islam* addresses this question.[2] Throughout the pamphlet Maududi's argument employs a transparent sleight of hand which is characteristic of him. Briefly, he expounds the admirable teachings of Islam and leaves it to be inferred that, in the main, Muslims and Muslim states conduct their lives in accordance with these teachings. By contrast, he cites all the undesirable features in the life of western states and their inhabitants and infers that these are in accordance with the principles they proclaim, and that where they are not, this merely proves that their high-sounding principles are sheer hypocrisy. The dishonesty of this procedure is obvious. The honest procedure would have been to examine both Muslim countries and western countries, and to examine *in both cases* both the proclaimed principles and the extent to which these are acted upon. It is worth nothing that his failure to do this, at any rate in this pamphlet, is in contradiction with the claim made for him by two of his admirers, Khurshid Ahmad and Zafar Ishaq Ansari, joint authors of *Mawlana Mawdudi: An Introduction to His Life and Thought.* Their words are worth quoting at length:

He urges that the Muslim heritage (which is naturally a complex composite of truly Islamic and non-Islamic, of healthy and unhealthy elements) should be subjected to critical examination and careful analysis. Thereafter only those elements which are demonstrably derived from the Qur'an and the *Sunnah* should be considered of permanent value. Likewise, the Western civilization should be subjected to a critical scrutiny and analysis. The Western philosophy of life, the Western standard of evaluation, and the corruptions and errors which have plagued the Western social life should definitely be discarded. But this should not prevent Muslims from abstracting the healthy achievements of the modern West.[3]

A comparative examination of the kind which Maududi's disciples tell us he himself considered necessary would have shown how strikingly similar are the declarations of principle of the two civilizations and how no less strikingly similar is the very general failure to live up to them. Maududi makes much of the fact that the proclamations of Islam precede by several centuries the United Nations Declaration of Human Rights. He fails to note that very many of the tenets of Islam in this field were also the tenets commonly accepted by the nations of the West, and had been so accepted centuries before the Quran was revealed to Muhammad. He also fails to note that

Islam never achieved the formulation of human rights and its formal joint acceptance by a number of nations, while the United Nations achieved this on a virtually world-wide scale. Maududi writes with heavy sarcasm:

> more often the rights which were given on paper were not actually given to the people in real life . . . the United Nations, which can now be more aptly and truly described as the Divided Nations, made a Declaration of Universal Human Rights, and passed a resolution against genocide and framed regulations to check it. But as you all know there is not a single resolution or regulation of the United Nations which can be enforced. They are just an expression of a pious hope. They have no sanctions behind them, no force, physical or moral, to enforce them. Despite all the high-sounding ambitious resolutions of the United Nations, human rights have been violated and trampled upon at different places, and the United Nations has been a helpless spectator. She is not in a position to exercise an effective check on the violation of human rights.[4]

All perfectly true—and if one substitutes for 'United Nations' 'Islam' or 'Muslim nations' the statement would be equally true. But Maududi, who knows perfectly well that this is the case, has nothing to say about it.

Before returning to the main argument it is worth noting some other examples of blatant dishonesty in the booklet. The continuation of the passage I have just quoted runs, 'Even the heinous crime of genocide is being perpetrated despite all proclamations of the United Nations. Right in the neighbouring country of Pakistan, genocide of the Muslims has been taking place for the last twenty eight years, but the United Nations does not have the power and strength to take any steps against India.' It is now not twenty-eight, but fifty years since the partition of the subcontinent—and today there are more Muslims living in India than there are in Pakistan. They suffer from widespread discrimination against them, but to describe this situation as 'genocide' is absurd.

Of the *dhimmis* (non-Muslim citizens of Muslim states) he declares: 'There is no difference at all between a Muslim and a non-Muslim citizen in respect of the civil and criminal law.'[5] And there is no mention of the fact that the *dhimmis* have to pay a tax which Muslims do not. He also writes that in the Declaration of Human Rights 'it is clearly implied . . . that these rights . . . have been framed for the white race alone.'[6] There is no such implication.

'The concept of sanctity of chastity and protection of women can be found nowhere else except in Islam.'[7] Such a claim leaves one speechless, as does the breathtaking claim on the same page that 'it has never happened that after the conquest of a foreign country the Muslim army has gone about raping the women of the conquered country.'

Having discussed human rights in general Maududi proceeds to set out the 'rights of citizens in an Islamic state'. But before coming to these let us take a look at what is undoubtedly one of the most basic documents for the study of Maududi's teachings. It is a pamphlet in Urdu—with no known English translation—entitled *Jamā'at i Islāmī kī Dāvat* (literally, the invitation [issued by] the Islamic Organization). 'Jama'at i Islami' is the organization which he formed in 1941 and continued to formally head until 1972 and thereafter informally until his death in 1979.

It is the text of a speech he made in May 1947 to a gathering in still undivided India of members and sympathizers of his Jamaat from all over the subcontinent, and without going so far as to rank him as one of his admirers does, as the greatest writer of Urdu prose of his day, one cannot fail to be impressed by the flow of his lucid, forceful, idiomatic Urdu.

It is worth remarking at this point that, like many other South Asian propagandists for Islam, when he speaks and writes in Urdu he does not pull his punches in the way in which he does when writing for an English-reading audience, and the arguments he presents are of the crudest kind.

In this speech we find the clearest statement of his root and branch condemnation of modern western civilization. He says that it has three basic principles, and that all of them are *fāsid*—that is, pernicious. These three principles are *lā-dīnī* (irreligiousness, which, for Maududi, is synonymous with secularism), nationalism, and democracy.

Like many unthinking religious people, he takes it as axiomatic that people who do not believe in God have no standards of morality. But he goes much further than that and asserts that in such irreligious societies individuals, families and communities all pursue naked self-interest in complete disregard of the interests of others. He ignores the easily observable fact that they are in general equally concerned, without sacrificing their own interests, to avoid sharp conflict with others wherever possible.

His argument on nationalism ends in a similar absurd conclusion. But here, as I indicated above, the premises from which he argues are ones which I whole-heartedly share. Let me quote at length.

We are not opposed to national feeling; that is a natural state of affairs. Nor are we opposed to the desire to seek the good of one's own nation, provided that it is not accompanied by a desire to harm other nations. Nor do we oppose the sentiment of love of one's nation provided that it does not assume the form of national prejudice, unwarranted partiality, and hatred of other nations. We also approve of the freedom of nations, because every nation has the right to manage its own affairs and it is not right that any nation should rule over another. What we do oppose, and in fact hate, is nationalism.

To me, all of this is not only not objectionable but positively good and inspiring. But once again he draws the untenable conclusion that nationalism necessarily results in constant aggression against other nations and ignores the general concern that rivalry should not escalate into aggression and war. He fails to note that for more than fifty years now (thirty-four up to the time of his death) the big western nations have not gone to war, and by contrast, notwithstanding the Islamist principles they all profess, the same period has seen war between Muslim West Pakistan and Muslim East Pakistan (leading to the establishment of Bangladesh) and of Muslim Iraq against Muslim Iran.

It is interesting to note in this connection a remarkable passage from another pamphlet. In it he praises the communists! He writes:

In this matter Muslims should display at least that amount of steadfastness which was shown by the followers of Marx at the outbreak of the Great War of 1914–18. When the war had started a great difference arose among the members of the Second International on this very issue of nationalism. Many socialists who had gathered on the Socialist International Front, seeing that their respective nations had plunged into the war, were swayed over by nationalistic sentiments and wished to join their national armies. But the Marxists said that they were pledged to fight for an ideology according to which the capitalists of all nations stood as their enemies and the labourers of all nations stood as their friends; therefore they could not support that nationalism which creates dissensions and divisions among labourers and brings them to opposite fronts in the company of capitalists. On this ground the Marxists separated from their comrades with whom they had relations of long standing. They could bear the break-up of the Second International but could not bear giving up their cherished principles. Nay, they proceeded further. Those who were true communists broke the idol of nationalism with their own hands. To defend their principles the German communists fought against Germany, the Russian communists against Russia, and similarly the communists of other countries fought against the governments of their own respective nations.[8]

He does not pause to reflect that this admirable steadfastness was the product of adherence to that principle of irreligiousness (indeed, in the case of these communists, *anti*-religiousness) whose perniciousness he so loudly proclaims.

On democracy he does not have much to say. It is a 'pernicious' principle because it means the absolute sovereignty of the people, whereas absolute sovereignty belongs only to God, and His subjects are not free to act in contravention of His commands.

Having disposed to his satisfaction of these pernicious principles he counterposes his own three *sālih* (sound) principles. But once again, before coming to these I want to examine his approach to the history of the countries which constitute the Muslim world.

He begins his survey with an account of the early period of Islam— the age of the Prophet and the first four caliphs who came after him to head the Muslim community. In common with most Muslims he regards this period as the golden age of Islam, when the conduct of the affairs of the community conformed in every respect to the precepts of Islam, in marked contrast to the age that had preceded it.

There are three things worth noting about his account. First, he feels it necessary to explain why the Arabs were the people chosen to receive and accept the message of Islam, and this involves him in the difficulty that besets most Islamic propagandists, although both he and they seem blissfully unaware that there *is* any difficulty. He has to argue first that

no other people were more suited to be endowed with this Prophet than the Arabs. . . The Arabs were a fresh and virile people. So-called social progress had produced bad habits among the advanced nations, while among the Arabs no such social organization existed, and they were, therefore, free from the inactivity, debasement and decadence arising out of luxury and sensual satiety . . . They were brave, fearless, generous, faithful to their promises.[9]

But he and other propagandists also wish to present a picture of the miraculous change which the coming of Islam wrought in an incredibly depraved nation. So, with hardly a pause for breath, Maududi goes on to describe these wonderful Arabs as follows:

It was a country without a government. Each tribe considered itself to be an independent sovereign unit. There was no law except the law of the strongest. Loot, arson and murder of innocent and weak people was the order of the day. Life, property and honour were constantly in jeopardy. Tribes were always at daggers drawn with one another. Any trivial incident was enough to spark off a ferocious war. Indeed, Bedouins from one tribe thought they had every right to kill people from other tribes.

Whatever notions they had of morals, culture and civilization were primitive in the extreme. They could hardly discriminate between pure and impure, lawful and unlawful. Their lives were barbaric. They revelled in adultery, gambling and drinking. Looting and murder were part of their everyday existence. They would stand naked before each other without any qualms of conscience. Even their women-folk would strip nude at the ceremony of circumambulating the Ka'bah. They would bury their daughters alive lest anyone should become their son-in-law. They would marry their stepmothers after the death of their fathers. They were ignorant of even the rudiments of everyday life such as proper eating, dressing and washing.

One is left wondering whether the 'bad habits' prevalent amongst the advanced nations were any worse than the bad habits of these 'brave, fearless, generous, faithful' people before the coming of Islam.

Next, on the golden age of the four Righteous Caliphs. Maududi makes absolutely no reference to the fact that many millions of the Shia sect of Muslims, comprising among others virtually the whole population of Iran and important minorities in Iraq, Pakistan and India, not only refuse to accept the first three caliphs as legitimate, but execrate them; and this loathing of the first three 'righteous' caliphs is still a motive for Shia-Sunni riots in Pakistan and elsewhere.

Finally, and astonishingly, he speaks of how 'The Companions of the Prophet took up the mission of the Prophet after his death. They *travelled to* [my italics—RR] distant lands to spread the Islamic teachings . . .' and greatly impressed 'the entire population of the countries they *visited*' [my italics],[10] If one did not know one could be forgiven for not realizing that these 'travels' and 'visits' were in fact the rapid conquest by Muslim armies of a vast tract of territory bounded by Spain in the West and India in the East.

The pamphlet just quoted does not continue its 'historical perspective' beyond that point. But elsewhere he goes on to take a long jump over several centuries and land at somewhere about 1800, from where he proceeds to discuss what happened, not in the Muslim world as a whole, but in those parts of it which fell under western imperialist rule. Khurshid Ahmad and Zafar Ishaq Ansari summarize Maududi's views:

Maududi's own analysis is that the Muslim society has gradually drifted away from the ideal order established by the Prophet (peace be upon him), which· had continued and developed along the same line during the period of *al-Khulafa' al-Rashidun* [the Righteous Caliphs]. The first important change in the body-politic of Islam was a change from *Khilafah* to a more or less worldly monarchy with very important consequential changes affecting the role of religion in the socio-political life. Gradually the very idea of unity of life began to be weakened, and consciously or unconsciously a degree of separation between religion and politics was brought about. There also developed a bifurcation of leadership into political and religious leadership, with separate domains and areas of influence for each.

The second major change occurred in the system of education. This had catastrophic consequences as it began to perpetuate the schisms and tensions that were shearing Muslim society and gradually sapped the springs of creativity which had ensured the vitality of the Islamic civilization in all the major realms of human effort.

As a consequence of the above changes, the moral life of the people began to deteriorate; their faithful allegiance and sincere devotion to Islam weakened, and a gap between theory and practice began to appear and widen . . . Widespread efforts were made throughout Muslim history to rectify this situation. But the rot continued till Muslims succumbed to the colonial powers of the West. During this period an alien system was imposed upon them in all fields of life, including the field of education. Because of this new system of education the separation of religion and politics in practical life gradually became an acceptable proposition for Muslim society. When the Muslims threw off the yoke of foreign dominance and began living as independent peoples, the leadership of the Muslim countries generally passed into the hands of those whose mental attitudes and life-styles had been shaped by the colonial system of education and their experience of political subjection. These are living, by far and large, under the spell of non-Islamic ideas and values. This is in addition to the several weaknesses inherited by Muslims from earlier periods of their history.[11]

It is understandable that Maududi devotes major attention to the deplorably corrupting influences on Islam resulting from long subjection to imperialist rule, because his own life was lived in India and Pakistan. But that is no warrant for neglecting to examine in similar detail the corruption of pure Islam in those Muslim countries which never fell under direct colonial rule. His favourite tactic of contrasting the precepts of Islam (and leaving it to be inferred that these are observed in Muslim states) with the practice of western nations (and leaving it to be inferred that these had never formulated precepts comparable to those of Islam) prevents him from drawing attention to the true state of affairs that has long prevailed in Muslim states. Here is a typical example:

Islam recognizes the right of every citizen of its state that there should be no undue interference or encroachment on the privacy of his life. The Holy Qur'an has laid down the injunction: 'Do not spy on one another' (49:12). 'Do not enter any houses except your own homes unless you are sure of their occupants' consent' (24:27) . . . . The Prophet has even prohibited people from reading the letters of others, so much so that if a man is reading his letter and another man casts sidelong glances at it and tries to read it, his conduct becomes reprehensible. This is the sanctity of privacy that Islam grants to individuals.[12]

To which he might have added that this is also the sanctity of privacy the traditional western liberal principles also grant to individuals. He continues:

On the other hand in the modern civilized world we find that not only the letters of other people are read and their correspondence censored, but even its photostat copies are retained for future use or blackmail. Even bugging devices are secretly fixed in the houses of the people so that one can hear and tape from a distance the conversation taking place behind closed doors.

To which again, he might have added that exactly the same thing happens in the countries of the Muslim world. He ends with the ludicrously exaggerated statement that 'In other words it means that there is no such thing as privacy and to all practical purposes the private life of an individual does not exist.'

This standard tactic of his releases him from any need, as he thinks, to look at Muslim states, to study their history, to assess the state of affairs prevailing there and formulate a programme of what true Muslims like himself need to do about it.

True, one finds the occasional vague general statement that all is not well in the Muslim world: 'Courts of Law in an Islamic State are established for the purpose of enforcing the Divine Code and not to violate it as they are doing at present in almost all the Muslim States'[13] and 'Even more painful than this is the realization that throughout the world the rulers who claim to be Muslims have made disobedience to their God and the Prophet as the basis and foundation of their government.'[14]

But this is about the sum total of what he has to say on this point. English readers might well have expected him to tell us more about how and why this state of affairs came about. Here we have countries that have always been Muslim, have never been subjected to western imperialist rule, countries which moreover had, according to Maududi, experienced the golden age of Islam. It was not subjection to western imperialism that corrupted them. So what *did* corrupt them? One might have expected a root and branch reformer like Maududi to make a fearless analysis of the situation that developed in these countries and then proceed to say equally fearlessly what needs to be done to eradicate the evils that prevail in them. But, to put it mildly, fearlessness is not evident in anything he has to say about that. Saudi Arabia is not exactly an exemplar of all the high principles of Islamic democracy, Islamic freedom, and Islamic human rights, but no one reading Maududi would ever know this. One is tempted to the cynical conclusion that this is because it is Saudi resources that finance the world-wide propaganda of Maududi's ideas, and you don't bite the hand that feeds you. And what goes for Saudi Arabia goes for all the other Muslim countries too. Where, for example, in all these Islamic countries with a continuous Islamic history is there a single one which can be called a democracy? And why is Saudi Arabia so wholly subservient to that perniciously secular, perniciously democratic and perniciously nationalist imperialist power, the USA?

As we have seen, Maududi speaks of the pain he feels when he considers that 'throughout the world the rulers who claim to be Muslim have made disobedience to their God and the Prophet as the basis and foundation of their government'. But one cannot avoid the conclusion that this pain is, shall we say, not a very acute one. A thoughful reader would have thought, 'He writes virulently against the rulers of states who are not and never have been Muslims and, therefore, obviously, could not be expected to rule according to Muslim principles. Surely he should attack even more bitterly rulers who profess loudly their devotion to Islam and at the same time violate all its basic principles?' But no. On the contrary he goes along with the attitude which in my experience is very generally found amongst Muslims. When non-Muslim rulers commit appalling crimes, Muslims roundly condemn them. But when Idi Amin, Khomeini, Saddam et al commit these same crimes their profession of Islam gives them full protection from Muslim censure.

And now let us see what in Maududi's view an Islamic state ought to be. He lists 'the rights of citizens in an Islamic state' as follows:

(1) The executive head of the government and the members of the assembly should be elected by free and independent choice of the people.
(2) The people and their representatives should have the right to criticize and freely express their opinions.
(3) The real conditions of the country should be brought before the people without suppressing any fact so that they may able to form their opinion about whether the government is working properly or not.
(4) There should be adequate guarantee that only those people who have the support of the masses should rule over the country and those who fail to win this support should be removed from their position of authority.[15]

Admirable! (And, incidentally, not only entirely acceptable for those nations of the West whose decadence and immorality Maududi deplores, but also put into practice there to a greater extent than in Muslim countries.) And again:

Islam gives the right of freedom of thought and expression to all citizens of the Islamic State on the condition that it should be used for the propagation of virtue and truth and not for spreading evil and wickedness. This Islamic concept of freedom of expression is much superior to the concept prevalent in the West. Under no circumstances would Islam allow evil and wickedness to be propagated.

Islam has also given people the right to freedom of association and formation of parties or organizations. This right is also subject to certain general rules. It should be exercised for propagating virtue and righteousness and should never be used for spreading evil and mischief.[16]

And who is to decide whether any person or any organization is using freedom of expression 'for spreading evil and wickedness' or 'evil and mischief'? Maududi does not suggest an answer to this key question.

Similar problems arise in relation to all the other 'first principles' he expounds.

The responsibility for the administration of the government, in an Islamic state, is entrusted to an *amir* (leader) who may be compared to the president or the prime minister in a modern democratic state. All adult men and women who believe in the fundamentals of the constitution [and who is to decide which of them do and which of them don't?—RR] will be entitled to vote for the election of the *amir*. The basic qualifications for the election of an *amir* are that he should command the confidence of the largest number of people in respect of his knowledge and grasp of the spirit of Islam; he should possess the Islamic quality of fear of God and be endowed with qualities of statesmanship. In short, he should have both virtue and ability. A *shura* (advisory council) is also to be elected by the people for assisting and guiding the *amir* in the administration of the state. It will be incumbent on the *amir* to administer the country with the advice of this *shura*. The *amir* can retain office only so long as he enjoys the confidence of the people and will have to relinquish his office when he loses this confidence. But as long as he retains such confidence he will have the authority to govern and exercise the powers of government in consultation with the *shura* [the advisory council—whose advice, however, as Maududi makes clear elsewhere, he is not bound to accept].[17]

Maududi spells out in more detail the qualifications which the *amir* should have. There are, he says four legal qualifications which determine a person's eligibility to the membership of the Consultative Assembly or to the post of the Head of an Islamic State'. These are that he 'should be . . . a Muslim, . . . a male . . . sane and adult, and . . . a citizen of an Islamic state'.[18] Verses of the Quran are quoted to testify to each of these requirements.

But that is not all. Far from it. He also declares that no one is qualified to fully understand what Islam commands unless he is 'a versatile scholar of Arabic (both modern and ancient)'. . . . aware of the meaning of 'the language and terminology used therein [in the basic texts of Islam and which are] so different from the terms in vogue today' and also well-versed in 'such modern subjects as Political Science, Economics, Constitutional Law and the problems arising therefrom'.[19]

And where are such paragons to be found? And who is to decide whether candidates for election have the qualifications which they declare they have? This decision, if you please, is to be taken by an 'Election Commissioner'[20] or 'an Election Tribunal or a Judge'.[21] And who is to appoint such a commissioner, tribunal or judge, having satisfied himself that he is qualified to undertake this task? No answer!

Furthermore, how does one proceed from the present unsatisfactory state of affairs to the realization of the ideal Islamic state? Maudui has only vague generalities to offer. And the study of some of his practical activities suggest interesting conclusions.

One should of course beware of thinking that if a man preaches a message which his practice does not match, this invalidates that message. But at the same time it is important to be aware of the fact that a man who proclaims so loudly and with such self-righteousness, if I may say so, the values of Islam which are to save the whole world, doesn't observe these values in his own life and activities. The most striking example of this incongruity occurred in Pakistan during the presidential election of 1964, when despite his insistence that only a male was eligible for election to Head of State, he openly supported the candidacy of Fatima Jinnah. But there are other examples too. He and his followers preach the virtues of the simple life which the Prophet and first caliphs lived. Well, in 1968 Maudui came to England, and I (doubtless among many others) was invited to meet him. And where? At the London Hilton. I asked one of his admirers, 'Why there? There are surely plenty of simpler places in Britain than the Hilton to which you could invite your guests and so demonstrate the consonance between your principles and your practice.' And he was forced to agree.

I have stressed throughout this article that Maududi and his Saudi backers have done a great deal to spread his message far and wide, and well beyond the bounds of Pakistan. There is a significant point to be made about the English-language publications through which this is done. The English versions of the pamphlets of Maududi which I have, bear on the title page the words 'translated and edited by Khurshid Ahmad' or [published by] 'The Islamic Foundation, Leicester' of which Khurshid Ahmad was, the back cover of *Mawlana Mawdudi: An Introduction* tells us, 'Director General from April 1973 to September 1978'. The degree to which this translating and editing modified the original text is not clear, but from Khurshid Ahmad's statement in his introduction to the 1980 edition of *Towards Understanding Islam* it seems that he has allowed himself quite a lot of liberty. He made a translation in 1959, of which he writes, 'Strictly speaking, I did not venture a literal, word for word translation of the original text. I tried to follow the original as faithfully as possible, but departed wherever necessary from a strictly literal rendering in the interest of a more effective communication of the meaning of the text.'[22] He tells us that Maududi went through this translation and approved it. However, the 1980 version is the product of a feeling that 'the translation needed further improvement'.[23] His 'improvement' has also produced quite extensive annotation to the text, and one receives the impression throughout that a major motive has been to tone down for the English reader statements which in their original undiluted form would not have been too readily accepted. Some of these annotations have the effect of highlighting glaring omissions in Maududi's arguments, but the attempts to remedy these omissions is sometimes quite laughable.

Thus Maududi's repeated ignoring of the Shias is 'remedied' by a note which tells us that the Sunni-Shia 'divergence of belief. . . has. . . no practical value now'.[24] Similarly at one point where the English reader might jibe at Maududi's implication that Muslim states implement the declared principles of Islam, a footnote tells us: 'Some of the points referred to here are to materialize when the Islamic state has attained its final form. As far as the transitory phase is concerned efforts will be made to approach them as early as possible.[25]

Maududi's main appeal has been to his fellow-Pakistanis, and here one should not draw too hasty conclusions from the fact that when in 1972 he decided that his Jama'at i Islami should participate in the election of that year and fielded 148 candidates, only four were elected. How far his influence has increased since those days I have no means of estimating, but he was greatly helped during the period of the Zia ul Haq regime when the slogans of the government echoed those of the Jama'at, and Khurshid Ahmad, in disregard of the notable lack of human rights, Islamic or otherwise, under that regime, was a minister in Zia's government. It is true that rural voters (who of course constitute the great majority of the Pakistan electorate) either disregard much of Maududi's teaching or are actively hostile to it, but his influence in the lower middle classes of the towns is very great, and their aggressiveness can do a good deal to intimidate their opponents. As an instance of this, Pakistani friends of mine who live in London but visited Pakistan last December, moved in circles who found it uncomfortable to give parties at Christmas because of the vociferous protests of the Jama'atis against the celebration of 'unIslamic' festivals.

The basis of his great appeal, as it seems to me, is a simple one. His arguments, such as they are, confirm his supporters in the strong, unthinking prejudices they already hold. We can summarize his way of proceeding thus:

He argues that one glance at the universe is enough to convince anyone that God exists.

Also that a proper, serious study of the life of Muhammad cannot fail to convince the reader that he is the Prophet of God, and that the Quran, revealed to him, is the word of God.

He knows that any serious religious thinker cannot fail to confront the problem of the existence of evil in a universe created by a God who is both all-powerful and all merciful, and the problem of how to reconcile predestination with free will. So he doesn't even mention these problems.

He tells us that the Arabs, the first recipients of Muhammad's message, were the finest people in the world and therefore the most fit to receive it.

Simultaneously he tells us that they were one of the most depraved people in the world, and the coming of the Prophet miraculously transformed them.

He tells us that the golden age of Islamic society was the period of Muhammad and the four Righteous Caliphs. The Shia don't approve of all the Righteous Caliphs. So he doesn't even mention the Shia.

The noble precepts of Islam have always been proclaimed by Muslim states, but he doesn't even *look* at what the Muslim states did since the end of the 'golden age'—and are still doing.

He asserts that the big nations of the West are decadent and immoral—as they are bound to be, because they are irreligious, and people who reject religion have no standards of morality. He doesn't even look at the noble principles they proclaimed, doesn't even mention for instance, that the American declaration of independence begins: 'We hold these truths to be self-evident, that all men *were created* equal, and were endowed by their *Creator* with certain inalienable rights' (my italics—RR).

All of these things accord with the preconceived prejudices of the average lower middle-class urban Muslim, who believes the Quran without, in the typical case, knowing what it says. He has learnt in childhood to 'read' it, in the sense of being able to pronounce correctly the sounds which its Arabic letters and diacritical marks represent. But he has never read it in Urdu or English translation. He just *knows* that whatever it says is right. And now here comes a man who has studied intensively the Quran, the Hadis, and all the basic texts of Islam—and Maududi has certainly done all this—and can *prove* that what they all along believed is correct. What more could one want? And that is why Maududi's movement needs to be taken seriously— and vigorously combatted.

Notes and References

1. Leicester: The Islamic Foundation, 1980, p. 37.
2. The edition I have was published by the Islamic Foundation, UK, in 1976, in co-operation with the Islamic Council of Europe and the King Abdul Aziz University, on the occasion of the World of Islam Festival. It is 'an English translation of a talk given by Mawlana Mawdudi at the invitation of Civic Rights and Liberties Forum ... [in] Lahore, Pakistan on 16th November, 1975.' The editors add, 'To put the discussion in perspective we are including an earlier talk of Mawlana Mawdudi [first broadcast in 1948 and here 'slightly revised'] on the political system of

Islam as chapter one to the present book. These two talks taken together would enable the reader to have a clear idea of the Islamic political framework and the nature and concept of human rights in Islam.'

3. Khurshid Ahmad and Zafar Ishaq Ansari, *Mawlana Mawdudi: An Introduction to His Life and Thought*, Leicester, The Islamic Foundation, 1979, pp. 16–17.
4. Maududi, *Human Rights in Islam*, pp. 13–14.
5. Ibid., p. 11.
6. Ibid., p. 18.
7. Ibid., p. 19.
8. *Nationalism and India* (Pathankot (Punjab)), 1947, pp. 7–9.
9. *Towards Understanding Islam*, p. 41.
10. *Islam: An Historical Perspective* (Leicester: The Islamic Foundation, 1974), p. 9.
11. *Mawdudi: An Introduction*, pp. 22–3.
12. *Human Rights in Islam*, p. 27.
13. *First Principles of the Islamic State*, 1952, 2nd (revised) edn. (Lahore: Islamic Publications Ltd., 1960), p. 35.
14. *Human Rights in Islam*.
15. *First Principles,* 1960, p. 37.
16. Ibid., pp. 31–2.
17. *Human Rights in Islam*, pp. 10–11.
18. *First Principles*, pp. 60–1.
19. Ibid., pp. 7–9.
20. Ibid., p. 52.
21. Ibid., p. 59.
22. *Towards Understanding Islam*, p. 15.
23. Ibid., p. 16.
24. *First Principles*, p. 45.
25. *Human Rights in Islam*, n. 5, p. 10.

⚜17⚜

INTER-FAITH DIALOGUE—
AND OTHER MATTERS

I t is commonly said that modern communications have brought
the peoples of the world into closer contact with one another
and so made possible increasing tolerance and understanding
between them. That is indeed the case, but no one who contemplates
what has been happening in country after country in recent years can
fail to see that these same modern communications have also brought
into closer contact with one another peoples and communities who
have not the least desire to foster mutual tolerance and understanding
and whose attitudes to one another range all the way from amused
contempt to hatred so virulent that, given the opportunity, they will
engage in mutual killing, taking advantage not only of modern
communications but also such achievements of modern technology
as the Kalashnikov rifle.

This is not a new phenomenon. The idea that encounters with
unfamiliar cultures encourage mutual understanding found expression
in the familiar saying that travel broadens the mind. If this was ever
true it was true of an age in which only the enlightened had the means
to indulge in foreign travel. If we look at recent British experience
this suggests a different conclusion. In Britain (and no doubt elsewhere)
it has become more and more common for people to take holidays
abroad. In the great majority of cases it seems that this experience, far
from broadening the mind, narrows it. Reaction to other people's

---

* Originally published in *A Journal of History, Indo-British Review* 1 xx (i): 38–40.

ways and other people's food have ranged from amusement to ridicule to indignation and contempt, almost as though these people had adopted their way of life as a deliberate affront to their British visitors. Those who catered for these British visitors soon realized that what the British wanted of them was good weather (which fortunately they had no difficulty in providing) combined with every facility for continuing in the British way of life, with proper provision for the maintenance of such essential British institutions as 'a decent cup of tea', fish and chips, and so on. Only then did their indignation simmer down. And one had to regretfully conclude that travel broadens travellers' minds only when they had already been broadened before they set out on their travels.

At that level mutual intolerance produces no great problem. But in it one can already see the beginnings of much worse things, with mutual dislike hardening into mutual hatred, and developing to the point where white people will kill black people simply because they are black, Sikhs will kill Hindus simply because they are Hindus, Hindus will kill Sikhs simply because they are Sikhs, and so on—the list could be extended almost indefinitely. And when matters reach this stage the situation confronts those of us who seek to promote mutual understanding and mutual love with very grave problems.

My own estimate is that mutual hatreds—between races, nationalities and communities (religious and otherwise)—have long been increasing at a greater rate than mutual tolerance and understanding, though such understanding has been increasing too. If that is so, the upholders of mutual understanding need to confront the situation, to exert themselves to concert their efforts, and to consider constantly whether they need to improve the way in which they go about their tasks. It is in the light of this understanding that I want to offer some friendly criticisms of current practices. I shall focus on inter-faith relations but I shall also have in mind the broader issues to which the same sort of considerations apply—for instance, those of racial, national, and cultural conflicts which are sharpening everywhere.

I have two quite strong reservations about what I have experienced of inter-faith dialogue. The first is that it is conducted in terms which in effect exclude many people whom it should not. For example, I am an atheist (and what used to be called a communist, though the latter word has now long since ceased to have any generally agreed meaning).

It would be stretching the meanings of words like 'religion' and 'faith' unacceptably to apply them to my beliefs. Yet my beliefs govern my conduct in life no less than the religious beliefs of Christians, Muslims, Sikhs, and Hindus. My own concept of the term 'communism' is one which sees it as something that derives from humanism and logically follows from it. I am, then, a humanist. I know that there are among my fellow-humanists some who think that humanism must necessarily be based on atheism. That is most emphatically not so. Humanism may also be based upon religious concepts. Our common humanism—my atheist humanism and others' religious humanism—ought surely to provide the basis for extending what is today called 'inter-faith' dialogue to include the irreligious.

Even more important than the irreligious is another category of people—the kind of people who would describe themselves as 'not particularly religious'. W. Cantwell Smith coined the word 'amelist' for such people (on the pattern of 'agnostic'—an agnostic being one who 'doesn't know' whether there is a God or not and an 'amelist' one who 'doesn't care').[1] Probably the great majority of people in the northern hemisphere now belong to this category, and writing which bears the label (so to speak) of 'inter-faith' dialogue has no appeal to them. Yet means to appeal to them must be found. The fact that they are neither religious nor irreligious does not in the least mean that they lack values in which they believe, even though they do not see any need to arrange these in a coherent system. For example, most are quite strongly committed to freedom of conscience, freedom of speech, and a rather vague sort of humanism, and these values are common to them and to the exponents of inter-faith dialogue (even if their practice, like that of the religious and the irreligious, does not always measure up to the principles they profess). We need to find the means to speak to these and to have them speak to us.

I can see that religious people engaged in inter-faith dialogue could respond to what I have said, 'We agree with you, but our own particular task is a more restricted one.' There is some force in this argument, but I would say that even if one accepts it one can still ask that they conduct their dialogue in terms that do not suggest, as they sometimes do, that only religious people have strong moral values, and that meaningful argument can fruitfully be addressed only to them. Thus Martin Forward wrote, 'When religions abandon their hold upon society, one of the costs is that faith has no means of expressing itself, no place to be nurtured, no capacity to mature.'[2] I would argue that this is far from being the case.

I feel another reservation about inter-faith dialogue. Its exponents seem to me to favour what Milton called 'a fugitive and cloistered virtue . . . that never sallies out and sees her adversary, but slinks out of the race', and I wholeheartedly agree with Milton in feeling that such a virtue is not to be praised. It seems to me that many of those who engage in Christian-Muslim dialogue make it a rule never to say anything that could give offence, and that this severely curtails the usefulness of what they have to say. They are committed to an approach which concentrates on seeking common ground between the adherents of the two religions, and this is a wholly admirable approach. But those who adopt it must be aware that there are millions of Christians and millions of Muslims who do not share it, and in my opinion those who do share it, on both sides, need courteously, but openly and vigorously, to criticize those in both religious communities who do not. To do this effectively, Christians who support inter-faith dialogue need to concentrate their fire mainly upon fellow-Christians whose stand is opposed to theirs; similarly, Muslims need to do the same in opposition to their adversaries in the Muslim community. (At the same time, both have a perfect right to express their opinions and criticisms of each other too.)

The exponents of Christian-Muslim dialogue need to state forthrightly that there is no *one* Christianity and no *one* Islam. In Christianity there is, for example the *opus dei* of the Jesuits who found Christian grounds for supporting the worst excesses of the Franco regime in Spain: and there are also those Latin American Jesuits who see Christian doctrine as one which demands support for the liberation struggles of the Latin American peoples. Similarly there is the Islam of Ayatollah Khomeini, which required him to condemn Rushdie to death, and the Islam of others who emphatically deny that their religion requires any such thing. Supporters of either of these opposed trends cannot express their views without giving offence to their opponents. But here one should bear in mind the words of St Jerome, quoted by Thomas Hardy in his Explanatory Note to *Tess of the Durbervilles:* 'If an offence comes out of the truth, better it is that the offence come than that the truth be concealed.' Dialogue both within and between faiths cannot be conducted without giving some offence, and while, obviously, one should always speak and write in a way which minimizes the offence given, effective dialogue requires that every participant in it says frankly and honestly what he/she thinks. This *must* sometimes give offence. The argument advanced by many in the controversy over Salman Rushdie's *The Satanic Verses*, that no one should be permitted to give offence to the adherents of any religion, is quite untenable. There are, in any case, in every religion fundamental beliefs which are in themselves deeply offensive to adherents of other religions. Well, too bad. Everyone must learn to live with that. I may remark in passing that my own beliefs, which I hold as deeply and sincerely as any religious person holds his or hers, have been assailed all over the world, and in the most intemperate language, for years together, but I have never felt that I had any right to demand that the writings of such assailants be banned.

It is worth dwelling for a moment on *The Satanic Verses* controversy. The failure of the exponents of inter-faith dialogue during that controversy to act upon the principles I have been discussing was very striking. Indeed, they seem to have been remarkably silent on this issue, which, more than any other in recent years, demanded their presence upon the scene, with clear statements of their view of the issues involved. Many of them who understand the feelings of the anti-Rushdie campaigners seem to me to have been saying to them, in effect, 'We recognize that devotion to Islam demands that you act as you do, and we respect your stand.' What they ought to have said was, 'We challenge the view that Islam sanctions your behaviour and your demands', and pointed to those doctrines of both mainstream Islam and of the Sufi trend in Islam which dictated a very different response. I did this in an article which (to my pleasant surprise) was published in the English pages of the London Urdu daily *Jang*.[3] But I have seen nothing on similar lines from either Muslim or Christian writers. The nearest response that I have seen was expressed in articles by Akbar S. Ahmad. These stressed the importance of the Sufi tradition in Islam with its doctrine of love for all humankind. What he did *not* do was tell his readers how forthrightly many of the adherents of this tradition had, over the centuries, attacked their bigoted co-religionists. Yet such a forthright attack cannot be avoided if the message of mutual understanding and mutual tolerance is to prevail.

NOTES AND REFERENCES

1. *Modern Islam in India* (Lahore: Minerva Bookshop, 1943), p. 334.
2. *Connexions, An Occasional Bulletin, Interfaith,* July 1989.
3. In instalments between 12 and 16 August 1989.

⚜ 18 ⚜

AN INFIDEL AMONG BELIEVERS

First the 'infidel' bit: I became an atheist in 1933, at the age of fifteen, and have remained one ever since. I could not, and still cannot, see any rational proof of the existence of God, and it seems to me that if you assert the existence of God the burden of proof is upon you, not upon those of us who make no such assertion. I also felt, and still feel, that the common view of God held by religious people, or at any rate by Christians and Muslims, that God is both all-powerful and all-merciful is totally irrational. He could be one of the other, but not both. (In later years a Jesuit friend of mine said that God is omnipotent, but that doesn't mean that He can do anything. For example, He can't create another God. It didn't occur to me until later, but this means that 'omnipotent' is a meaningless word.) As for His alleged all-kindness, when Milton wrote (and Christians still sing today) 'All things living He doth feed' he wrote something which he knew perfectly well was not true. And if, as Mrs Alexander said, God created 'All things bright and beautiful' He also created all things dark and ugly. So I abandoned belief in God and looked for belief in something else. The something else I discovered was humanism, though I didn't know that word at the time. And humanism led to communism, and I joined the Communist Party. In those days sensitive and intelligent people knew pretty well what you believed in if you called yourself a communist, but that, of course, has long ceased to be the case. A time came when I had to explain that I was not a 'Soviet' communist, or a 'Chinese' communist, or an 'Italian' communist, but just a *communist* communist. Here it will be enough to say that I am still content to call myself a communist, but I have never accepted, and do not now accept, any version of communism which is not in accord with humanism and respect for human rights.

At one time, I believe, you could not be admitted to membership of the Communist Party unless you were an atheist. Certainly this was once the case where the Communist Party of the Soviet Union was concerned. There existed in the Soviet Union a League of Militant Atheists, and I expect there was one in other countries too, though I never encountered any in Britain. It attacked religion head-on, as did the nearest thing to it in Britain that I was aware of, the Rationalist Press Association (RPA). I never saw much point in doing that. For the already converted there was material for amusement in the RPA 164-page book, *The Bible Handbook* (first published in 1888) with its chapters on Bible Contradictions, Bible Absurdities, and so on, but there was no point in using it against anyone but those small number of Christians who were as aggressive and bellicose as any militant atheist could be—and not always even against them. In relations with people who wore their religion more lightly or more calmly this kind of approach was, and is, useless. In my early days in the communist movement—what I may call the People's Front days—most communist parties no longer barred religious people from membership, and I think they were right not to do so. For myself, I think I had already, in practice, begun to operate on the principle, admirably articulated in later years by Sam Aaronovitch, a Communist Party organizer whom I much admired, as 'He who is not for us is partly for us', with its corollary that one builds on what common ground one has and in normal circumstances attaches more importance to that than to the areas, no matter how extensive these may be, where no such common ground exists. This doesn't mean that I reject the better-known principle of 'He who is not for us is against us'. That too is true and one shouldn't try to evade this by pretending to be what one is not. Thus I have never, except in exceptional situations of short duration, concealed the fact that I am an atheist and a communist or hesitated to defend my beliefs—calmly and good-humouredly, I hope—against anyone who cares to attack them. But I won't generally initiate such discussions.

In the eight years from 1934 to 1942 the religious believers I came into contact with were all Christians, but in 1942, when I was a conscript in the British army, I was posted to India and stayed there for three and a half years—from March 1942 to August 1945. There, of course, I encountered people of other religious faiths. One of my fellow lieutenants was a Muslim (a Pathan) and another was a Sikh. Most of the hundred or so men under my direct command were Hindus, but there were Muslims and Christians too. I count myself fortunate that my first encounter with the religious diversity of India was in a situation where communal antagonism was almost non-existent. The British authorities, experts in 'divide and rule', had found it was not practicable to divide and rule their south Indian soldiers, known in those days as 'Madrassis', and while in north Indian army units there were separate kitchens for Hindus and Muslims, in ours everyone ate from the same kitchen. And we officers too, five white British, one Sikh and one Pathan Muslim, all dined together.

In those days the language of the Indian Army was Urdu, and I learnt it. And by a series of fortunate accidents, after I returned to England and was a year later released from military service, I became a student of Urdu (with Sanskrit as my subsidiary subject) at the University of London's School of Oriental and African Studies, and in 1949, immediately after taking my degree, a member of its teaching staff, which I remained until my two-years-early retirement in 1981. During that period, between 1949 and 1965, I was granted three separate years of study leave in India and Pakistan, with leave for shorter periods in the years after that. Study leave was given specifically for work in Urdu, and during those years I never went further south than Hyderabad. Since Urdu, or at any rate literary Urdu, despite some nationalist claims to the contrary, is now almost exclusively the language of Muslims, it was amongst Muslims that I spent most of my time—Muslim writers, scholars and students of Urdu literature. But since what I like most in life is relating to *people* (not countries, places, books and other things) I have always talked readily with anyone who could talk Urdu with me, high and low, educated and uneducated, delighted to profit by the readiness of South Asians in general to communicate on almost any subject, to ask you questions which no Englishman would dream of putting to you, and to answer similar questions in return. With Hindus, other than English-educated secular-minded Hindus, for whom Hinduism is little more than a vague cultural tradition, I have had very little contact—a fact which I regret. With Sikhs, and with Muslims both in India and Pakistan, I have had much more. Personal relations with all of them have, with very, very few exceptions, always been friendly, and with some—one Hindu, one Sikh and several Muslim—I have formed close friendships of in some cases more than forty years standing.

Some of these close friendships have been formed with deeply religious people, Muslims and, in later years, Christians. (By 'deeply religious' I emphatically do *not* mean those who shout loudest about their religion.) One, whom I will call Bashir, since I don't know whether he would want to be identified, was interested in seeing the way I taught Urdu to English students. He was present on one occasion when I was reading with them a passage about Allah. In traditional style it enumerated all the blessings Allah had conferred upon humankind. I paused and said, 'Yes, and He made plague and cholera and malarial mosquitoes, didn't He, Bashir Sahib?' 'Yes,' said Bashir. 'Why?' I asked. '*I* don't know,' he said—and quite clearly he wasn't in the least perturbed. He believes that God *is* all-merciful, and if this cannot be proved by rational argumant, that makes no difference. God is all-merciful: that, to him, is a fact. He believes, and I don't, and that is the end of the matter. That's no ground for any mutual hostility. I go along with that. Two of my favourite nineteenth-century Urdu writers, the proto-novelist Nazir Ahmad and the poet Akbar Ilahabadi, men of widely differing views, were united in their belief, which I share, that for religious people it is necessary to recognize that rationality can take you only so far, and beyond that it is all a matter of faith. And about faith there can be no argument. Either you have it or you don't.

Nazir Ahmad has a brilliant article about God's creation of Adam and His decision to make humankind his khalifa (vicegerent) upon earth. Nazir Ahmad speaks of His doing both these things 'for reasons which He alone knows'.[1] And Akbar writes: 'God is beyond the range of telescopes' and

Why all this concentration on the problem?
You ask What God is? God is God. What else?[2]

Among my own contemporaries the Muslim to whom I have felt closest was the late Mufti Raza Ansari, of Firangi Mahal. I first met him in Aligarh, where he lectured in the Department of Theology, and I have several cassettes of my recorded interviews with him, a selection of which I should one day like to publish. A more courteous, considerate and tolerant man it would be difficult to find. Secure in his beliefs, which *were* beliefs and not mere prejudices, he could talk calmly, attentively and with respect about my often very different views. I found the same qualities later in Jesuit priests. (One of them learnt Urdu from me, and through him I met others.) What they and I have in common is a humanist morality, though theirs is religiously based and mine is not.

As one who has spent most of his life in studying and teaching Urdu, and is now (in Urdu-speaking circles!) quite famous, it is with Muslims that I have had most occasion to discuss, and often to dispute, the validity of what they think their religion teaches them. This has been especially relevant since Khomeini's *fatwa* condemning Salman Rushdie to death.

Obviously, if you want to be taken seriously by Muslims you need to be reasonably well-versed in Islamic beliefs and practices, and so able to meet Muslims on their own ground, and in my article 'Salman Rushdie, Islam and Multiculturalism' I attempted to do this.[3] To which I should add that in confronting Muslims whose attitudes I reject, I attempt, without in any way concealing my own beliefs, to build upon common ground between me and them. And that, I think, is why I, an infidel among believers, not only survive, but evoke, if I may say so, affection and respect.

NOTE AND REFERENCES

1. The article is summarized at length and with substantial quotation in Ralph Russell, *The Pursuit of Urdu Literature* (London and New Jersey: Zed Books/OUP, 1992), pp. 119–20. The original (in Urdu) is reprinted in Iftikhār Ahmad Siddiqi, *Nazir Ahmad* (Lahore: Majlis i Taraqqi e Adab, 1971), pp. 444–6. The Urdu original of the words quoted is on p. 444.

2. Quoted on p. 144 of Russell, *The Pursuit*. The Urdu originals are in *Kulliyat II*, p. 26 and *Kulliyat I*, p. 534.

3. Chapter 15 of this volume.